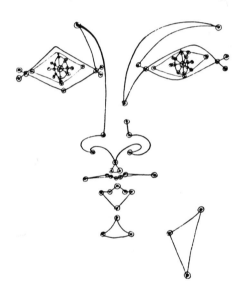

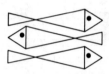

Farrar, Straus & Giroux

NEW YORK

Professional Secrets

AN AUTOBIOGRAPHY OF

Jean Cocteau

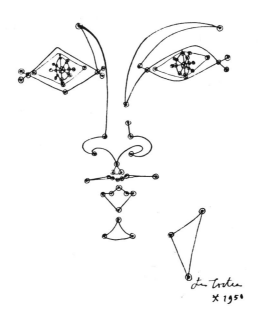

Drawn, from his lifetime writings, by
ROBERT PHELPS

Translated from the French by
Richard Howard

© 1970 by Farrar, Straus & Giroux, Inc.
All rights reserved
Library of Congress catalog card number 70-82626
First printing, 1970
Printed in the United States of America
Designed by Patricia de Groot

The translations from the works of Jean Cocteau were made with the
kind permission of the following publishers: Editions Stock, for *Lettre à
Jacques Maritain, Opium, Orphée,* and *Le Rappel à l'ordre;* F. Bruckman
Verlag, K.G., for *Démarche d'un poète;* Editions André Bonne, for *Entretiens autour du cinéma;* Editions Gallimard, for *Maalesh, Discours de réception de l'Académie-Française, Le Discours d'Oxford, Mon premier voyage,
Poésie Critique I,* and *Poésie Critique II;* Librairie Plon, for *Le Cordon
ombilical* (Copyright Librairie Plon, juin 1962); Calmann-Lévy, Editeur,
for *Jean Marais* (Copyright Calmann-Lévy, Paris, 1951); Editions Grasset,
for *Corrida du 1ᵉʳ Mai, Journal d'un inconnu, Colette, Reines de la France,
Lettres aux américains,* and *Portraits-souvenir;* Editions du Rocher, for *Le
Sang d'un poète, La Difficulté d'être,* and *Le Journal de La Belle et la Bête;*
Librairie Jules Tallandier, for *Jean Cocteau: Entretien avec Roger Stéphane*
(© 1964 RTF et Librairie Jules Tallandier); New Directions, for *The
Knights of the Round Table* (*Les Chevaliers de la Table Ronde*). The
translation from *Le Livre Blanc* is by permission of M. Edouard Dermit,
sole legatee of Jean Cocteau of l'Académie-Française.

For Monroe Wheeler,
Cocteau's oldest friend in America;
and for Jean-Cégèste and Stephane-Orphée Dermit,
his newest friends in France

CONTENTS

Remembering Cocteau, by Robert Phelps   ix

PART 1   *Le Prince Frivole*   1

CALENDAR: 1889–1900

  1   *My Grandfather's House*   8
  2   *At the Circus*   13
  3   *Theatre*   18
  4   *Dargelos*   23

CALENDAR: 1900–1914

  5   *Les Monstres Sacrés*   31
  6   *Le Beau Monde*   39
  7   *Les Ballets Russes:*
       Diaghilev—Nijinsky—Stravinsky   49
  8   *Rilke's Lamp*   55

PART 2   *Le Rappel à l'Ordre*   59

CALENDAR: 1914–1923

  9   *Montparnasse: Apollinaire and Picasso*   70
 10   *Le Coq et l'Arlequin*   79
 11   *Le Numéro Barbette*   90
 12   *Raymond Radiguet*   94

CALENDAR: 1923–1929

13   *Villefranche: A Letter to Jacques Maritain*   104
14   *Le Livre Blanc: Notes on Homosexuality*   117
15   *Opium: Journal of a Disintoxication*   125

PART 3   *Le Sang d'un Poète*   133

CALENDAR: 1929–1936

16   *Le Sang d'un Poète*   142
17   *Around the World in Eighty Days*   148

CALENDAR: 1936–1940

18   *Of Criminal Innocence*   185

CALENDAR: 1940–1946

19   *Making La Belle et la Bête*   195
20   *My Room in the Palais-Royal*   235

PART 4   *La Difficulté d'être*   239

CALENDAR: 1946–1963

21   *A Letter to Americans*   253
22   *Working in the Theatre*   258
23   *Three Friends: Bérard—Gide—Colette*   273
24   *La Corrida of May 1*   283
25   *Diary of an Unknown Man*   293

A Jury of His Peers   317
Sources and Asides   323

Remembering Cocteau

All his life he was a *Wünderkind*, an eager, trusting, enchanted (and enchanting) child. He believed in fairy tales, in secret signs, in *"monstres sacrés,"* and in emblematic destinies like those of Oedipus, Orpheus, Antigone, and his own *"enfants terribles."* At the same time, he was the sort of child who urgently needs to please, to hold the attention of the grownups, to feel himself noticed, cherished, forgiven, remembered, loved. In a sense, everything he wrote was an effort to delight or seduce. He would produce an article or a drawing for almost anyone who asked, and a large part of his lifework was created at the request of friends. On the very day which was to be his last, French radio listeners heard his recorded voice praising Edith Piaf, who had died a few hours earlier, and for whom he had once written cabaret songs and a play.

Encyclopedias are always a little baffled as to how to classify him, since there is hardly an expressive medium in which he did not make something. He was a writer, of course: of novels and plays and poems, essays and journals, criticism and memoirs, in formats of his own design, often with his own illustrations. But he also made paintings and sculpture (the earliest with pipe cleaners), as well as ballets, movies, stage sets, tapestries, potteries, Christmas cards. He "tattooed" an entire house, an outdoor theatre, four chapels. He wrote dozens of letters daily, usually short and festooned with drawings ("half telegram, half valentine," said Glenway Wescott), and always signed with his trademark star and rooster name. He was an ardent friend, a robust narcissist, a tireless Pied Piper to half a century of flossy Parisians. He talked, dazzlingly, and like Ireland's G. B. Shaw, he had a genius for public relations as well as for literature. Fashion illustrations and perfume ads were not at all beneath him, nor was he ever caught without a memorable press release, whether about himself, or flying saucers, or his newest protégé.

Like Walt Whitman and Gertrude Stein, he will be remembered for his face as much as for his books. He complained about his celebrity, but his nature found it impossible to remain invisible or obscure. *C'était plus fort que lui.* His hands, his hair, his speaking voice, his most personal habits and predilections, all had to get into his creative act, and whether we like it or not, there they are fixed, indiscreet but numinous, alluring to the memory, teasing the imagination, forever renewing their promise to reveal something to us—something about ourselves —which we shall not be able to discover by any other, less equivocal means.

To contain Cocteau's complete works, Auden once said, it would take not a library but a warehouse. Yet today, less than a decade after his death, it already appears that it will be less by his works per se, however various, than by his personality and his legend, that he will remain longest with us. He was a maker, yes; and few twentieth-century writers have a better-wrought product to offer. But it is not with the great impersonal artisan-poets of French literature that he is most readily classed—not with Molière and Racine, Balzac and Flaubert, Mallarmé and Valéry. He belongs rather to that other tradition, equally long and important, whose heroes include Villon and Montaigne, Rousseau and Stendhal, Gide and Jouhandeau, and whose deepest instinct is to record the minutes of its own meeting.

If this is true, then what is the Cocteau Story? By what interpretation does he become more than the spoiled, rich, gifted child, mischievous and frivolous and even dangerous, whom he is sometimes reduced to by people who dislike him? What does his personal history (as touched up in his own presentation, of course, since it was Cocteau after all who said, "I am a lie that always speaks the truth . . .") have to tell us?

Essentially, I think, it is a cautionary tale, a fairy story, about another young Prince Charming who realized one day that the secret of life may lie beyond the classic ideal of Knowing Thyself; that, on the contrary, self-*unknowing* is closer to the heart of the mystery; and that a man's truest self-realization might require him, above all, to learn to close his eyes: to let himself be taken unawares, to follow his dark angel, to risk his illegal instincts, to trust his non-reasonable, "invisible," given self. So the Prince "puts himself to sleep" and begins a new life, dangerous, imprudent, often misunderstood by others and not necessarily understood by himself, but obstinately dedicated to showing us that a man can never know his own truth, but can only embody it, accept it. "*Je ne me lève jamais sans me dire: 'Tu n'y peux rien: accepte . . .'* Every morning I tell myself, 'You can do nothing about it: submit . . .'" The poet is not only a man who makes memorable phrases; he is also someone in whose image, somehow, sooner or later, the rest of us recognize behavior or values for which we would otherwise lack an example. By his embodied existence, he enables us to see.

One of Cocteau's most original plays is a cabaret-farce-*cum*-morality-pageant called *The Knights of the Round Table*. At the climax, Sir Galahad reveals the Holy Grail to King Arthur's court, and as everyone exclaims in wonder, Galahad quietly asks what it looks like.

> KING ARTHUR: Galahad, why do you ask us to explain the Grail? . . . Is it not you who should be explaining it to us?
> GALAHAD: I cannot see it. . . . I shall never see it. I am the one who makes it visible to others.

This is Cocteau's basic view of all art, all artists. The creating man is not so much an entertainer, or even a maker, as he is a priest. Cocteau saw his own life as a living parable, and in some of his later books there even appear chronologies, with the dates of his significant encounters and turning points. It is as though he were at once Orpheus and his own Bulfinch. The poet takes Picasso to Rome; he meets Raymond Radiguet; he quarrels with Stravinsky. He is betrayed in love; he finds consolation in opium; he moves to the South of France. He makes his first film; he travels around the world; he suffers a dozen psychosomatic illnesses—all so many stages on life's way, as full of import and allegory as *Pilgrim's Progress.*

It looks like narcissism—excessive, obsessive, unrelenting narcissism. In a way, it is. (A poet's strengths are inseparable from his weaknesses.) But it is also something more. For Cocteau believed (or trusted) that his own history was as emblematic as that of Orpheus, his own encounters as fatal as those of Oedipus, his own beloveds as heroic as Eurydice or Hippolytus. And just as we no longer have Orpheus' own poems, only his myth and the meanings we continue to read into it, so Cocteau implies that his personal trajectory of suffering and choice may remain in human memory, and usable to human speculation, longer than his created works of art.

A strange, childlike assumption, certainly. Only a funambulist as nimble and self-loving *and* courageous as Cocteau would have dared to propose it. In the light of common sense, everyday living—and especially in the context of our own half of the century, in which Cocteau's Europe may well be, as Valéry declared in 1945, *fini*—it seems preposterous. But then, to his contemporaries, Kierkegaard seemed preposterous, as did Joan of Arc and Socrates and Oscar Wilde and the original Orpheus himself to theirs. Meanwhile, less than a decade after Cocteau's death, he is already a semi-mythic presence in twentieth-century civilization. No single play or novel or poem or drawing or film he ever made is quite as memorable, curious, and portending as

Cocteau himself. His best pages—for instance, the Sphinx's speech in *The Infernal Machine*—seem like so many "lines" which Bulfinch-Cocteau recorded from Orpheus-Cocteau's flashing table talk. And then, like the last eloquent line of a sonnet sequence, there is his tomb.

On the outskirts of Milly-la-Fôret, the village near Fontainebleau where Cocteau settled after 1947, he found a neglected chapel which had been used, centuries before, by a colony of lepers, who had supported themselves by selling medicinal herbs. It was called Saint-Blaise-des-Simples, and it was as tiny as a chapel could be, much taller than it was wide or deep, more like a shallow cistern, though with exquisite proportions. With permission from the local authorities, Cocteau proceeded to have it cleaned and then to annotate its walls with his own "handwriting," as revealing and unofficial as doodles on a telephone pad. Over the altar there is a risen Christ, surrounded by body-builder guards and rapt angels; on the walls there are slender botanical drawings of herb flowers—belladonna, valerian, saffron, spearwort, arnica, henbane; and near the door, straddling Cocteau's signature, there is a wistful cat, gazing up at the angels as though he imagined they were so many meadow larks.

It is the most personal tomb a poet has ever had—far from the congested pomp of Père-Lachaise or Montmartre; comparable only to Chateaubriand's lonely island in Saint-Malo bay, though less remote and austere. Outside, there are farmer's fields, swallows in the Ile-de-France sky, motorcars shifting gears in the distance. Inside, it is quiet, intimate, homemade. Cocteau's body lies just below the stone floor, with his own last promise—at once generous and eager—inscribed above: "*Je reste avec vous* . . . I remain with you."

Not only his works, then, but something closer to himself, closer to his own image and voice and life's mystery, is what he has left us.

ROBERT PHELPS

*. . . ne plus envisager l'art
comme une distraction,
mais comme un sacerdoce . . .*

. . . no longer to consider art
as an amusement,
but as a priesthood . . .

I

Le Prince Frivole
1889–1914

*Un jeune homme ne doit pas
acheter de valeurs sûres*

A young man must not make
safe investments

Jean Cocteau and his mother

Dargelos

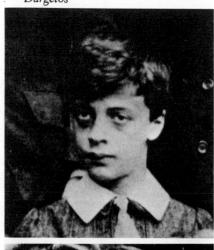

Cocteau in school

Sarah Bernhardt

Mistinguett

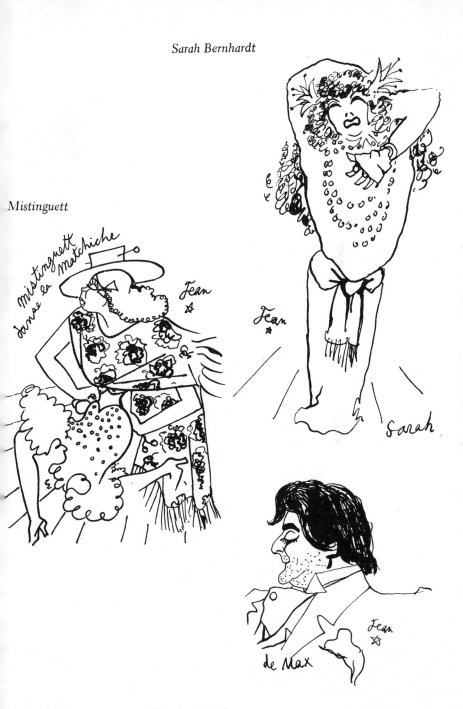

Edouard de Max

ove: Cocteau, as caricatured by Sem, 1912

posite: Cocteau at his architect's writing table, about 1916

low: Stravinsky, as caricatured by Cocteau, 1913

Cocteau at the time he met la Comtesse de Noailles

CALENDAR

1889–1900

Today, as it was eighty years ago, Maisons-Laffitte is a suburb of Paris, about twenty miles downstream on the left bank of the Seine, a little beyond Bougival, where Turgenev once built a house, and adjoining the 10,000-acre forest of Saint-Germain. The Cocteau family house is gone, and what was once its garden has been broken up into small building lots. But otherwise the village remains unchanged. There are private estates, mostly belonging to Paris financiers. There are racing stables, and along the river front there is a track for steeplechase racing. There is a model château, the masterpiece of the great seventeenth-century architect François Mansart, which the government acquired in 1904 and has since turned into a museum.

Here, in his Grandfather Eugène Lecomte's house on the Place Sully, Jean-Maurice Cocteau was born very early (3:50 a.m.) on the summer morning of July 5, 1889. "He weighs seven pounds," wrote his grandmother proudly. "He's well made, a truly handsome infant, with very thick black hair and the best-shaped head I have ever seen on a newborn child. He's not at all ugly. In fact, he's a lovely little old man . . ."

My Grandfather's House

> *"I prefer the mythologist
> to the historian . . ."*

Often memories are nothing. As though a window curtain were to remain intact during a fire, the silliest image comes down from the attic of recollection, while momentous ones remain there. One of my great memories is of having filched out of my grandfather's bedroom, after he died, a package of dreadful cigarettes, Nazilles or Nazirs, I can't remember which, and some kind of cigarette holder. I pocketed them all, and can still see myself at Maisons-Laffitte, among the paths and tall grass of the Place Sully, smoking that cigarette with the sovereign awareness of disobeying. I was happy.

*

Mine was the childhood of all children. My brother and sister were much older than I; my real brother and sister were my cousins Pierre and Marianne Lecomte. One day Marianne led me out to the coachhouse (We also had a kitchen garden, a continual wonder! The old gardener had given his children strange names he found in some old books my grandfather had thrown away: he baptized his daughter Iphigénie and his son Antoride); there, she made me climb into the big carriage that took us to Mass on Sunday mornings, and she told me: *Now I know everything, there are grownups who go to bed in the afternoon, the men are called bunnies, the women pussies, and if you tell I'll hit you with the shovel till you're dead. Uncle André is a bunny.* That is childhood! We had been given a mechanical swimming toy which had broken, and all that was left of it was the spring; when the spring was stretched taut it was the *Moscovi*, and when it was released it was the *Moscova*—and that would send us into fits of hysterical laughter! . . . My family was driven mad by our *fous-rires!* But what is beautiful in childhood is precisely that kind of absurdity, that purity of childhood which is truly absurd.

*

In Paris—Rue La Bruyère—we lived during my whole childhood in an *hôtel particulier* whose courtyard adjoined the Jardins Gaveau. My grandparents lived upstairs, in an apartment the architect's whim had so arranged that you had to walk along corridors, climb up and down steep stairways in order to get from one room to another—an ideal apartment for the ghosts and gallops of childhood. So often have I constructed and elaborated that apartment in my dreams that I can no longer put it back where it belongs. The apartment has left the building and floated free, like a Montgolfier balloon. I remember our own apartment, our own rooms, and very very far away another world, an unreal and fabulous region, the apartment where my grandfather kept a silver bathtub that rang like a gong, full of shoes and books, and where he collected Greek busts, Ingres drawings, Delacroix paintings, Florentine medals, autographs of cabinet ministers, masks of Antinous, teardrop *flacons*, and Stradivarius violins. There was even an old box with a wig of Rossini's in it.

When my mother was a little girl, her family had lived in the same house as the composer, and my mother would be sent with eggs, which had been brought fresh from the country, to Rossini. Madame Rossini dared not enter her husband's bedroom, for he had a terrible temper; my mother would creep in, glimpsing on the piano a series of wigs destined for the monumental egg emerging from the sheets and eiderdowns. These wigs, on their stands, ranged from short hair to long. The maestro wore them one after the next, until the barber's imaginary visit.

One of these wigs, in its oval green box, became a fetish of my childhood, the goal of secret forages in my grandfather's closet. But I preferred the cabinets of masks and violins. Behind their glass, the Antinous masks with their enamel eyes, pale terra-cotta cheeks and necklaces of beard, were arranged in tiers on red velvet, like an opera box by Manet. The violins decorated the billiard room. They were kept in cases lined with royal-blue velvet on top of an ebony cabinet whose drawers contained resin, extra strings, and billiard chalks. For these treasures were used. Even the sacred Stradivariuses, which resonate when another Stradivarius is played *anywhere,* vacated the blue velvet on the evenings the quartet assembled: Sarasate, Sivori, Gré-bert, and their host, the amateur Eugène Lecomte. On those chamber-music evenings, my cousins and I played a special game which consisted in creeping up the formal staircase which connected the two floors and which, as I have said, by means of that magic locating the upper apartment outside space, became a site in and of itself, autonomous, closed off at the top landing by a gate installed by my grandfather to keep us from falling downstairs.

The game, then, consisted in waiting for Sarasate's arrival, hidden behind a red-plush lantern halberd we used for playing "poor prisoner," and then, as soon as he stopped to arrange his hair in front of the hall mirror, shutting the gate and thereby creating the tableau: *the lion tamer caged!*

With his huge mustache, his gray mane, his frogged Prince Albert, his watch chain, and his trousers strapped under tiny patent-leather boots, we considered Sarasate, behind the bars, as a lion in lion tamer's costume, a result which satisfied our longing, before the fact, for animated cartoons and for high caricature.

But the real spectacle, the show we most enjoyed, was put on during vacations at Maisons-Laffitte, a kind of racing grounds strewn with villas, gardens, avenues of lindens, lawns, flower beds, and fountains in the squares. Here thoroughbreds and bicycles prevailed, and we played tennis at each other's houses in a bourgeois world divided by the Dreyfus affair. The Seine, the track, the tiny gate in the wall round the Forêt Saint-Germain, the empty lots where we played detective, the campsite down the slope, the outdoor restaurants with their arbors, the village carnival, the fireworks, the feats of the firemen, Mansart's château with its overgrown bushes and busts of Roman emperors—all this created for childhood a realm calculated to flatter its illusion of living in places unique in all the world.

The trainers lived high. Max Lebaudy, known as the "little sugarbowl," washed his barouches in champagne and organized *corridas.* At one of these we saw Mme du Gast, president of the Society for the Protection of Animals, arrested for disturbing the peace. There were gymkhanas with sack races and ladies exercising beribboned rabbits on leashes.

Sundays at dawn, in the Place Sully, which sported in its center a gas lamp and a bed of begonias, my grandfather would post himself in a tussore jacket and a straw hat on backwards, a little bunch of primroses in one hand, peering down the lanes to the race track. Suddenly, under an implacable sun, the virtuosi arrived. They arrived in an open fiacre, without a coachman. The fiacre of the virtuosi! Melpomene or some instrumental allegory must have been enthroned, invisible, upon the box.

Sarasate, right foot on his left knee, shoulders pressed against the deep upholstery, wearing a Prince Albert, an opera hat, and red leather gloves, held the reins and drove the pair from the inside banquette. Once they had reached our house, the exhausted horses were unharnessed and served a mash of hot burgundy and carrots, and the virtuosi dined. Sivori was a dwarf. At table, my grandmother ensconced him on a stack of scores. *Not on Beethoven, madame!* he would exclaim, *not on*

Beethoven! and spear another strawberry with his toothpick. My grandfather cut his meat with the same gesture he would use, in a little while, on the music, his bow frisking over the phrases. Indeed, that chamber music was not meant to be heard, to please, but to be executed, measured, nodded out by the leader. A sport, an exercise like any other: fencing, rowing, boxing. It offered everyone satisfaction, brought old friends together, kept them from quarreling, insured our unpunished forays into forbidden rooms, affording us charades and *fous-rires.*

Grébert played the cello. Each time my grandmother, at the other end of the room, tiptoed past, holding her knitting, he would stand up and bow, still playing, tilted over the void.

After the quartet, our virtuosi dressed up in whatever costumes they could find and went off to serenade a neighbor on the Place Sully, the lady doctor Mme Gache-Sarrothe, inventor of the strait jacket. Evening was falling. The Great Bear lit up over the garden. The sprinkler system inspired the heliotropes. Dinner was served—to the children in a separate dining room said to be for "minor offenders," where my Cousin Pierre refused to eat except from the plates with Napoleon's initials. After dinner the gentlemen seasoned their meerschaums, and Sarasate described his conquests of Europe. He exhibited at the end of his watch chain a tiny gold coffin containing an infinitesimal and quite realistic violin presented to him by the Queen of Spain. One evening the infinitesimal and realistic violin fell into a stein of beer. Attempts were made to fish it out with a straw. Amid general consternation, Sarasate clutched his hair in both hands and shrieked with a tremendous rolling of *r*'s: *Le violon de la Reine! Le violon de la Reine!*

Such moments have no interest save to illuminate the angle from which a child glimpses the grownups, on all fours, behind pantry doors and on staircases, with eyes that admit only poetic intensity.

At the Circus

"There are poets and grownups."

Childhood has its smells. I remember, among others, the paste of the scrapbooks we made when we were sick, the lindens of Maisons-Laffitte that went wild at the approach of thunder, the delicious gunpowder stuck to the carcasses we picked up in the grass the day after the fireworks, the arnica for wasp stings, the mildewed paper of an old file of *La Revue des Deux Mondes*, the upholstery of our big carriage, kept in the cool shed where a chaos of stakes, sprinklers, croquet sets, and badminton nets clustered around it. I should add the heady fragrance of the compost heap and of the ground spattered with white droppings under the tree where the greengages split their sides falling. Not to forget the smell of the geranium pots in the cold frame and of the pond with its dead frogs posing like opera tenors, one hand over the heart. Later I was to discover the smell of Marseilles which inspires hope, of ambergris which comes to life on the skin and makes you blush, of the crushed lilies of alcoves, and of the opium which betrays a China of exquisite manners and slow tortures.

But none of these, profound and even solemn as they were, approached the smell of the Circus, the smell of the Nouveau-Cirque, the great marvelous smell. Of course you knew it consisted of horse manure, tanbark, stables, healthy sweat, but it also contained something indescribable, a mixture which escaped analysis, an amalgam of expectation and excitement that caught in your throat, that habitually preceded the show instead of a curtain going up. And the deep richness of my childhood compost heap reminds me that this circus smell is a kind of weightless compost, a flying golden dung-dust rising under the glassed-in dome, rainbowing the light globes, haloing the acrobats' exertions, then subsiding, sinking back to fertilize the motley clowns, helping them to bloom.

No sooner had I emerged, escorted by the usher and Fraülein Josephine, at the top of the little stairs to one of the hatchway entrances, than this vibrant dust caught my eye, aureoling with a kind of apotheosis the rigging, the poles, and the band perched in mid-air; the huge nave exploded into laughter around me, into a music of trumpets, trombones, drums, and golden cymbals. The acrobats and clowns were the best part of the show for me, features of the program like the Augustes who fill the gaps between acts and help roll up the tarpaulins. And to their act itself, I preferred the acrobats' bird-catching gestures, the slippers they rubbed with resin, the towel they would shrug off their shoulders, the entire family's final salute, then their reappearance, known as the *rentrée gracieuse,* at a run and a leap! then the sudden stop, hands high, smiling from the tips of their toes to the roots of their hair. The net was a no-man's-land, between heaven and earth. For the motion-picture camera had not yet proved that the crudest, the most aggressive spectacle contains a vanishing angel, a departing fume, once the slow-motion shutter checks the rhythm of life.

The orchestra stopped short. The crowd waited, gaping, and a drumroll accompanied the acrobats' fall. The acrobats dropped. They dropped, languidly they died and languidly stood up again, walking languidly across the net with great strides, a post-mortem gait. Released from the blood's burden, they set their feet in a slow, nightmare soil, like the globs of phosphorescence caught between the dark meshes of a fish net.

One act we loved, aside from our clowns and acrobats, was the Mexican Sharpshooters—the term "cowboy"was still unknown. Men and women in fringed leather trousers put their lassos through calisthenics which ended, on Monday, at home, with furniture broken, tearful scenes, and a session in the closet.

Footit and Chocolat came in the second part. A tiny pony galloped around the red-velvet rim of the ring, the *Entr'acte* placard on its back. The audience stood up, walked around, went backstage. Grooms in pale-blue uniforms with brass buttons dismantled the poles, hoisted the trapezes, put away the marksmen's targets, the jugglers' stands, the conjurers' tables; hawkers of mints, caramels, and lemon drops droned their litanies; children turned somersaults on the matting; the Augustes served lemonade; and the intermission ended, bringing me closer to the sinister finale, to the end, to the exit where you couldn't find your overcoat sleeve because of a last despairing glance at the empty ring.

But we are not there yet. Footit and Chocolat are about to come onstage. No, what am I saying? They would never make the mistake of coming onstage, of performing in a music hall. They come *into the ring*, not at all the same as coming onstage. One must not confuse a medal with a statue, and I am amazed that today's clowns consent to perform in profile, on a mere stage. It seems that the danger of not being funny, or danger itself, can loom up from nowhere with all the cunning of a bull, obliging the circus performer to make his countless Spanish twirls. The obstacle of the footlights and the orchestra pit, the trap of the wings and the dead end of the backcloth betray him. High-wire artists and the great clowns are consecrated, I think, to the arena, to that ring surrounded by eyes. If only by the style of their costumes which already links them to the bullfighter.

Footit had the bullfighter's sequins, his grace, charm, glory, and glamour. He won that glory and that glamour from children, the most difficult audience in the world; he managed that tour de force of entertaining grownups as well, giving them back their childhood. Childhood identifies itself with that

nervous excitement of the clowns when they learn a new trick
and decide to try it out on one of themselves, with the scolding
of the ringmaster, the refusals to work, the insubordinations
and mistakes in syntax. Chocolat, a slow-witted Negro in black
silk tights and a red tail coat, was the scapegoat of endless
tongue lashings, cuffs, and kicks.

With his tasseled shorts, his huge naked calves, his starched
collar, his Goldilock curls, his cruel grease paint, the grimace of
his gory lips, his pointed hat which emitted, at each drubbing, a
cloud of flour, his sequined breast band, his mad-duchess
voice—in short, by a mixture of nurse, baby, and English lady-
in-waiting (his hairdo was part Sarah Bernhardt, part Queen
Alexandra), Footit brought into the ring an atmosphere of
Satan's nursery, in which the children recognized their secret
skirmishes and whose grandeur subjugated the grownups themselves.

The main attraction of the program was the nautical pantomime. The Rising of the Waters fills me, still, with poignant
regret. No trick, no movie montage, will replace that marvel:
cleared of its matting, the green ring sinks with a muffled roar.
Tiny plumes of water spurt up between the planks. And the
whole circus is transformed into a pool, another world. Water-
lily leaves on which an organdy ballerina pirouettes, a transparent mill whose rooms are filled with ghosts, a stag pursued
by hounds into the depths, Footit who lures a floating calf's-
head by offering olive oil and vinegar, and then the China of
Papa Chrysanthème, a number in which Chocolat returns from
Paris in a beige bowler, bawling out the popular refrain:

> *Ta-ra-ra-BOUM-di-hé,*
> *La grammair' ça m'fait suer!*

That was the Nouveau-Cirque when we were seven. And that
same Nouveau-Cirque was to become, five years later, in 1904,

the site of a historic theatrical event: the advent of American rhythm.

All of a sudden, the cakewalk came, and everything else turned pale and fled. Spotlights exploded from the soffits of the Nouveau-Cirque, red-white-and-blue silk streamers were draped around the entrances, the first Negroes (poor Chocolat was all we had known) solemnly introduced *le Cake*, a tidal wave of elegance broke over the rows of women covered with pearls and feathers, of monocled men with cropped hair or gleaming heads, the orchestra attacked, with all its brass and its drums, an unfamiliar music whose rhythms evoked the marches Souza had conducted here with a punctuation of pistol shots, the spotlights converged like ballerinas between the hedges of blue grooms, and Les Elks appeared.

Spotlights do not work in every case. Sometimes they pick out some poor wretches merely to emphasize their solitude. Rare are the artists who glow, who shimmer under the shower of light. Monsieur and Madame Elks possessed this privilege of diamonds and of stars. The house rose stamping to its feet, and in the very center of that delirious public, Monsieur and Madame Elks danced. They danced: skinny, crooked, beribboned, glittering with sequins, spangled with gaudy lights, hats raked over their eyes, their ears, knees higher than their thrust-out chins, hands twirling flexible canes, wrenching their gestures from themselves and hammering the artificial floor with the taps on their patent-leather shoes. They danced, they glided, they reared, they kicked, they broke themselves in two, three, four, they stood up again, they bowed . . . And behind them the whole city, the whole of Europe began dancing. And following their example the rhythm seized the New World, and after the new the old, and that rhythm spread to machines, and from machines returned to men, and this went on and on, and Les Elks are dead, Chocolat and Footit dead, the Nouveau-Cirque dead, and dead or alive the procession is still dancing, led by the tiny canes and the beribboned skeletons of Les Elks.

Theatre

I want the kind of readers who remain children at any cost. I can tell them at a glance: loyalty to that first enchantment guards better than any cosmetic, than any diet, against the insults of age. But alas for such readers, who would huddle safe and sound in the asylum of their credulous enchantment as if in the womb—our enervating century offends them by its chaos, its fidgets of light and space, the host of its excuses for dividing, for rending oneself from others and from oneself.

The child wants a room, in which to collect his toys, his loves. He detests what disperses, is partial to the kind of diseases that cluster and close up tight. I carried this loathing of leavetakings, of places where you cannot visualize those you love, to the point of idolizing thunder. The gentle bowling of an April's thunder, that cooing Sunday thunder which rearranges the furniture of heaven—I still worship it, for such thunder was the signal that there would be no expeditions, that the family would stay home, that my cousins and I would play with my blocks, that the nursemaids would sit sewing in a circle, that I would hear the quartet and then the billiard balls clicking downstairs, testifying to the childishness of grownups.

Accursed were the occasions which, on Sunday, forced me out of my snug dreams, out of my lair, my refuge. Accursed, except for two: one of which resulted from the dissatisfaction of grownups, one from their satisfaction. These two exceptional occasions provoked what we called "the little death," an exquisite and inextricable anxiety coveted, concealed, longed for, dreaded, in which the pride or shame of being rewarded or punished played no part. The first occasion prolonged the dream of a Sunday in the country, the second of a Sunday in

town. Both released me, in a sense, substituting for my intimate
methods of enchantment an accidental and unpredictable kind.
This was the first: clutching a smelly cup in my right hand, a
mint drop in my left, I would refuse the Sunday-morning laxative. Coaxed, I would refuse. Threatened, I would refuse.
Implored, I would refuse. No sooner had my mother's already
terrible eyes sprung the trap of her still-charming voice, no
sooner had the slap brushed my cheek, than *the little death*
began.

Well as I knew the scheme, *the little death* always managed,
when it appeared, to take me by surprise. It took me over its
shoulder, in a sack. Pierre Barère, my grandfather's sidewhis-
kered servant (he ate snails alive, crunching the shells), would
dress up as Mère Lachique. After a brief realistic scene, he
thrust me into the sack and ran up and down the house until I
was dizzy and no longer knew where I was. I believed everything, savored my terror. My heart pounded, my tongue went
dry, my ears buzzed, and I came out of the sack drunk on
darkness and dreams, ready to refuse the laxative, having really
crossed the river of the dead and squeezing in one hand, by way
of a funerary obol, a half-melted mint drop.

In town, *the little death* resulted from a reward: theatre
tickets! We were going to the theatre! No sooner had I heard
the great news than the mechanism started up: a dim endless
corridor, a corridor of the little death, opened in my fevered
sleep, crossed Sunday morning and ended in broad daylight,
opposite the tribunal of black-robed matinee ticket takers at the
Châtelet or the Nouveau-Cirque.

La Biche au Bois, Le Tour du Monde—first shows, first rap-
tures! Later, when we know the actors, the directors, the wings,
when the newspapers and our own work put us in contact with
the stage, it is too late to be in the house. We know where we
are. There is no more to it than that. And never will the dying
Tristan's lament as he stares out to sea supplant in our souls

Phileas Fogg's "Twenty-thousand pounds for you, Captain, if we reach Liverpool tonight!"

*

Often, too, my Lecomte cousins and I would put in a modest appearance at the Palais de Glace on the Champs-Elysées. I don't think the décor has altered much. The monumental mint drop covered with ice shavings by the sudden stops of the figure skaters who bear down, bent double, cigarette held behind their back, and who abruptly about-face, rigid, dead-pan, upright, against the barrier, amid tiny screams from an onlooking female admirer, the band shaking its Basque tambourines, catching up the beats of the skaters' waltz with all the sonority of a cathedral, the white dust silvering that band the way the Nouveau-Cirque's aerial manure gilded the acrobat families—no, except for the tunes in favor, it seems to me that the azure plush of the draped mirrors, the rosettes and canopies of the barrier, the slender cast-iron alcazar of the boxes, pillars, and arcades must be about the same.

At five, the Palais de Glace, as though under a spell, emptied out its students, its adolescent cousins and family groups, making way for the feathered ladies of the fashionable world. This was the hour of the *grandes cocottes* who no longer exist, and of the half-beavers. In the dressing room, we unscrewed our skates, and the attendants scolded us when we lagged behind as we always did, postponing our departure as long as we possibly could. What we wanted was to cheat the schedule and stay late enough to watch the entrance of the cocottes and the actresses.

Then appeared a creature whose very name, in that place, was a masterpiece: Polaire! A yellow serpent's flat head balancing the Portuguese oysters of her eyes that twinkled with nacre, with salt, with cool shadows, her features drawn tight, lashed to the nape of her neck by a huge black Percheron knot, the inverted brims of her felt toque riding her bangs, a Lalique jewel for a belt buckle, the slit skirt revealing black stockings and high-buttoned shoes on cruel blades, the actress, violent as an insult in Yiddish, stood poised at the rink's edge, rigid, upright, in the posture of a *crise de nerfs*.

A child's eyes register fast. Later he develops the film. I see again as if it were yesterday the frogging on the olive-green tunics of the instructors in their caviar caps, their dressmaker's boots. They are waltzing. The cocottes are named Liane de this, Liane de that, and all these lianas coil round the olive-green instructor. Fur muffs down, they dash forward, circle, sway, bend, uncoil, rise again, imitating the noble curves of the Métro entrances, and cross the rink, eyes lowered. Between numbers, silver blades screwed into the Louis XVI heels, they limp toward the washrooms or perch, in dry dock, around tables.

One of these tables grouped Willy, Colette, and her bulldog. Willy, his huge mustache and imperial à la Tartarin, his eyes sharp under their drooping lids, his lavaliere, his top hat glistening above its pasteboard aureole, his bishop's hands clasped over the knob of his stick. Beside him, our Colette. Not that sturdy Colette who serves us succulent salads with raw onion in them and does her marketing at Hédiard's . . . but a slim Colette, this one, a kind of tiny fox in cycling clothes, or a fox terrier in skirts and a black spot over one eye, a knot of red veiling tucked above one temple.

*

My mother and my father would go to the Comédie-Française or to the Opéra, and on those evenings I was the audience for my mother's toilette. A cloud of perfume and mauve rice powder embalmed her bedroom, the penumbra between the chintzes with their motley foliage (exotic trees and tropical birds). A door ajar on the intense gaslight of the bathroom illuminated the mirrored cabinet in which the scene was reflected—lovelier, deeper. It was in that mirror that I followed the preparations. My svelte mother, monumental and foreshortened from my seat between the dressing table and the fireplace, seemed to be supported by the long, stiff, red-velvet gown embroidered with jet beads, a gown from Chez Raudnitz with puff sleeves out of which the pale arms, shoulders, and décolleté emerged above a fringe of the same red velvet trimming a very simple bodice, décor appropriate to the classic scene at the box rim: tortoiseshell-and-black-lace fan fluttering, mother-of-pearl lorgnette raised, discreet applause. Such, at least, was the pantomime I imagined during the ceremony of the long gloves, so difficult to pull on, dead skins which came to life, gradually taking shape until the successive effort of each finger and the adorable final rite which consisted in buttoning over the wrist, with a crucially feminine gesture, the tiny circlet where I kissed the bare palm. That was the end of the show, prologue to the real spectacle for which all these graces were devised, and the wardrobe mirror showed me my mother, or indeed that madonna encased in velvet, choked by diamonds, beplumed with a dusky aigrette, standing tall and bristling with brilliance, like a glittering horse chestnut, distracted, torn between last-minute instructions to be good and a final glance in the mirror. The prostrate chambermaid, spreading the train, conferred upon my mother the final nobility of a Spanish Virgin. Then a fur cape hid all the bouquets and luminous daggers, Maman bent down, kissed me quickly, and left for that ocean of murmurs, jewels, feathers, and bald heads into which she would cast herself like a red river and mingle her velvet with the velvet of the box, her scintillation with that of the great chandelier.

For a long time I was not allowed to go to the theatre, and I knew about it only from the programs my mother forgot in my room. When my brother Paul was taken to the opera—*Samson et Dalila,* I think it was—I consoled myself somewhat with the thought that one of us had now embarked upon the red river, and that it would soon be my turn to know those forbidden great gold rooms. When I had scarlet fever or German measles and was kept in bed—and also when I faked appendicitis to stay home from school—I would design scenery for my toy theatre. My Fraülein Joséphine sewed the costumes. We hammered, cut, pasted, and painted; we made footlights out of candles, and a collapsing prompter's box. I think that was when I caught the red and gold disease of the theatre, from which I have never recovered.

Dargelos

*"Since childhood he had longed
to be those he found beautiful,
not to be loved by them."*

Among these memories, I cannot pass over my *lycée* in silence —to my great shame. For I was the typical bad student, incapable of learning, of retaining anything. Prizes in gymnastics, German, and drawing merely emphasized my misconduct—surrounded it with a gold frame. If I close my eyes, my school memories are vacant, even sinister: guillotine awakenings, tears, squalid notebooks, ruler swats across the fingers, squeaking chalk, Sunday detentions, empty classrooms stinking of gas, tiny prison desks on which I copied out a thousand times "eight and eight do not make fourteen" in a handwriting flabbier than blotters; suburban stations, grim departures and grim returns, autumn trains in which the older boys trussed us up and pitched us into the baggage nets.

I could describe other tortures: dormitories at dawn, mortal terrors of being questioned, attempts to crib from one's deskmate protecting himself behind walls of dictionaries, deluges of threats, discovery of indecent caricatures, cold sweats until the deliverance of the bell which provoked a happy pandemonium and set my heart beating again. My poor family despaired and

tried everything . . . the Petit Condorcet, the Grand Condorcet, Fénelon, private tutors! But it is no use, when a head
empties as fast as it is filled, when a boy, set apart for secret
tasks, tries to preserve his somnambulist's sleep only to be
roused with a start at the far edge of his dream by well-meaning
murderers.

*

At the Lycée Condorcet, our senses wakened uncontrollably
and grew like weeds. Everyone had a hole in his pocket, a damp
handkerchief. Art classes especially inspired us, concealed behind the rampart of our drawing boards. Sometimes, during the
other classes, a sarcastic master would suddenly call on a
student at the point of orgasm. The boy stood up, cheeks
flaming, and stammered whatever came into his head, trying to
turn a dictionary into a fig leaf. Our laughter increased his
embarrassment.

The classroom reeked of gas, chalk, and sperm. This amalgam
revolted me. It must be said that because what the others regarded as a vice was nothing of the kind to me or, to be more
precise, was merely a crude parody of a form of love my instincts already revered, I was the only boy in the school who
seemed to condemn this state of affairs. Which resulted in
perpetual taunts and onslaughts on what my schoolmates took
for modesty.

But Condorcet was a day-boy lycée, and these practices did
not ripen into love affairs; they scarcely exceeded the limits of a
clandestine game.

One of the boys, named Dargelos, enjoyed tremendous prestige because of a virility far beyond his years. He exhibited
himself cynically enough, and capitalized on a spectacle granted
even to boys of other grades in exchange for rare stamps or
cigarettes. Seats near his desk were in great demand. Rivalry for
his favor spawned intrigues worthy of the memorialists of
Versailles.

He was handsome, let me add: he had the beauty of an animal, of a tree, of a stream, that insolent beauty which is only heightened by filth, which seems unaware of itself, which turns to advantage its every resource and needs merely to appear in order to persuade. This robust, devious, obvious beauty bewitched precisely those surest of being insensitive to it: the headmaster, the monitor, the masters, tutors, proctors, even the porter. Imagine the chaos Dargelos provoked—cock of the walk, ringleader, unpunished rebel, with his dark shock of hair over slanting eyes, his proud, scraped knees—in these grubs so greedy for love, so unversed in the riddle of the senses, and utterly defenseless against the terrible damages inflicted upon any sensitive soul by the supernatural sex of beauty.

I have always assumed that Dargelos was conscious of his privilege and exploited it. He was the school vamp. He dazzled, disdained, despised us all from the vantage of his endowments, developing in us that overrated but indisputable *inferiority complex* which even more than pride is the cause of so many miseries.

His presence made me ill. I avoided Dargelos, and spied on him. I dreamed of some miracle which would draw his attention to me, dissolve his pride, reveal the meaning of my attitude, which he must have taken for absurd prudery and which was merely an insane craving to please him.

My emotion was vague: I could not clarify its meaning beyond an alternation of torment and rapture. All I was sure of was that it had nothing to do with what my schoolmates felt.

One day, unable to endure it any longer, I confided in a boy whose family knew mine and whom I used to see outside of school. "How stupid you are," he told me. "It's so easy! Ask Dargelos over one Sunday, take him behind the bushes, and that will do the trick." What trick? There was no trick. I stammered that I didn't mean a pleasure easy enough to take in class, and vainly struggled with language to give a form to my dream. My friend shrugged. "Why make such a fuss about it?

Dargelos is stronger than we are (he used other words). The minute you flatter him, he does what you want. If it matters that much to you, you can have all you want of him."

The crudity of this judgment stunned me. I realized it was impossible to make myself understood. Even supposing, I mused, that Dargelos accepts such an invitation, what would I say to him, what would I do? I didn't want to play with him for five minutes, I wanted to live with him forever. In short, I worshipped him, and resigned myself to suffer in silence, for without giving my suffering the name of love, I realized that it was the contrary of the schoolroom exercises and that it would meet with no response.

This adventure which had no beginning came to an end. Urged on by the friend in whom I had confided, I asked Dargelos to meet me in an empty classroom after the five-o'clock study hall. He came. I had counted on a miracle to show me what to do. In his presence I lost my head. All I could see were his muscular legs, his knees blazoned with scabs and ink.

"What do you want," he asked, with a cruel smile. I guessed what he was thinking, and that my request had had no other meaning for him. I blurted out the first thing that came into my head.

"I just wanted to tell you the monitor's out to get you." This was a ridiculous fib, for Dargelos had bewitched all our masters.

He ducked his head and made a face. "The monitor?"

"Yes," I went on, drawing strength from my own terror, "the monitor. I heard him telling the headmaster, 'I'm keeping an eye on Dargelos—he's gone too far this time.' "

"Gone too far!" he said. "Listen, boy, I'll show him how far I can go—I'll show him during drill; and as for you, if you come bothering me like this again, I'm warning you, next time you'll get your ass kicked in."

I can still see his brown skin. From his very brief shorts and the way he never pulled up his socks, you could tell he was proud of his legs. We all wore the same kind of shorts, but

because of his manly legs, only Dargelos looked *naked*. His open
shirt revealed a powerful neck. A thick tangle of hair overhung
his forehead. His face with its rather thick lips, slanting eyes,
and snub nose offered every feature of the type which would
become my downfall: the wiles of dissembling fate afford us the
illusion of freedom, yet in the end always lead us into the same
trap.

*

Now Dargelos has left my personal Olympus, and like the
gypsy violinist who detaches himself from the orchestra to play
among the tables, he serves the dream to a host of unknown
readers. I have not changed his name. Dargelos was Dargelos.
The name is pride's program. Where does he live now? Is he
alive? Will he show himself? Shall I see his sarcastic ghost
appear, my book in his hand?

Perhaps I would be astounded to encounter another Dargelos
now, humble, sluggish, timid, stripped of his legend and regret-
ting, through me, what he must have taken, ultimately, for
faults, and perhaps managed to overcome. Perhaps he will ask
me to restore his power to him, and the secrets of his prestige. I
prefer him to remain in the dark where I have substituted for
him *his constellation*, to remain for me the type of all that is
not taught or learned or judged, of all that is not analyzed or
punished, of all that is singularized in a person, the first symbol
of the wild forces which inhabit us, which the social machinery
tries to extinguish, and which beyond good and evil maneuver
the individuals whose example consoles us for living.

CALENDAR

1900–1914

Cocteau's father died when Jean was ten years old ("My father was a painter, and now whenever I smell turpentine I see him . . ."). The next year, 1900, he entered a private school, the Petit Condorcet, and proceeded on to the Grand Condorcet in 1902. In 1904 he was expelled and for a time he studied privately at the pension of a M. Dietz, but he soon ran away and, according to his own account, ended up in Marseilles:

"An old Annamese woman found me absolutely lost and wandering up and down the waterfront. I told her lies, that my family was monstrous, that I never wanted to go home again. So she took me to the Old Quarter of the city and there I stayed for a year—my best period!—working with the boys who showed tourists the local sights and took them dancing at night. I even lived under a false name. A boy had been drowned and I had his identification papers. But finally my uncle sent two policemen after me and I was marched back home . . ."

A little later he fell in love with an actress named Madeleine Carlier. "I was seventeen or eighteen, and Madeleine was thirty, but she passed for twenty. There was a family council, and my mother threw up her hands, crying, 'Poor Jean—with an old woman!' I've used this story in Le Grand Ecart, which is why I have always said this novel is almost an autobiography."

About this time, too, he was taken up by Edouard de Max, then the reigning tragedian on the Paris stage. De Max rented

the Théâtre Femina for the afternoon of April 4, 1908, and before a fashionable invitation audience, he and a number of other
actors read from Cocteau's fledgling poems. It was a chic debut
for a not quite nineteen-year-old boy, and after this, Jean went
everywhere, knew everyone, charmed everyone. Mistinguett later
told a friend that he had "done me the honor of giving me his
virginity." He met Proust, who had recently lined his room with
cork and begun to write A la Récherche du Temps Perdu, and
who described him as "remarkably gifted and intelligent:—with
his fine fishbone nose and his fascinating eyes, he has the air of
a sea siren, also something of the seahorse." He became an
intimate friend of the formidable Comtesse de Noailles, a
Rumanian-Greek aristocrat who wrote love poems in French. He
was presented to the dowager Empress Eugénie, widow of
Napoleon III.

Then, in 1909, the Ballets Russes came to Paris. Like everyone
else, Cocteau was dazzled. Soon he had met Diaghilev and
Nijinsky and was designing posters for the company. He even
wrote the libretto for an exotic ballet called Le Dieu Bleu, with
music by Reynaldo Hahn. At the same time, two things happened which were to influence him for the rest of his life. He
met fresh, fierce, twenty-seven-year-old Stravinsky, his first encounter with a creator who was more than a salon pet (Stravinsky: "I remember someone calling my name in the street—'C'est
vous, IgOR?'—and turning around to see Cocteau introducing
himself . . ."). And then, one evening in 1912, he was crossing
the Place de la Concorde with Diaghilev and Nijinsky. "We
were returning from supper after the performance. Nijinsky was
sulking, as usual, and walked ahead of us. Diaghilev was making
fun of some ridiculous antic of mine. When I asked him why
(I was accustomed to being praised), he stopped, adjusted his
monocle, and said: 'Etonne-moi. Astonish me.' "

Les Monstres Sacrés

Expelled from the Grand Condorcet for insubordination, I crammed for my *bachot* with Monsieur Dietz, a tutor who astounded us by the contrast between his Protestantism and his odalisque poses. (He sprawled, drooped, coiled and uncoiled, languidly advanced an arm here, a leg there, peering at us over his pince-nez and shaking with sarcastic laughter.) His son acted at the Comédie-Française under the pseudonym Garry, and his nephew Pierre Laudenbach was preparing to become Pierre Fresnay. Sundays and Thursdays, I ran off to join my accomplices René Rocher and Carlito Bouland (the latter's resemblance to Coquelin had encouraged him to learn by heart all the *tirades* in the master's repertoire); we pooled our resources and engaged, quite cheaply, stage box II at the El-dorado. I ought to mention that we took along a basket of violets in order to bombard our favorites—a clumsy, wet, cold bombardment which divided its victims between a smile and a scolding.

That stage box had an importance all its own: it participated in the show, being squeezed halfway between footlights and spotlights. It was cheap because from it you could see only a corner of the stage through the scrolls of the double basses and the bald heads of the double-bass players. But what mattered was the proscenium area where the music-hall singers performed their numbers. Behind a zone of luminous dust, the teeming house was invisible to us, all but the pale-blue plush at the edge of our box and the orchestra leader, Monsieur Dédé, a woolly, mustachioed Negro who wore enormous spectacles and conducted in white gloves.

The orchestra attacked the maxixe, and under the hail of our bouquets, one fist on her hip, her sombrero cocked, and a

Spanish shawl draped around her slit skirt, Mistinguett made
her entrance. After the maxixe and

> *La femme torpille*
> > *pille*
> > > *pille*
>
> *Qui se tortille*
> > *tille*
> > > *tille,*

she left the stage under a new salvo of bouquets. Then began
the dares and the drawing of straws to determine which of us
would visit her backstage, braving the watchman in his sinister
alley. Dates with our "songstresses" took place at the Taverne
Pschorr; but no amorous reality equaled the minute-long con-
fabulation near the watchman's stool, our star clutching her
flowered robe and affording us the surprise of her *bicyclettes*,
the blue spokes of a wheel she painted round each eye till the
end of her life.

Years later, visiting her son Léopold, I leafed through the
family album. The first thing you see is an almost ageless
peasant woman nursing a baby. "My mother," Leopold said.
Then with each photograph the peasant woman grows younger,
winning her race with time. The album must be read in the
opposite direction to our bourgeois albums; for his mother,
younger and younger, more and more elegant, perfects the
famous countenance of Mistinguett—her huge joyous mouth,
her eyes of an animal that cannot smile, her chestnut curls and
her silken legs.

Not long ago Mistinguett telephoned to invite me to her
latest revue. She had reserved for me, at the Folies-Bergère, the
stage box corresponding to stage box II. So that it was from the
perspective of my own youth that I saw her emerge from a
forest of ostrich feathers, wearing a simple tailored suit and no

jewelry, advancing on the audience, beyond the footlights, and there, her eyes flickering over every seat, singing Villemetz's verses:

> *Oui, c'est moi*
> *Me voilà*
> *Je m'ramène.*

There is more than one patriotism. I try to toughen the skin which in all of us is victimized by military marches, but why should I toughen that deeper skin which would make Mistinguett's voice intolerable in exile, and which makes me hear her the way a Scotchman hears bagpipes, a Spaniard castanettes, a Pole the piano? Whether she sings her urchin's laments, standing beside a big dog like one of Velàzquez's young lords, or whether she explains to the house:

> *On dit que j'ai la voix qui traîne*
> *Quand je chant' mes rengaines*
>   *c'est vrai—*

tears fill my eyes when I hear that voice so long apprenticed to the school of street cries and newspaper vendors, that voice which is in complicity with complaint, one more stare from a face put together out of slaps.

At intermission, I took one of the loveliest girls I know to her dressing room. No sooner were the introductions made and the visitor seated than this phenomenon occurred: beauty and youth extinguished by a woman who in a moment would return, in a long fiery gown, to a stage of snow and ice, eclipsing her escort of boyish gigolos . . . "Come now," one of my feminine readers will object, "you speak of Mistinguett as if she were Duse! What part can she play? What playwright can she serve? Which are her heroines?" I don't know. She incarnates herself. She expresses the best of my city. She flatters the patriotism I am not ashamed of. And how I respect her determination to glitter by that light which takes so long to reach men and which is the attribute of the stars!

*

In our theatre-mad youth, two great figures predominated: Sarah Bernhardt, Edouard de Max. For what had they to do with tact, with restraint, with proportion, with anything *comme-il-faut*, this royalty of the *comme-il-ne-faut-pas*, these tigers who licked themselves and yawned in front of everyone, these forces of artifice at grips with that force of nature, the public?

Mounet-Sully was in his dotage. The old blind lion drowsed in a corner of the menagerie. Sometimes he would raise one paw in a magisterial swat: *Oedipus Rex*. Bernhardt and de Max frequently performed together, and I can never forget our delirium when the golden curtain parted after the play and the tragedienne took her calls, the talons of her left hand thrust between her breasts, her right, at the end of its long stiff arm, leaning on the proscenium arch. Like some Venetian palazzo, Sarah listed under the weight of her chokers and her fatigue, painted, gilded, prosthetized, and propped amid a columbarium of applause. *La Sorcière! La Samaritaine! Phèdre! Andromaque!* . . .

Her body was like that of some splendid rag doll. The broad breastplate, gleaming in the uniform of the Duke of Reichstadt or under the turquoises of Théodora, ended at the thighs with a sash which lashed her together behind and in front gathered itself in a huge knot that trailed down over boots or a train. Endlessly, she bowed: at her entrance, at her exit, at the end of each act; and her sublime acting, which exploded every convention, was one long swoon broken by screams of rage.

The last time I was lucky enough to see her, she was doing Athalie. One leg had been amputated. Negroes carried her onstage in a sort of sedan chair. She recited the dream. When she reached

Pour réparer des ans l'irréparable outrage

she smiled, shook her head, flung her arms wide, struck her chest with a bejeweled fist, bowed, taking the line to herself and apologizing to her public for appearing yet again. The audience gave her a standing ovation.

Those were spectacles of the theatre inconceivable to our times, when we are so ridiculous as to suppose we have a sense of the ridiculous and take as an insult to ourselves the first unfamiliar sign of greatness.

Madame Sarah Bernhardt was like those tragediennes without a theatre, whom I have often mentioned and who invent for themselves a character and a décor in the void, in life. As if their inability to represent heroines exalts them, inspires them to their extremity. But Madame Sarah Bernhardt presented the phenomenon of living at the extremity of her person in life *and* on the boards. By her extraordinary power of swooning she filled the arms of the world. She was said to be tubercular, doubtless because of the countless handkerchiefs she kneaded and crushed against her mouth, because of the red roses she chewed during her love scenes. And then, all at once, she would break off the swift flow of her automaton's voice to emphasize some salient truth all the more striking in that it occurred unrehearsed.

I recommend to those who cannot admit the existence of sacred monsters of this order that they go to New York and see the film of Madame Sarah Bernhardt, preserved at the Museum of Modern Art. At sixty, she acts the part of Marguerite Gautier. One is reminded of a famous Chinese actor who said, at the same age, "I'm beginning to be able to play ingénues."

What actress will play the great *amoureuses* better than

Sarah in this film? None. And when it is over, we find ourselves back in modern life, like the diver who returns to the surface after having come face to face with a giant pink devilfish in tropic seas.

*

De Max was a tragedian of genius. Like Isadora, like Sarah, he knew nothing of codes, formulas. He invented, he foraged. He embarrassed you. He went too far. You felt responsible for his mistakes. You dared not look at your neighbors. Then all at once you were ashamed of your shame. The last laugh in the house was indignantly shushed. De Max, with a furious grip, mastered ridicule, rode it out. His vainglory prevailed and carried you off at a gallop. (I can never forget his Nero in *Britannicus,* an operetta Nero, peering through an emerald monocle and wearing a robe with a train, a Nero to end all Neros.)

René Rocher knew de Max (whom my Uncle Raymond Lecomte, a stickler for the correct use of the particle, never called anything but *the actor Max*). He had rung the actor's bell, I believe, at his house in the Rue Caumartin, a few steps from our school, opposite the Passage du Havre where we bought itching powder and stink bombs. De Max never closed his door to anyone. He admitted Rocher into his circle, and Rocher, intoxicated with pride, brought me along.

Like the ocean, whose gestures and reverberations he shared, down to his glaucous eyes, de Max was *"redouté des mères à genoux"*—dreaded by imploring mothers, all but mine, who trusted him, and rightly so. "Your son knows de Max—he's lost!" That was the leitmotiv and inaccuracy itself. No black masses, or pink ones; no snares for the young. The intimacy of Edouard de Max suggested instead the tribal interior of a gypsy caravan, and his bedroom that of Louis XIV, where he received his courtiers, his favorites of either sex, including a veritable harem of ravishing women.

From that first visit, I still keep a signed photograph: "To your sixteen years in bloom, from my forty in tears," and the recollection of a curious dedication scrawled on a picture of Mounet-Sully which decorated the bedroom: "To de Max, from his admirable admirer." De Max had the agelessness of felines: this commander, this emir, this monstrous Siamese cat, this black panther would curl up in the dim light among filthy cushions and furs where our quick glances recognized the costume of Hippolytus.

For the bric-a-brac of the Rue Caumartin consisted of stage props and furniture from old productions. The diadem of Heliogabalus served as the chandelier. One was obliged to sit, or not sit at all, on Nero's throne or the X of Ximène.

The chaos of de Max's establishment was his style, his *business*, the caprice of an Oriental nature as generous as it was impulsive. In that derided and dreaded apartment which showed the very contours of his soul, we were shown nothing but instances of nobility.

Marie, the ancient housekeeper with the gray fringe of Guanhumarah, opened the vestibule door. The guest passed through a series of rooms which had something of the dressing room of the Fratellini clowns about them, something of the taxidermist's parlor, and something of the laboratory of Dr. Coppelius or Faust. On an upright piano enameled pale green and carved with pink rambler roses were piled books by Verlaine, Baudelaire, Verhaeren, Gide, all in heavy leather bindings—so many missals. One had to sidle between wreathed columns, Gothic chests, cathedral tapers. Four stairs led down to the fake-Pompeian bath; to the right, a bay window revealed a lugubrious little Parisian yard: the dead snake of a hose, a dead lawn, a dead wall. An archway separated the bedroom from the writing alcove: here de Max dipped his pen into the mouth of a pottery toad and wrote his letters with violet ink in a tall, spiky hand, drying them with gold dust. A tiny cup contained his fortune, which he distributed to those poorer than he.

If he went out, he sported a velvet suit with pearl-gray lapels, thrust a gray pearl into his black-satin cravat, cocked the huge gray pearl of his bowler over his left ear, pulled on pearl-gray gloves, powdered his gray double chin until it was pearly, moistened his dark-ringed eyes with saliva, and in tiny patent-leather boots with pearl-gray tops he crossed the courtyard, stepped into the show window of his pearl-gray "electric," and sitting bolt upright, offering numismatists the medals of each profile, drove in silence toward the Bois de Boulogne. Here he made the circuit of the lake, motionless, eyes fixed on the heavens, mouth bitter, one mole punctuating his face just under the left nostril, and returned by the same route. At night he performed in the eight-act plays of Ferdinand Hérold and Paul Vérola: *Bouddha, Ramses II,* and the rest—every hero, every legend galvanizing his mania for costumes, for postures.

Now I shall tell you about the scandal of the costume ball given by Robert d'Humières at the Théâtre des Arts, of which he was the director. De Max, the most naïve creature in the world, had taken it into his head to attend with an escort: Chiro Vesperto (a model), my schoolmate René Rocher, and myself. Our naïveté exceeded his own, for we regarded the occasion as no more than an excuse to dress up.

Imagine, then, the pearl-gray electric under the porte-cochere of the Boulevard des Batignolles and the dismayed stare of Robert d'Humières, disgorging de Max with an eagle on his helmet and swathed in an Arab veil, Vesperto and Rocher dressed, or undressed, as Arcadian shepherds, and myself as Heliogabalus with red curls, an overwhelming tiara, a train embroidered with pearls, rings on each finger and toe, and painted toenails.

It did not take us long to realize our mistake. Robert d'Humières quickly parked us in a stage box, where we were laughed out of all countenance. Sarah Bernhardt dispatched her companion, Mlle Seylor, to me: "If I were your mother, I would send you home to bed." I sniffed back my tears. The grease paint began to run and burned my eyes. De Max realized his blunder. He took us away, cleaned us up, and drove us home.

Nor is that my only recollection of a festivity in which de Max played a part. This great heart, among other faults of taste, committed that of admiring my first poems, and of attempting to gain them a hearing.

He organized, out of his own pocket, a matinee at the Théâtre Femina devoted to my verses. The most famous actresses were pressed into service. Laurent Tailhade combed his gray crest that looked so much like the Canon Mugnier's, screwed in his glass eye, his monocle, and read out an introduction that was a veritable massacre of the poets of the day. I was the only one left standing . . .

The fact remains, nonetheless, that my career dates from that matinee, and that my subsequent efforts to cause it to be forgotten suffice to render it, for me, unforgettable. But, in the long run, de Max helped me. He read deeper than my follies, divined within me a hidden strength, obliging me to conquer myself and teaching me by his example that greatness is often hard put to adapt to mere nuance.

Le Beau Monde

> "I am a Parisian, I speak Parisian,
> I pronounce Parisian."

The Comtesse de Noailles

At table, she wanted the guests to listen to her and stop talking. I have often quoted Baudelaire's remark: "Hugo plunges into one of those monologues he calls a conversation." The Count-

ess, even before reaching the dinner table, collared conversation
in this way and never again relinquished it. Not even to take a
drink: holding a glass to her lips, with her other hand she
motioned to the guests not to interrupt. And the guests obeyed.
Hostesses "offered" her, repeated the refrain: "Oh, that Anna,
she's a wonder—a wonder!" The Countess continued. From her
upstairs maid to George Sand, from her butler to Shakespeare,
she somersaulted, juggled, rope-danced, changed trapezes in
mid-air. It would be only fair to add that she was known to
cheat, that now and then she lifted cardboard weights, fell off
the wire. Some people never noticed, others laughed up their
sleeve, others suffered. I suffered, pitying as I watched her
flounder, tangled in her own tangents. Anything rather than
silence! Hypertrophy of utterance, a kind of verbal vertigo kept
her from understanding what she was doing. After several
experiments (sometimes she managed to keep her balance,
carried it off) I decided against such public encounters, prefer-
ring to meet tête-à-tête.

And yet . . . I remember one occasion of profound success.
It was at the Princesse de Polignac's. I love the Princess, I love
the way she wheedles irrevocable verdicts to destruction with a
gossamer smile, swaying her head from side to side like a sly
baby elephant; I love her superb profile—a cliff eroded by the
sea . . . and it is doubtless to the fact that our evening ended
at her house that we owe the good fortune of an Anna de
Noailles in full possession of her means.

The soirée was over. Music stands and gilt chairs littered the
pale Savonnerie carpet. Suddenly, among this flotsam of the
concert, I noticed, sitting among a group of ladies, the Comtesse
de Noailles. She was engaged in some sort of extraordinary
exercise. Before it sings, the nightingale practices. It croaks and
squawks, it howls and squeaks, and those unfamiliar with its
methods stand dumbfounded at the foot of its nightly tree.
Such was the Countess's prelude. I watched her from a distance. She sniffed, sneezed, burst out laughing, sighed as if her

heart would break, loosened her Turkish necklace, dropped her scarves. Then she puffed out her throat, quickly compressed and loosened her lips, and began. What did she say? I no longer know. I know that she talked, talked, went on talking, until the great room grew crowded and the young people sat on the floor and their elders made a circle in the armchairs around her. I know that the Princesse de Polignac and her sister the Princesse de Caraman-Chimay, standing one on each side, seemed acolytes in some imaginary boxing ring. I know that the black-liveried servants and the powdered footmen ventured as near as the open doorways. I know that through the windows, thrown wide that June, the Countess's words, like the waltz in a Lubitsch film, bewitched the trees, the plants, the stars—that her words penetrated neighboring houses, suspended quarrels, embellished the sleep of men, and that everything, everyone from star to tree, from rooftops to the chauffeurs of the waiting limousines, murmured: "The Countess is talking . . . the Countess is talking . . . the Countess is talking . . ."

It was glory she idolized. Glory, her *idée fixe!* "Failures, that's all you care about, failures!" she told me. To no avail, I contended that the privilege of our country was, precisely, to possess a secret glory, illustrious men whose very existence was unsuspected by the average Frenchman. Rimbaud scarcely at all. Verlaine only just. Hugo! Glory was the number of squares, streets, avenues . . . His fame, Rome, and the number of His temples constituted, in the Countess's eyes, one of the proofs of the existence of God. "Anna," I told her, "you want to be immortal—a bust in your own lifetime, only with legs." She insulted me, I returned the compliment. Our disputes ended with my flight from the field. I left the table. One evening (the argument concerned my *Letter to Jacques Maritain*) the Countess, brandishing a chair, chased me, in her long chemise, out onto the landing. She leaned over the railing as she clutched it, shrieking: *"Besides, it's simple. If God exists, I'd be the first to be told!"*

The Empress Eugénie

How many treasures I owe Lucien Daudet! Beyond that of his friendship, and of having found a second family of my own in his, it was Lucien who introduced me to the Empress Eugénie, and to Marcel Proust.

Lucien presented me to the Empress at Cap Martin, where we were staying in the hotel with our mothers. The most moving and the most displaced woman of the century, the Empress owned the Villa Cyrnos, one of the steep gardens at the sea's edge, infested with croaking frogs.

Youth, entering, meets departing age at the door. It is an endless moment, a ghastly minuet figure, a sounding of the abyss. This contact of hands forms a never-ending chain. I had to overcome my timidity, my sloth, and let myself be guided by Lucien, a veritable page at this little court of Cyrnos, to the Empress herself. I remember how hot it was that day. The cicadas were singing like fever, like quinine. The sea shimmered, licking itself around the edges.

We are told that Tarquin the Proud attacked poppies, slicing off their heads with his sword. That is a symbol of activity. The Empress detested flowers: she cudgeled them with her straight-handled cane, beat them out of her path. So that it was a dry garden we walked through, all rocks and cactus—a true Spanish garden whose stiff plants bristled with all the daggers of the Madonna.

I was beginning to quail, to dread the apparition (the Empress was out for a stroll, and we were walking toward her) which would inevitably suggest Winterhalter's *Decameron*, the famous painting of the Empress among her ladies-in-waiting, a thousand times less reassuring than the Grenadiers of the Guard—when the encounter took place, swift, unexpected, black, and tiny as an accident. And, as in an accident, I had plenty of time to see the obstacle approaching in slow motion, to control my nerves, to feel no emotion, to keep my head.

The Empress turned out of a winding path. Mme de Mora and Count Clary accompanied her, appearing a moment later. She clambered up the slope wearing a kind of cassock, a priest's hat on her head, leaning on her cane—like some goat-goddess. The first thing that struck me was the insignificance of the space she occupied, her size reduced like those mummified heads shrunken by the Zulus who had killed her son: no more than a blot, there in the bright sun. All that was left of the great fire-balloon of the painting, I realized, was this goblet of charred fuel, this black heart of the poppy. What had kept me from recognizing this woman was what was missing around her, the crinoline, the flounces, the mantle, the huge straw hat dangling from a ribbon, the garland of field flowers, the tiny Chantilly parasol.

The face was the same, retained its delicate oval. As if, merely, an unhappy young woman had buried her face in her hands once too often, and the lines on her palms had left their imprint there. The eyes kept the same celestial blue, but the gaze was diluted: a blue water inspected you.

The Empress stopped, the blue water looked me up and down. Lucien introduced me. "I can no longer decorate poets," she said. "Here, I'll give you this"—and with a sudden gesture she tore off a white sprig of daphne, offered it to me, watched me put it in my buttonhole, and continued her promenade. "Come along." I walked beside her. She questioned me about dancing—Isadora Duncan, the Ballets Russes. She described some fireworks the night before off the Cap-d'Ail. She stopped sometimes and burst out laughing. That voice, that broken laugh too big for her body—where had I heard them before? A memory of the bullring: they were the laugh, the chatter of young Eugénie de Montijo, the laugh, the chatter which must have terrified and fascinated a timid Napoleon III, the laugh, the chatter of all young Spanish girls, goat-feet stamping, fans beating applause for a matador at the kill.

"Preceded by her followers": the old joke would have fallen

flat at Cyrnos. The Empress exhausted her suite, strode ahead, marveled if others complained of fatigue, suggested that she walk back with me some of the way.

When I took my leave and she invited me to return soon again, I saw a flash of youth run through that face, that tiny black-gowned body, like the lizard's sudden spurt that brings ruins to life.

I saw the Empress once again—at the Hôtel Continental, where fools censured her for taking up residence opposite the Tuileries. What was left of the past that could affect this woman dead several times over? A habit. The habit of a neighborhood, most powerful of all.

The Continental kept up a certan style: electricity was masked by the gas globes of the lampadaries. Lucien Daudet guided me through the vestibules, past Boulle furniture, velvet sofas. A door opened, chestnut with gilt moldings. At the far end of an enormous salon, the Empress was seated beside the fire, framed by the old Comtesse de Pourtalès, the old Duc de Montmorency. Threadbare, cadaverous, moss-grown, his crush hat under his arm, the Duke was a prodigy of elegance.

The Empress had heard that women were wearing dyed wigs—all colors. She questioned me. I replied that this was indeed the case but that I rarely frequented the places where they were to be seen. The Comtesse de Pourtalès protested: "Dyed wigs! Lunacy!" At which the Empress turned on her, exclaiming, "My dear, we had our own!" And when the ancient lady objected, to the degree that she might contradict her sovereign, the Empress, implacable, raucous, suddenly young, began to recapitulate the list of *their* lunacies: crinolines inspired by Goya's Infantas, lace pantalettes below the hem, tasseled boots—nothing was spared. And to conclude: "*You,* my dear, had a carriage with mirrored doors and roses painted on them!" The Countess choked: "Roses! . . . Roses painted on the doors!" The Empress was tremendously amused. She furnished details. She insisted. The Duke followed her lead and fetched up old scandals, old *fous-rires*, old eccentricities. And I held my breath, I did not stir, I trembled lest I interrupt, by some clumsy gesture, this amazing scene, lest I close too abruptly the Empress's drawer, wake the cock whose crow would scatter these shadows, these ghosts.

Marcel Proust

Marcel Proust's bedroom, in the house on the Boulevard Haussmann, was the first darkroom in which I witnessed almost daily, or to be exact almost nightly, for he lived by night, the development of a great work. He was still unknown, but we acquired, from our first visit, the habit of regarding him as an illustrious writer. In that stifling room, filled with benzene fumes and the dust which covered the furniture like gray fur, we watched a toiling hive in which the thousand bees of memory manufactured their honey.

*

I cannot remember first meeting Proust. I see him, with a beard, on the red banquettes at Larue (1912). I see him, without a beard, at Madame Alphonse Daudet's. I see him again, dead, with the beard from the beginning. I see him, with and without a beard, in that cork-lined room cluttered with medicine bottles; I see him in his sordid dressing alcove, buttoning up a lavender velvet vest over a wretched squat torso that seemed to contain no more than machinery; I see him lying down, *gloved*; and I see him standing up, eating a plate of noodles.

I see him among dust covers, one for the chandelier, one for each armchair. Mothballs gleamed in the shadows. He leaned against the mantelpiece of the salon of this Captain Nemo's *Nautilus*, like a character out of Jules Verne, or else, lounging in full dress near a crepe-draped frame, like the dead Carnot.

Once, heralded by Céleste's voice on the telephone, he arrived at three in the afternoon to take me to the Louvre with him to see Mantegna's *Saint Sebastian*. In those days the canvas was in the same salon with *Madame Rivière*, *Le Bain turc*, and *Olympia*. Proust seemed like a lamp turned on in broad daylight, a telephone ringing in an empty house.

Another time he was surely (perhaps) coming around eleven at night. I was visiting a neighbor on the floor below, and I had asked to be told of his arrival. At midnight I went back upstairs and found him on my landing, sitting on a bench in the shadows. "Marcel!" I exclaimed. "Why didn't you at least wait for me inside? You know the door's always open."

"Dear Jean," he answered in that voice he scrubbed at as he spoke until it became something between a giggle and a wail, "dear Jean, Napoleon once ordered a man shot who waited for him *inside*. Of course I wouldn't dream of reading anything except your Larousse—but there might have been letters lying about, etc. . . ."

Someone has stolen the book in which he had written me verses—I still remember one couplet:

Tel un sylphe au plafond, tel sur la neige un ski,
Jean sauta sur la table auprès de Nijinsky.

But, for all the letters we exchanged, we stopped seeing each other after a ridiculous scene: I had appeared quite informally at his house on the Boulevard Haussmann, without hat or coat. When I came in, I said: "I don't have a coat, I'm freezing."

He wanted to give me an emerald. I refused it. In a day or two, I had come down with a cold. Whereupon a tailor arrived to take my measurements for a fur-lined coat. The emerald was supposed to have made possible this purchase, among others. I sent away the tailor, and Proust never forgave me. With his letter of grievances came another of some dozen pages which he instructed me to send on to the Comte de B. . . . . This endless indictment ended with a postscript: *"As a matter of fact, don't mention it to him."*

Everything about Proust evinced an unassignable site, a locale with which he corresponded by magic. In that country he possessed incalculable wealth, and the oddest security police. How often we would receive long letters studded with loving reproaches for transgressions we certainly had no knowledge of, but which we had committed, he assured us, and which our coarse senses had not registered.

Here we come within reach of the poetry of Marcel Proust. For with Proust, as with others, poetry is never where you expect to find it. His hawthorns and his steeples are so much décor. His poetry consists of an uninterrupted series of card tricks, shifting speeds, the play of mirrors.

To underline and thereby expose the ubiquity of this kind of poetry, I shall tell one little anecdote—a very great one.

We came out of the Hôtel Ritz together. Proust had distributed tips, as he always insisted on doing, until he had no more money in his pockets. When we reached the doorman, Proust realized his predicament and asked him for a loan of fifty francs. "As a matter of fact," he added as the doorman eagerly took out his wallet, "keep them. They were for you."

What did Proust die of? A health fad, a change in his habits, an open window in the alchemist's laboratory? (After all, Marcel had once told me that he could never hear *Pelléas* again, for a certain phrase describing the spring breezes passing over the sea was enough to bring on an asthma attack.)

But the morning after he died, it was no longer a question, alas, of whether I went to the house in the Boulevard Haussmann with a high heart or a humbled one, knocked at the door, disobeyed orders and walked in despite Céleste, who tried to make sure you had not, yesterday, "touched someone's hand who might have touched a rose" and thereby caused another attack.

No, that day all we could do, Lucien Daudet and I, was to walk into a room we knew with the blinds down and the lamps dim, but which had become alien, even alarming, because we were there in the morning, at an hour when Marcel Proust never received.

We walked from the vestibule into the rooms of a stranger. Death received for him. The blinds of this *Nautilus* where mothballs crunched underfoot, where Proust once lounged among the dust covers, covering himself with beards, with wigs, with gloves and fur-lined coats—the blinds were open, and they revealed a kind of ransacked villa. Friends stood about in the attitudes lightning gives its victims, for it was lightning indeed, this mourning which had struck the whole of literature and a few partial hearts.

Céleste took us in to her master. The bedroom was empty. In it reigned that silence which is to silence what shadows are to ink. Something definitive yet light, something formal. Without benzene or eucalyptus fumes, the room was *bare:* Proust lay on his child's bed in his cork-lined sentry box, presenting an admirable vizier's profile. He was wearing that beard behind which he had giggled as though behind a lace fan, and which, on his corpse, became the attribute of a magus, of a king.

And suddenly, turning our eyes from this spectacle which overwhelmed us all, we saw on his left side, at the far corner of the dusty fireplace, a huge, uneven stack of school copybooks. The stack loomed in the shadows, in that darkness so gently illumined by that pale profile, as though by a white porcelain night light; and we remembered that these were the copybooks Marcel shuffled and jumbled when he wanted to read us some chapter. This tall, uneven stack of school copybooks was, in all deference to the lovers of catastrophe, the *opera* or, to be grammatical, the *opus* of our friend.

That pile of paper, on his left side, went on living like the watch on a dead soldier's wrist.

Les Ballets Russes

Diaghilev and Nijinsky were two free men who lived in order to speak their piece, to cry their cry.

I met Serge Diaghilev at Madame Sert's. From that moment, I became a member of the troupe. I no longer saw Nijinsky dance except from the wings or from the box where Diaghilev, behind Madame Sert's Persian aigrette, watched his dancers through a tiny mother-of-pearl lorgnette.

That was in 1910. Nijinsky was dancing *Le Spectre de la Rose*. Instead of watching the performance from out front, I stood in the wings, where there was a better one. After kissing the girl, the Spectre of the Rose leaps out her window . . . and lands among the stagehands, who squirt water into his face and scrub at him with towels, like a boxer between rounds. What grace coupled with what brutality! I still hear the thunder of that applause, still see that young man smeared with grease paint, sweating, panting, one hand pressing his heart and the other clutching a stage brace. He collapsed on a chair, and in a few seconds, slapped, drenched, pummeled, he walked back out onstage, bowing, smiling.

Nijinsky was shorter than average height. In body and soul, he was an extreme case of vocational distortion. His Mongol head was joined to his body by a very long, very thick neck. The muscles of his thighs and calves stretched the cloth of his trousers so that his legs seemed to be bowed . .,. backward. His fingers were short, as though sliced off at the first joint. In other words, you would never believe that this balding little monkey in his long overcoat and a hat perched on the top of his skull was the public's idol.

But he was, and rightly. Everything in Nijinsky was organized to be seen at a distance, under the lights. Onstage, his excessive musculature became sinuous. His height increased (his heels never touched the floor), his hands turned into the foliage of his gestures, and his face—his face glowed.

A metamorphosis of this kind is almost inconceivable to those who never witnessed it.

For several days before the première of the *Faune*, he startled us at supper at Larue by moving his head as if he had a crick in his neck. Diaghilev and Bakst were alarmed, questioned him, received no answer. Afterwards we discovered he was preparing himself for the weight of the horns. I could cite a thousand examples of this perpetual study, which made him abstracted and surly.

At the Crillon (Diaghilev and he migrated from hotel to hotel, pursued by the dispossessed fate of all vagrants) he wrapped himself in the turkish-towel robe from the bathroom, pulled the hood over his head, and scribbled his choreography all day long.

I saw him create every one of his roles. His deaths were heartbreaking: the one in *Pétrouchka*, when the puppet turns into a man, reduced (or enlarged) us to tears; the one in *Schéhérazade*, when his body thumped the stage like a fish in the bottom of a boat . . .

*

Serge Diaghilev seemed to be wearing the tiniest hat in the world. If you put it on, it engulfed your ears. For his head was so enormous that anything he wore on it was too small.

His dancers nicknamed him *Chinchilla* for the one white lock he did not dye jet-black like the rest. He stuffed himself into a fur-lined coat with an opossum collar, and sometimes fastened it with safety pins. His face was a mastiff's, his smile a baby crocodile's, one tooth always outside. Sucking that tooth was the sign that he was pleased, or frightened, or angry. He gnawed at his mouth under its tiny mustache as he watched his artists

from the back of his box. And his watery eyes slanted down-
wards in their sockets like oysters. This man conducted across
the world a company as mixed, as motley as the Nijni-Nov-
gorod fair. His only luxury was to discover a star.

*

It was in that penumbra, between blue-gel spotlights, that I
met Stravinsky, who was then completing *Pétrouchka.* He told
me about it in the roulette room at Monte Carlo, surprising
that world which nothing surprises by his gesticulations, his
grimaces, his barbaric jewelry. But we saw very little of each
other until the famous première of *Le Sacre du Printemps.*

It would be interesting to trace, in the monolithic totality of
this work, the responsibility of each of the collaborators: Stravinsky the composer, Roerich the designer, Nijinsky the choreographer.

Musically, Impressionism was the order of the day. And then,
suddenly, among those charming ruins, grew the tree Stravinsky.

All things considered, *Le Sacre* is still a Fauvist work, a
Fauvist work which has been *organized.* Gauguin and Matisse
usher it in. But if the period's musical backwardness, compared
with the achievements of its painting, necessarily kept *Le Sacre*
from coinciding with other disturbing manifestations, the work
provided nonetheless an indispensable dynamite. Moreover, we
must not forget that Stravinsky's tenacious collaboration with
Diaghilev and his apprehensions for his wife, ill in Switzerland
at the time, kept him somewhat out of the center. His audacity
was therefore quite gratuitous. In any case, as it stands, the
work was and remains a masterpiece; a symphony instinct with
savage melancholy—the sounds of earth in parturition, of
plowed fields and primitive camps, tiny melodies rising from the
depth of time, the lowing of cattle, profound convulsions—
prehistoric Georgics.

Roerich was a mediocre painter. On the one hand, he
costumed and set *Le Sacre* in a style not really alien to the

work, but on the other he attentuated it by the flabbiness of his accents.

There remains Vaslav Nijinsky. Returning home—that is, to the various palatial hotels in which he camped out—this young Ariel sulked, leafed through folio volumes, and revolutionized the syntax of gesture. He was poorly educated, and his modern models were not the best. Having known only too well the triumph of grace, he rejected it, systematically seeking the reverse of what had brought him glory; to escape old formulas, he imprisoned himself in new ones. But Nijinsky was a moujik, a Rasputin; he bore in himself that fluid which maddens crowds, and he scorned the public (which he did not scorn to please). Like Stravinsky, he transformed into strength the weakness of what nourished him; by all these atavisms, by the lack of culture, by cowardice, by *humanity*, he escaped the German danger, the system which desiccated a Reinhart.

I have often heard *Le Sacre* without the dances; I would like to see it with the dances. In my memory, impulse and method balanced each other in the choreography, as in the orchestra. The defect consisted in the parallelism of music and movement, in their lack of interplay, of counterpoint. Here we had the proof that the same chord, often repeated, is less fatiguing to the ear than the frequent repetition of a single gesture to the eye. People laughed at a monotony of automatons rather than at a breakdown of attitudes, and at the breakdown of attitudes rather than at the polyphony from the pit.

We may distinguish, in the choreographer's work, two parts: one dead (example: the position of the dancers' feet when not in motion, a simple desire to contradict the traditional points-out pose) and one vital (example: the storm and the dance of the chosen maiden, a naïve, mad dance, the dance of an insect or of a doe fascinated by a boa, the dance of a dynamited factory—indeed, the most overwhelming spectacle I can recall in the theatre).

The various contributions of these three men therefore

formed a whole both homogeneous and heterogeneous, and what was defective in details was dissolved, uprooted by irresistible temperaments.

Thus we first came to know this historic work amid such an uproar that the dancers no longer heard the orchestra and had to follow the beats Nijinsky was stamping and calling out to them from the wings.

Le Sacre du Printemps was performed in May 1914 in a new theatre, a hall without patina, too comfortable and too cold for a public accustomed to emotions elbow-to-elbow, to a warmth of red velvet and gold. Not that *Le Sacre* would have been more correctly received on a less pretentious stage; but this luxurious house symbolized at first glance the misunderstanding which brought into collision a work of youthful strength and a decadent public. A spent public, supine among Louis XVI garlands, Venetian gondolas, the languorous divans and cushions of an Orientalism for which we must blame the *Ballets Russes* themselves.

The house was packed. To a trained eye, all the raw materials for a scandal were on hand: a fashionable public, lapped in pearls, aigrettes, and ostrich plumes; and side by side with these tail coats and tulles, the business suits and bright bandeaux of that race of aesthetes which acclaims the new for no better reason than its hatred of the boxes (the latter's sincere jeers being far less offensive than the impotent accolade of the former). Add to this the feverish musicians, as well as a flock of Panurge's lambs torn between fashionable opinion and the prestige of the Ballets Russes. And of course we should anatomize the thousand nuances of snobbery, super-snobbery and counter-snobbery requiring a chapter to themselves.

It may be useful to indicate one aspect of the audience on that occasion: the almost complete absence of young painters and of their masters. An absence motivated, I learned much later, for the former by their ignorance of these ceremonies to which Diaghilev, not yet having sniffed them out, did not invite them—and for the latter by a prejudice against *le beau monde*. This scorn of luxury, which a Picasso makes into a cult, has its good side and its bad. I welcome the cult as an antidote, but perhaps it shrinks the horizon of certain artists who avoid contact with luxury more from envious hatred than from a genuine apostolate. The fact remains that Montparnasse knew nothing of *Le Sacre de Printemps*, that *Le Sacre du Printemps* performed by Monteux at one of his regular concerts suffered from the bad press of the Ballets Russes, and that Picasso first heard of Stravinsky in Rome, with me, in 1917.

*

Let us return to the audience in the Avenue Montaigne, waiting for the conductor to tap his desk and for the curtain to rise on one of the noblest events in the annals of art.

The audience played the role it had to play; it rebelled at once. People laughed, shrieked insults, hissed, imitated the cries of animals, and might have wearied of this sooner or later, if the crowd of aesthetes and a few musicians, carried away by excessive zeal, had not insulted and even manhandled the public of the boxes. The tumult degenerated into a tussle.

Standing in her box, tiara awry, the ancient Comtesse de Pourtalès brandished her fan and screeched until her face turned purple: "This is the first time in sixty years anyone has dared insult me!" The good lady was sincere; she believed it was all a hoax.

*

At two in the morning, Stravinsky, Nijinsky, Diaghilev, and I crowded into a fiacre and told the driver to take us to the Bois de Boulogne. No one spoke; the night was cool and mild. By the scent of acacia, we recognized the first trees. Once we reached the lakes, Diaghilev, stuffed into his opossum, began muttering in Russian; I could tell Stravinsky and Nijinsky were listening, and when the driver lit his lamp I saw tears on the impresario's cheeks. He was still muttering, slowly, indefatigably.

"What is it?" I asked.

"Pushkin."

There was a long silence, then Diaghilev mumbled another short phrase, and the emotion of my two neighbors seemed to me so intense I did not resist my impulse to discover its cause.

"It's hard to translate," Stravinsky said, "very hard; it's too Russian, too . . . Russian. But it goes something like this: 'Come with me, come with me to the islands.' Yes, that's it, it's very Russian, because you see, with us, you go to the islands the way we're going to the Bois de Boulogne tonight, and it was going to the islands that we first imagined *Le Sacre du Printemps*."

For the first time, an allusion had been made to the scandal. We returned at dawn. You cannot imagine the sweetness and the nostalgia of those men, and whatever Diaghilev may have done subsequently, I shall never forget, in that fiacre, his huge, tear-stained face, reciting Pushkin in the Bois de Boulogne.

Rilke's Lamp

It was my good luck, around the same period, to be living in a vast gallery with five French doors overlooking some twenty acres of wilderness in the middle of Paris, on the Boulevard des Invalides, at that pretentious age when nothing seems worthy of our genius, when no miracle amazes us, when we are certain that Fate promises and preserves for us nothing less than exceptional abodes. I should say: my bad luck. For it is a pity that a fortune so insolent no longer favors us once we become capable of measuring it, of savoring its privileges.

Cutting school one day, I ventured into the monumental courtyard of the mansion which stands at the corner of the Rue de Varennes and the Boulevard des Invalides and asked the

concierge if I could explore the place. I discovered that the
mansion was called the Hôtel Biron, that it had latterly been a
Convent of the Sacred Heart, and that since the "separation" it
had been in the hands of a liquidator of state property, that
Rodin lived in the central pavilion, that the other rooms were
rented out, and that if I would take the trouble to follow the
concierge he would show me those premises which were still
available. If any of them suited me, I need merely make an offer
to Monsieur Ménage, the liquidator. That same evening I
possessed the gallery I have mentioned (formerly the nuns'
dancing and solfège classroom). A year's rent would have lasted
a month in the fleabag hotels of the neighborhood. A door, to
which I possessed the giant key, opened onto a portico and the
portico led down to the garden. Garden, park, farm, ranch, for
all I know . . . Nothing, I repeat, but the blasé eyes of an un-
grateful age could keep me from falling on my knees in rapture.
Was it possible that Paris lived, labored, trafficked, trudged
around a silence so vast? For if it existed only by contrast, this
silence nonetheless prevailed, sacrificing ear to eye, emanating
grass and trees, extinguishing the uproar of a city by the power
of a habit which makes silence into the privilege of overgrown
gardens. It was, if you will, a *spectacle of silence*, a phenomenon
deriving from an old routine of the sense of hearing which the
sense of sight almost always supplants. I mean that music dis-
tracts us less from a spectacle than a spectacle keeps us from
hearing, and that the visual emotion of being a thousand miles
from Paris, in the middle of the countryside, thereby trans-
ported you into the middle of a silence.

To the right of the portico, you walked through a tiny, empty
chapel, decorated with lilies and doves, into the room with tall
French doors. A stove, a piano, a studio bed, a packing case
covered with shawls, a few chairs and oil lamps quickly made
the old classroom habitable, and from one day to the next I
invited my stupefied guests into an enchanted realm which
skirted on the left the gardens of the Rue Barbet-le-Jouy and on

the right the Boulevard des Invalides, as far as the deconse-
crated church where Count Osnovitchin organized Russian
celebrations. I shall never forget Catulle Mendès deciding he
would pay a visit to some garret poet (after the luncheon in the
Boulevard Malesherbes) and entering, one summer evening,
this décor à la Capitaine Fracasse. He kept repeating *Nom de
Dieu! Nom de Dieu!*, switched his legs and my furniture with
his cane, passed a pianist's hand over his face and his yellow
curls, and declaiming the hemistichs of one of his recent works,
aimed his belly framed in an unbuttoned waistcoat between the
clumps of shrubbery and the wrought-iron gates. My girlfriend
of the period, Christiane Mancini, had gone out—in a black
velvet gown with a train—to buy beer and sandwiches in the
Rue de Bourgogne. And we had invited Mendès! The moonlight, as Madame de Sévigné says more or less, was arranging its
washing, its statues, its penguins, and its dead nuns. A fabulous
mass of reeds and rubbish perfumed the air, clustered in the
center of a kind of circle of sand and weeds. This was the only
place which brambles and fallen branches had not invaded. The
rest formed a minor virgin forest, an inextricable vegetable
knot. The moss-grown steps, the façade with its green windowpanes, the sundial of what is now the Musée Rodin loomed
over this disorder. On the other hand, my own French doors,
difficult to open because of the thick carpet of forget-me-nots,
overlooked veritable tunnels of verdure leading to the unknown.

If I tell you how luck secured my tenancy in a domain which
suggested the Hôtel Pimodan and Baudelaire's parties there, I
do so first of all because it seems to me to mark the end of the
discoveries Paris once reserved for explorers, a kind of flea
market of domiciles. And second because Fate willed that this
site of poetry should be saved by a poet. For one morning, in
the concierge's lodge, I happened to hear the liquidator discussing an allotment of the grounds and the extension of the Rue
de Bourgogne as far as the Hôtel Rohan . . . I summoned the
press. Hallais, Abel Bonnart, Chaumeix, Nolhac paid visits to

learn at one and the same time that this treasure existed and
that it was about to vanish. Their articles proved our case.
Cabinet ministers came in their turn and marveled. In short, I
had saved the gardens of the Hôtel Biron, and I boast of that
achievement to this day. I boasted less, at home, of possessing a
fairy-tale realm, for such bachelor quarters would have drawn
maternal thunderbolts down upon me. A silly episode gave the
show away. My mother belonged to the Société des Amis du
Louvre. The society decided to visit the Hôtel Biron and requested my mother to intercede with her son in order that the
friends of the Louvre could make use of my portico. My mother
informed the president that he must be mistaken, that her sons,
etc., etc. . . . Letter after letter, interrogations, and discovery
of the mystery. My mother put a good face on a bad moment
and carried her indulgence to the point of serving cakes and
orangeade on my packing cases, the day of the visit. But I was
then obliged to forego the luxury of possessing another domicile
than my courtyard room in the Avenue Malakoff.

Long, long afterwards, I was to learn about the lamp which
burned every night behind a corner window. It was the lamp of
Auguste Rodin's secretary, Monsieur Rilke. I believed I knew a
great many things in those days, and I lived in the filthy ignorance of my pretentious youth. Success put me on the wrong
track, and I did not know there exists a kind of success worse
than failure, a kind of failure worth all the success in the world.
And I did not know that one day the far-off friendship of Rainer
Maria Rilke would console me for having seen his lamplight
without realizing it was signaling me to come and burn my
wings in it.

2

Le Rappel à l'Ordre

1914–1929

Ce que le public te reproche,
cultive-le, c'est toi

What others criticize you for,
cultivate: it is you

Cocteau—by Modigliani, 1916 (Collection Edouard Dermit)

Cocteau—by Picasso, Easter Sunday, 1917 (Collection Edouard Dermit)

top: "Les Six" (left to right): Darius Milhaud, Jean Cocteau, Georges Auric (a drawing), Arthur Honegger, Germaine Taillefere, Francis Poulenc, Louis Durey

above: Cocteau, at Pramousquier, 1922

left: Cocteau during the 1914–1918 war

Cocteau, as the angel Heurtebise, in his play Orphée

Raymond Radiguet

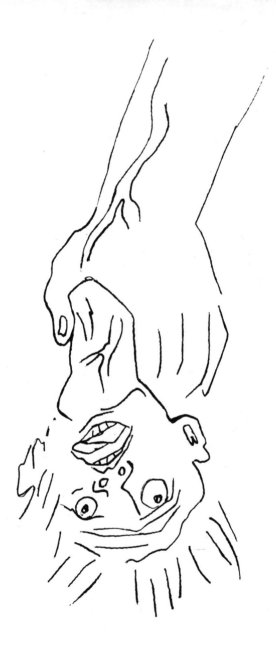

*Three self-portraits made during an opium disintoxication cure
in Saint-Cloud, 1928*

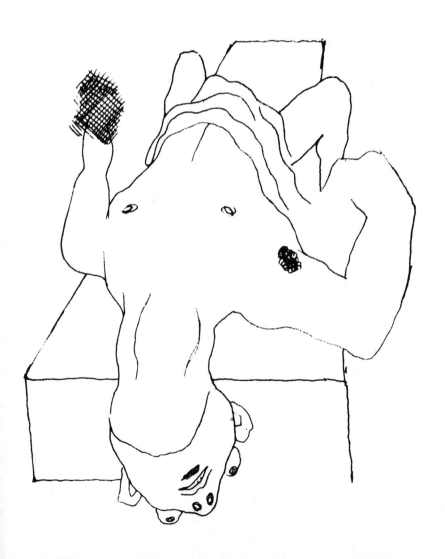

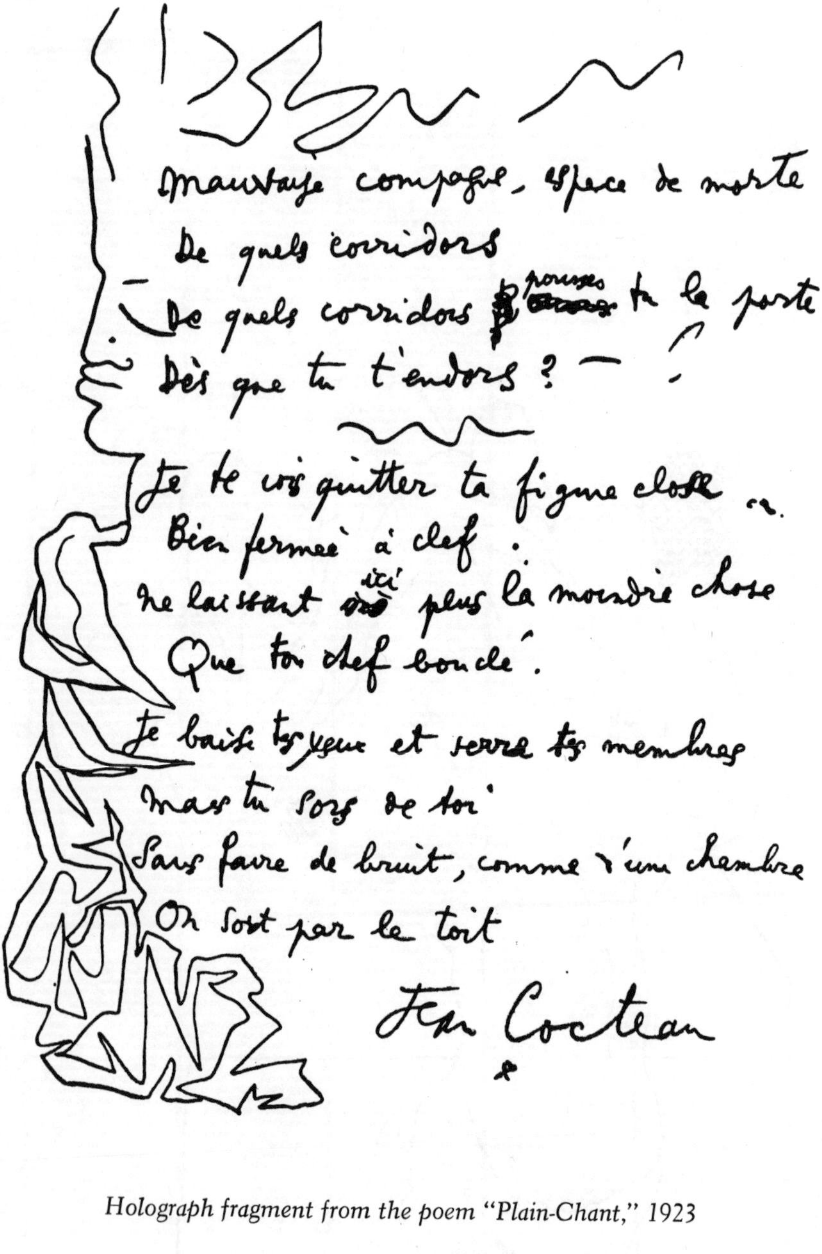
Mauvaise compagne, espèce de morte
De quels corridors
De quels corridors pousses-tu la porte
Dès que tu t'endors ?

Je te vois quitter ta figure close
Bien fermée à clef.
Ne laissant ici plus la moindre chose
Que ton chef bouclé.

Je baise tes yeux et serre tes membres
Mais tu sors de toi
Sans faire de bruit, comme d'une chambre
On sort par le toit

Jean Cocteau

Holograph fragment from the poem "Plain-Chant," 1923

CALENDAR

1914–1923

In the spring of 1914, Cocteau visited Stravinsky and his family in Switzerland, where he finished what he came to regard as his first book, Le Potomak. Not published until 1919, it is part diary, part aphorism, part fever chart. Almost one third of its pages are devoted to an album of cartoons. The subject is Cocteau's self-reckoning, with mea culpa and auto-da-fé mixed: his realization that to be a true poet, to serve his own gifts as worthily as Stravinsky was serving his, he must radically alter his life. "At nineteen, flattered and feted, I had become ridiculous and squandering, a chatterbox taking my own banter for eloquence and my wastefulness for prodigality." He returned to Maisons-Laffitte and "cloistered myself, tormented myself, questioned myself, insulted myself . . . I decided to consume myself and be reborn."

But in the middle of this immolation, war broke out, and for a time Cocteau resumed his familiar role of Prince Frivole. With Misia Sert, who kept one of the smartest salons in Paris, he formed an ambulance corps with a uniform designed by Poiret, and with Madame Sert's Mercedes-Benz leading the way. On August 20, André Gide joined him at a tea shop in Paris and, as usual, disapproved: "He is incapable of seriousness, and all his thoughts, his witty words, his feelings, all the extraordinary brio of his habitual conversational manner shocked me, like a luxury product on display in a time of famine and mourning. He talked about the fighting at Mulhouse in amusing epithets and mimicries; he imitated the sound of the bugle, the whistling of the shrapnel, and then, because he could see that I was not amused, he said he was sad. He wants to be sad because I am sad. He takes up my sadness and explains it to me . . . Next he is talking about a woman at Red Cross headquarters who shouted on the staircase: 'I was promised fifty wounded men this morning. I want my fifty wounded men' . . . The odd thing is, I believe he would make a good soldier . . . that he would be courageous. He has the insouciance of a street urchin. Next to him, I always feel clumsy, heavy, moody."

Cocteau did not actually serve in the armed forces, though for a time he wore a uniform (as a Picasso drawing of him shows). One of his earliest biographers, Roger Lannes, refers to his "entering into contact with a regiment of marines who adopted him, letting him share their extraordinary existence, in which danger was mixed with magical freedom—a marvelous life of night patrols with officers who were charming heroes . . ." But Cocteau's presence was illegal. He was arrested and returned to civilian life in Paris in 1915. There he met Roland Garros, a young aviator who in 1913 had been the first to cross the Mediterranean and who now took Cocteau up in his plane, inspiring part of a long poem, "La Cap de Bonne-Esperance." With Paul Iribe, he briefly published a magazine called Le Mot, to which he contributed drawings signed with the name of his dog, Jim. Then he discovered the world of Montparnasse.

Heretofore he had known only the Right Bank, Proust's beau monde, and the fashionable boulevard theatre. Now he crossed over to the Left Bank, visiting Picasso's studio and the Café de la Rotonde, where Modigliani was the star. He also felt the prevailing wind of what Apollinaire was soon to call "l'esprit nouveau," the new wave, the new temper, Modernism. Gertrude Stein had been living near the Luxembourg Gardens for over a decade (Cocteau had presciently mentioned her in Le Potomak, which made him "the first French writer to speak of her work"), and then one day, as she tells it, "Picasso came in and with him and leaning on his shoulder was a slim elegant youth. It is Jean, announced Pablo, Jean Cocteau and we are leaving for Italy."

This was in 1917, a little before Easter. In Rome, they worked together with Diaghilev's company and Leonid Massine to prepare a new ballet called Parade. Picasso designed the sets, Erik Satie wrote the music, and Cocteau conceived the action (as well as the use of typewriters called for in the score). It was about a troupe of traveling players trying to entice a midway public to come in and see their show. The Paris opening in May was a disaster, which perhaps dampened Cocteau's spirits at the moment but in time only demonstrated the good uses of scandal, for when Parade was revived a few years later it was a success, and half a century later, though still unperformed, it remains a robust legend.

By the time the war was over, Cocteau's activity was manifold. He wrote a weekly column in which he reported on everything new in the arts or near-arts. With Blaise Cendrars, he founded his own publishing house, Editions de la Sirène, and issued not only his own books (Carte Blanche, Le Coq et l'Arlequin, Le Cap de Bonne-Espérance, Vocabulaire, etc.) but musical scores by Stravinsky, Satie, and a group of very young composers known as Les Six:

> Auric, Milhaud, Poulenc, Tailleferre, Honegger,
> J'ai mis votre bouquet dans l'eau d'un même vase . . .

The "vase" was another ballet, Les Mariés de la Tour Eiffel, to which they all contributed the music. There was also a mime-show (with music only by Milhaud), called Le Boeuf sur le Toit and featuring Cocteau's favorite circus clowns, the Fratellini brothers, in the cast, as well as a swift, severe adaptation of Sophocles' Antigone, with sets by Picasso, Cocteau himself playing the chorus and Antonin Artaud as Tiresias. In 1920, there were four issues of a "little magazine" called Le Coq and printed on large, folded sheets of pink paper. And there were essays, poems, two novels (Thomas l'Imposteur and Le Grand Ecart), and even an album of drawings, dedicated to Picasso ("Poets do not draw, they simply unravel their handwriting and retie it into new knots").

These were also the years of Raymond Radiguet, the fifteen-year-old poet who entered Cocteau's orbit by way of Max Jacob in 1918 and who became the most important influence his life and lifework were ever to know—"the pupil who became my master." Stravinsky saw young Radiguet frequently in 1922 and has given us a vivid portrait: "He was a silent youth with a serene, rather childlike look, but with something of the young bull in him, too. He was of medium build, handsome, rather pederastically so but without pederastic manners . . . He immediately struck me as a gifted individual and he also had the other intelligence, the machine à penser kind. His opinions were immediate and they were his . . ."

Radiguet died in 1923, at the age of twenty, leaving Cocteau desolate, at the age of thirty-four.

Montparnasse

"France between 1914 and 1924
presents the spectacle of
an incredible literary revolution."

Then came the war. In Paris, there was room for doubt; we furnished that room. In 1916, our revolution began.

All of us lived in Montparnasse—lived a life of poverty unencumbered by political, social, or national problems of any kind. When asked to name the great French artists of my time,

I could answer: Picasso, forgetting he was Spanish; Stravinsky, forgetting he was Russian; Modigliani, forgetting he was Italian. We formed a common front where contention was ordinary enough but where a kind of international patriotism prevailed. Such patriotism is a privilege of Paris and renders the city, more often than not, indecipherable to the world outside.

In 1916, Montparnasse was the provinces. We seemed to be stranded there, but we were not stranded—not with Modigliani,* Kisling, Lipschitz, Brancusi, Apollinaire, Max Jacob, Blaise Cendrars, Pierre Reverdy, André Salmon: men who almost unconsciously revolutionized literature and painting and sculpture.

This revolution was effected in extremely odd circumstances —in the middle of the First World War, a war so strange that our common front, as I have called it, extended from the front in Paris to the front lines: we circulated between them. It was this circulation which exhausted Apollinaire and left him a dead man at the Armistice, when it seemed to us that the whole city hung out its flags in his honor and in honor of our artistic patriotism.

Guillaume Apollinaire, when I met him, was wearing a pale-blue uniform, his head was shaved, and a scar shaped like a starfish crept down his temple from under a turban or helmet of bandages and leather straps. That little helmet apparently concealed a microphone which transmitted broadcasts, to him alone, from an exquisite world. He transcribed its messages, though some of his poems do not even supply the code. We

---

* When Modigliani painted my portrait, he shared a studio with Kisling, in the Rue Joseph-Bara. He sold me this huge canvas for five francs, but unfortunately I could not afford to have it carted home from the studio. Kisling owed the Café de la Rotonde eleven francs. He suggested giving its owner this portrait to cover the debt. The owner agreed, and the canvas began an odyssey which ended in America after some 17 million francs had changed hands. I have a color photograph . . .

would watch him listening—receiving. He lowered his eyelids, hummed, dipped his pen. A drop of ink gathered at its tip, trembled, and fell, starring the page. *Alcools, Calligrammes,* so many hieroglyphs of a secret language.

Only Villon and Apollinaire, so far as I know, unfailingly keep from falling by . . . faltering. Halt but not halting, only they advance into that disablement from which poetry is made and not even imagined by those who suppose they invoke its powers by writing verses.

Rare words (and he used many) lost their unfamiliarity in Apollinaire's hands. Ordinary ones turned unlikely. And he mounted those amethysts and moonstones of his, he set those emeralds and agates the way a knife grinder works, sitting on a chair on the sidewalk. No street artisan was ever more modest, more alert than that blue soldier.

He was plump, not fat, and his pale face had something Roman about it, with a tiny mustache above the mouth which uttered each word with an almost pedantic grace, a kind of breathless exactitude.

His eyes laughed at the gravity of his face, and his priest's hands accompanied his words with the two gestures sailors use for raising a glass, for taking a leak.

The laughter never left his mouth, but accumulated all over his body: it invaded him, jolted and jerked his limbs, imprinted its convulsions upon his flesh. Afterwards this silent laughter emptied out through his eyes, and his body pulled itself together, purged.

His thighs squeezed into army breeches, he padded in stocking feet across his little room on the Boulevard Saint-Germain, panted up a few steps to the tiny closet whose walls were covered with paintings by friends. In addition to Rousseau's portrait of him behind the hedge of sweet-williams and the angular damsels of Marie Laurencin, there were Fauvists, Cubists, Expressionists, Orphists, and a Larionov from the Machinist period that Guillaume called "the gas meter." He was a wild enthusiast of schools, and had learned, probably from Moréas at the Closerie des Lilas, the virtue of the names they bear, the names people murmur to each other, suggestively, mysteriously.

His wife's face looked like the bright globes of goldfish that hang in shops on the Quai de la Mégisserie opposite the book-stalls by which, he once wrote, the Seine is kept between its banks.

The morning of the Armistice, Picasso and Max Jacob came to 10 rue d'Anjou, where I was living in my mother's apart-ment. They told me they were worried about Guillaume, that fatty deposits were weakening his heart, and that we must telephone Capmas, my friends' doctor. We called Capmas. It was too late. Capmas begged the sick man to help him, to help himself, to try to live. He no longer had the strength: the charming breathlessness turned tragic. Guillaume was choking to death. That evening, when I joined Picasso, Max, and André Salmon in the apartment on the Boulevard Saint-Germain, they told me Guillaume was dead.

His little room was full of shadows, and of shades: those of his wife, of his mother, of ourselves, and of others who moved about in it or mourned stock-still and whom I did not recognize at all. His dead face illuminated the pillow beneath it with a laureate beauty—radiant as if we were looking at the young Virgil. Death, in Dante's gown, was tugging him, like a child, by the hand.

*

I can still see him sauntering through the hopscotch squares chalked on the streets of Montparnasse, favoring the fragile arsenal of his head, spouting one piece of abstruse information after the next. For instance, remarking that the Bretons were originally Negroes; that the Gauls never wore mustaches; that *groom* was a corruption of *gros homme* as pronounced by the boys who replaced Swiss *portiers* in London.

Sometimes he would stop, raise one marquise's finger, and say (for instance): "I have just reread *Maldoror*. The young owe much more to Lautréamont than to Rimbaud." I quote this remark rather than a thousand others because it reminds me of a scene Picasso once described to me: Picasso, Max Jacob, and Apollinaire, all very young at the time, walking in Montmartre, racing down the stairways, shouting at the top of their lungs, "Long live Rimbaud! Down with Laforgue!"—a demonstration infinitely more significant, in my opinion, than those which precede referendums.

One morning in 1917 (Picasso, Satie, and I had just weathered the scandal of *Parade*), Blaise Cendrars telephoned to say he had read a poem over my signature in the magazine *SIC*—a poem he was amazed not to recognize, though it was not at all in my style; he wanted to read it to me over the phone so I could tell him whether or not I had written it. The poem was a forgery. And out of that forgery Apollinaire made a whole drama. He exercised a certain jurisdiction over letters and set great store by his magistracy. From café to café, from Montparnasse to Montmartre, from editor's office to composing room he unearthed clues, questioned suspects, accused everyone—except the culprit, who much later confessed to the hoax. It consisted in sending a poem to Birot, the editor of *SIC*, baited with my signature so that it would be printed without verification. The poem was an acrostic; its capital letters spelled out: POOR BIROT.

*

Which takes me in the wrong direction. I shall instead describe, since it can do no one any harm, an incident which occurred the night of the first performance of *Les Mamelles de Tirésias*, at the Théâtre Renée Maubel.

Apollinaire had asked me to contribute a poem to the program. This poem, called *Zèbre*, used the word *rue* in the sense of *ruer*, to rush. The Cubists, led by Juan Gris, understood this particular *rue* of mine in the usual sense and, that night, after the performance, insisted upon an explanation of what that street was doing there. It didn't belong.

In this dock where we figured side by side, Apollinaire shifted from the role of judge to that of defendant. He was charged with having caricatured and compromised the Cubist dogma by entrusting his sets and costumes to Serge Ferat. Gris and I were fond of each other, all of us loved Apollinaire. But I recount the episode because it shows what hairs we were capable of splitting, what pinheads we danced on. The slightest deviation or indiscretion was suspect, subject to judgment, and likely to end with a sentence. "It was I," Juan Gris once said, "who introduced the siphon bottle into painting." (Nothing but Anis del Oso bottles had been permitted.) And Marcoussis, leaving the show of Picasso's *"fenêtres"* at Paul Rosenberg's, declared: "He has solved the problem of the window hasp."

This was no laughing matter. It is a great and noble period when such nuances preoccupy men's minds. And Picasso is quite right to say that a government which punished a painter for using the wrong color, for drawing the wrong line, would be a great government.

*

Picasso is the pope, the Borgia pope of a church whose *peintres maudits*, Van Gogh leading the way, were its first martyrs. When I met Picasso, he was living in an apartment overlooking the cemetery of Montparnasse. The prospect was less than cheerful, but Picasso has never bothered about appearances, except to reap them. For, whatever he does, Picasso harvests. He is a rag picker of genius: king of the rag pickers. As soon as he goes out, he gathers up all he finds and brings it back to his studio, where he raises it, no matter what it is, to the dignity of use. Nor does he collect unexpected objects with his hands alone: his eyes gather the merest, the meanest spectacle. And if you consult his work attentively, you can always recognize the neighborhood he lived in when he painted any one canvas, for it reveals precisely the elements which the inattentive fail to notice: graffiti chalked on sidewalks, shopwindows, posters, lampposts spattered with plaster, the plunder of garbage pails.

In the earliest so-called Cubist paintings, you can reconstruct the painter's daily route between the newspaper kiosks and peddlers' stalls of Montmartre. Out of everything old he makes the New, which may surprise but which holds you by its *realism*. Let me explain what I mean by the word. Strictly speaking, there is no such thing as abstract painting, for each picture represents an idea of the painter's or, in the long run, the painter himself. Picasso has never claimed to have painted an abstract picture. Savagely he tracks down resemblance and captures it to such effect that the object or figure at the source of his work often loses power and character beside its representation.*

In his studio, chaos ruled; drawings lay everywhere among the litter. When one of the first rich collectors visited Montparnasse he bent down, picked up a drawing from under a table, and asked how much it would cost. Picasso answered, "Fifty francs." And this collector, seeing a great number, exclaimed, "Why, you have a fortune, right here on the floor!"

It is a question when Picasso, victimized by visitors, ever finds time to work. He works on the sly, when you are eating,

---

* Many people who think they love painting love the model, the painter's pretext for painting his self-portrait. Still-life, nude, landscape—it is always his own portrait which results; and here is the proof. When you see a Virgin by Raphael, you don't say "Look, there's the Virgin." You say "Look, Raphael!" When you see Vermeer's *Girl in a Blue Cap*, you don't say "Look, there's a girl in a blue cap," but "Look, Vermeer!" When you see some anemones by Renoir you don't say "Look, anemones," but "Look, Renoir!" And when you see a woman whose right eye is in the wrong place, you don't say "Look, there's a woman whose right eye is in the wrong place"; you say: "Look, Picasso!"

telephoning, sleeping, when your distractions leave him free to organize the world his way, not yours. He never abets your vision, for he never abandons his own. To a lady who asked, "What does that represent?" he replied, "That represents a million." And he told another lady, who had asked if his works were hoaxes, "All works are hoaxes, starting with masterpieces."

And Picasso adds: "How can I do better than God Himself, who makes one mistake after another?"

*

Picasso's great friends have been, myself apart, Apollinaire, André Salmon, Max Jacob, Gertrude Stein, Pierre Reverdy, Paul Eluard. Poets. Is it not significant that he prefers to live with poets rather than painters? For he is a great poet. What he paints speaks, reflects the poet's exactions. His syntax is visual, comparable to a writer's. Apparently each of his canvases tries to conform to what Apollinaire called the *poem-as-event*.

Yet we must never forget that Picasso is a Spaniard. When he magnificently insults the human face, it is not an insult. He insults it the way his compatriots blaspheme the Virgin when she does not grant them what they have asked. Picasso always asks something, and the external world, matter itself, must obey him.

He is very short, with charming feet and hands, terrible eyes whose beams sink into the surface—and into the center. Intelligence squirts out of him like water from the nozzle of a sprinkler. It is cold, sometimes, under that shower, but the result is always salutary.

Nietzsche speaks of certain men as *mothers of Being*, men who continually give birth, who escape the critical spirit because they are devoured by the creative. It is a prophetic portrait of Picasso, who moreover, like all great creators, is both a man and a woman. *Drôle de ménage*, as we say: certainly no household I know of boasts so many broken dishes.

At the end of 1916 I took Picasso to Rome. Influenced by the hostile reaction of Montparnasse, Diaghilev adopted our groups and freshened his explosives. He had brought only Russian artists to France: Bakst, Alexandre Benois, Larionov. Now he annexed Picasso, Braque, Derain, Matisse, Laurens. He even tried to annex Renoir, but the old master was too infirm for the task.

Montparnasse was scandalized to see Picasso crack the Cubist tables-of-the-law and join me in Rome, where we would create, for Erik Satie's music, the ballet *Parade*.

We announced our departure to Gertrude Stein as if we had become engaged. Taking Picasso to Diaghilev was like taking Monsieur Renan backstage at a cabaret.

The Italian Futurists collaborated with us, under Marinetti's leadership—Prampolini, Balla, Carrà—and their help in constructing the carcasses of Picasso's costumes made our work possible. We were convinced the ballet would please everyone because our work pleased us and because it seemed only natural that others would share our pleasure. We did not suspect that *Parade* would be, in 1917, a great event and a great scandal in the theatre. It was first performed at the Châtelet, and for once Diaghilev, ordinarily so brave, blanched as he listened to the raging audience. With some reason. Picasso, Satie, and I could not get backstage. We were recognized, threatened, and if we were not lynched at the exit it was only because Apollinaire was there in uniform and wounded on the temple, and because this wound, prefigured in the Chirico portrait, obliged him to wear bandages inspiring respect from a naïvely patriotic public. Without him, women armed with hatpins would have poked out our eyes. He saved us from the crowd, but only just. Once calm was restored—several performances later—we heard one gentleman say to another: "If anyone had told me it would be so silly, I'd have brought the children."

Some time later, Strauss's *Josephslegende* scored a triumph in Paris. Diaghilev and I were sitting in a box with Hofmannsthal, who had written the ballet's scenario. At the tenth curtain call,

Hofmannsthal leaned over and murmured to Diaghilev, "I'd have preferred a scandal." And Diaghilev, in his "astonish me, Jean" voice, answered: "Alas . . . it's not that easy."

Le Coq et l'Arlequin

"We harbor an angel
whom we ceaselessly offend.
We must be that angel's guardian."

I admire the Harlequins of Cézanne and Picasso, but I do not love Harlequin. He wears a mask, and a motley costume. And at cockcrow, having reneged, he hides. He is a cock of the night.

But I love the true cock, truly motley—feather by feather, who stares, unwinking, unmasked, into the sun; who never reneges or hides, who is not afraid to love or to defend what he loves.

The cock says Cocteau twice, and lives on his *own* farm.

Long live the Cock! Down with Harlequin!

*

Thoughts of the canvas on which the painter is creating a masterpiece: "He is defiling me, he is abusing me, he is concealing me." Just so, man resents his splendid destiny.

*

The recent canvases by Henri Matisse shown at Bernheim Jeune are very curious. The sunlit Fauve has become one of Bonnard's kittens. The gallery is drenched in the atmosphere of Bonnard, Vuillard, Marquet: the window in a Vuillard bedroom opens onto a Marquet sea. We look for Matisse and we find, if I may say so, a case of occupational deformity.

The Impressionists blinked in the sun. Then came Matisse. He braved the sun which hoaxes us by filling our eyes with green when we have stared at red. Freely, joyously, boldly, Matisse painted pictures which make life an appetite.

What has happened?

Matisse works without profound disciplines, without those hidden geometries of Cézanne and the old masters whose vestiges our young painters pursue and which, unfortunately, too often substitute for painting on their canvases. So Matisse doubts, gropes, hesitates instead of heightening his discovery. Does he know the real value of that discovery and why it delights us? I sense, behind the work, a *beaux-arts* graduate, the kind of "professional" who would tell his son that painting is "one hell of a profession," etc., etc., opposing the grace which granted us his earlier canvases.

Leaving this exhibition, I found myself humming "The Crayfish" from Apollinaire's *Bestiaire*, which Francis Poulenc has just set to music:

> *Incertitude, ô mes délices,*
> *Vous et moi nous en allons*
> *Comme s'en vont les écrevisses,*
> *A reculons, à reculons.*

> Uncertainty, O my delight, the two of us advance
> The way that crayfish go—backward, backward.

*

Charlie Chaplin or Charles Chaplin or Charlot or Karl or Chap, depending on your country and class, deserves a long study to himself—which I hope to write one day. This comedian, tragedian, mime, acrobat performs everywhere at once. His art derives neither from that filmed theatre which makes the spectator feel he has gone deaf, nor from the Western which dilutes landscape with drama, nor from the serial in which mysterious men—sons of Eugène Sue, Dumas, and Edison—do their good or wicked deeds under Rudolph's cape, with Monte Cristo's fortune.

Chaplin is our modern Guignol. He speaks to every age, every nation. Esperanto laughter. Each of us is entertained by Chaplin for different reasons. With his help, the Tower of Babel would certainly have been finished. Since he never overstates any of the effects he continually creates, quick minds enjoy them while the rest are content with his pratfalls.

His latest film, *Shoulder Arms*, would be a kind of masterpiece if its clowning were not reduced by imputing the action to a dream.

There is no use describing this film which moves like a drumroll, in which setting and characters play their part without a single false note. But let us salute in passing the very fable of war: Charlot, camouflaged as a tree, goes out on reconnaissance. He is discovered. He escapes, a formidable enemy at his heels. The runaway tree hopping through the forest, playing hide-and-seek with that huge pursuing Wotan, is epic art. We have seen the spirit of lightness conquer the spirit of weight.

*

Erik Satie was an unspeakable man—speech, I mean, being insufficient to account for him. Honfleur and Scotland were his paternal and maternal origins; from Honfleur he inherited the style of Alphonse Allais's sketches, whose secret poetry bears no resemblance to the usual smut that passes for an anecdote; from Scotland he inherited a dour eccentricity.

In appearance he was a petty official, wearing a goatee, pince-nez, bowler, and carrying an umbrella.

Egotistical, cruel, obsessive, he would listen to nothing alien to his dogmas, and raged against whatever interfered with them. Egotistical because he thought of nothing but his music; cruel because he defended his music; obsessive because he polished his music. And his music was tender. So was he, then, in his way. For several years Erik Satie visited me, mornings, in my room at 10 rue d'Anjou. He kept on his immaculate overcoat, his gloves, his hat tilted over the pince-nez, his umbrella in one hand. With the other he sheltered his tortuous lips when he talked or laughed. He had walked all the way from Arcueil, where he lived in one little room, in which, after his death, under a mountain of dust, every letter his friends had ever written him was found. He had not opened one.

He kept himself clean with pumice stone. He never used water.

*

In a period when music spread in waves, in emanations, in effluvia, Satie, acknowledging Debussy's genius but fearing his despotism (they outraged and propitiated each other till the end), forsook his school and became, at the Schola Cantorum, the singular Socrates whom we knew.

Sickened by the vague, the melting, the superfluous, by padding and by modern hocus-pocus, often tempted on the other hand by a technique whose ultimate resources were well within his grasp, Satie deliberately *did without* in order to do more: to remain clear, simple, luminous.* But the public loathes candor.

People often ask why Satie tricks out his loveliest works with comical titles which baffle even the least hostile audience. Not only do these titles protect his work from persons possessed by the "sublime" and legitimize the laughter of those who are not; they also correct the Debussyist abuse of "precious" titles, of literature. With good-humored bad temper, Satie denatures all the *Lunes descendant sur le temple qui fut,* all the *Terrasses des audiences du Clair de lune,* and all the *Cathédrales englouties.*

*

The four-hand piano score of *Parade* is from start to finish a masterpiece of architecture, incomprehensible to ears corrupted by the nebulous, by *frissons.* First a fugue dislocates itself, giv-

* Satie wanted to create a theatre for dogs. The curtain goes up. The scene represents a bone.

ing birth to the quintessential rhythm of carnival melancholy.
Then come the three dances. Their many motifs, as distinct
from each other as objects, succeed without development, without interference. A metronomic unity presides over each, a
unity superimposing the role's contour and the reveries it provokes. The Chinaman, the Little American Girl, and the Acrobats release certain unsuspected nostalgias achieved with expressive means signally loyal to their ends. Rejecting spells, charms,
reprises, underhand caresses, fevers, miasmas, Satie never stirs
up the swamp. This is the poetry of childhood recovered by a
technician.

*

Genius, like electricity, is not to be analyzed. You have it, or
you don't have it. Stravinsky has it, and therefore never concerns himself with it. Never hypnotizes himself with it, never
entrances himself. He does not yield to the danger of auto-
intoxication, of making himself beautiful, or ugly. He transforms raw power, devising for its use apparatus ranging from
factory to flashlight.

How to describe Stravinsky without describing this latest
stage? Rings, spats, scarves, Norfolk jackets, ascots, stickpins,
wristwatches, mufflers, charms, pince-nez, monocles, spectacles,
watch chains—no help at all: they simply prove, superficially,
that Stravinsky pays no attention to anyone. He composes,
dresses, talks the way he pleases. When he plays the piano, he
and the piano fit: one object; when he conducts the *Octet*, he
turns his astronomer's back on us to solve this magnificent instrumental problem with silver figures.

From Rimsky-Korsakov he inherited the work habits he dis-
torts to his own purposes. On Rimsky's desk, the rulers, ink
bottles, penholders must have betrayed the bureaucrat. On
Stravinsky's, the order is alarming: a surgeon's instruments,
arrayed.

The composer fused with his craft, dressed in it, his works

harnessed to him like the old one-man band; shedding, thickening the rind of music around himself—Stravinsky is utterly united with the room he lives in. To see him in Morges, in Leysin, in Paris at Pleyel's, is to see the animal in its carapace. Pianos, tom-toms, snare drums, metronomes, cymbalon, staff markers, pencil sharpeners, music stands are all an extension of himself, the pilot's cockpit, the weapons bristling about the insect as we see it on film, enlarged a thousand times, during the mating season.

*

One of the noblest positions: that of Calchas, in Shakespeare's *Troilus and Cressida*. Loving justice, he joins the Greeks. The Trojans watch the traitor from their walls; the Greeks suspect him of spying. Impossible to feel more alone in the world than this man.

*

Picasso says that everything is a miracle, that it is a miracle we do not dissolve when we take a bath.

The night before the opening of *Antigone*, in December 1922, we were sitting out front—actors and author—in Dullin's Théâtre de l'Atelier. Crumpled canvas the color of blueing made the stage into a cavern, with openings on either side; in the center, high up, a hole behind which the chorus declaimed, through a megaphone. Around this hole I had hung the masks of boys, women, and old men painted by Picasso or executed from his models. Beneath the masks hung a white panel on which was to be painted the makeshift décor which sacrificed both the literal and the suggestive—equally expensive—to a sign language for a day of scorching heat.

Picasso walked back and forth across the stage.

He began by rubbing a stick of red chalk over the boards, which, because of the unevenness of the wood, turned to marble. Then he took a bottle of ink and began drawing, darkening certain areas with masterly assurance: three columns appeared. The existence of these columns was so sudden, so surprising that we burst into applause.

As we left the theatre, I asked Picasso if he had calculated their approach, if he had closed in on them, or if he, too, had been surprised by them. He answered that he had been surprised, but that you always calculate unconsciously, that the Doric column results, like the hexameter, from an operation of the senses, and that perhaps he had just invented such a column in the same way the Greeks had discovered it.

*

At seventeen, charged with electricity—I mean with shapeless poetry, incapable of constructing a *transmitter*, diverted by suspect praise and bad books—I kept turning, round and round, over and over, like a sick man trying to sleep. I wasted my time, throttled by absurd pride, sick at heart, thirsting for death. The Comtesse de Noailles infected me with her love of life. Her whole being uttered Jeanne du Barry's cry: "One moment more, Monsieur Executioner." But Anna de Noailles's was the cry of a queen.

Gradually I fell asleep—a somnambulist's sleep, which became my normal state—and I shall sleep it out, surely, to the end.

*

Stravinsky once told me that you must make allowances for your listeners—if he himself had seen his latest work a year ago, he would have shrugged his shoulders.

*

On October 12, 1492, Columbus discovered America. The foundling has come a long way. In recent years, our own artists have worked under its influence. Composers use its ragtime, painters its landscapes of iron and concrete, poets its advertising and its films. Its machines, skyscrapers, ocean liners, and Negroes were certainly the source of a new and excellent direction. They marched upon Capua like Hannibal's army of elephants.

The curve, the garland, the rebus, all our precious dissonances gave way to a more brutal disorder.

Fierce contacts. Art grew virile. Fauvism, in all its savagery, was upon us, a new age.

The jazz band can be considered the soul of these forces. They crystallize in it, singing their cruelty, their sadness.

I listen to a jazz band at the Casino de Paris: high in the air, in a kind of cage, the Negroes writhe, dandle, toss lumps of raw meat to the crowd in the form of trumpet screams, rattles, drumbeats. The dance tune, broken, punched, counterpointed, rises now and again to the surface.

The hot hall full of painted girls and American soldiers is a saloon in some Western film. This noise drenches us, wakens us *to do something else*. It shows us a lost path. No use making a bad imitation of a fox-trot. The lesson of rhythm sticks our nose in our own flabbiness. But if we let this cyclone sweep us away, that is merely another kind of flabbiness.

Never do what a specialist can do better. Discover your own specialty. Do not despair if your specialty appears to be more delicate, a lesser thing. Make up in finesse what you lose in force.

*

Style cannot be a point of departure. It is a result. What is style? For many, a complicated way of saying simple things. For us, a simple way of saying complicated things. A Stendhal, a Balzac even (the Balzac of *Père Goriot*, of *Cousine Bette*), tries above all to hit the bull's-eye. Nine times out of ten they succeed, somehow. It is that *somehow*, quickly appropriated, which they adopt according to the *results*, that way of taking aim, of firing fast and unfailingly, which I call style.

A Flaubert thinks only of taking aim. The bull's-eye is insignificant. He oils his gun. The lady of the shooting gallery, *with her back to the targets*, is watching him. What a splendid figure of a man! what a hunter! what style! What does it matter to her if the marksman hits the target, so long as he takes aim masterfully, gracefully, and above all, not too quickly!

How far Flaubert's so-called realistic scenes are from reality. *Madame Bovary*, for instance, in which the consciousness of taking aim swaggers on every page, swarms with unrealities. A series of salon tableaux.

*

To write, above all to write poems, is the same as to sweat. The poem is a perspiration. It would be unhealthy to walk, to run, to play, to be an athlete without sweating. Only the way a man walks and the man himself interest me. That is why few works by the living touch me. In the work of a dead man, in the perfume of his sweat, I look for evidence of activity. The Louvre is a morgue; we go there to identify our friends.

Rimbaud, at Harrar, affords the example of an athlete of poetry who does not sweat. But he no longer moves. Once you move, granted you accept the disadvantages of motion, you must sweat as little as possible; you must, so to speak, sweat dry.

*

A good writer always strikes in the same place with different hammers made of different materials and of different sizes. The sound changes. He nurses his nail: the *same* hammer would end by crushing it, driving the point no farther in, making the sound of dead wood. That is the sound of our great men.

The public does not expect what the true poet gives. The public is disappointed—it feels he has not kept his promises.

What did I promise you? You must learn that a good book never gives what you are entitled to expect of it. It cannot be an answer to your expectation. It must riddle you with question marks.

*

What men call genius rarely includes intelligence. Now, as I see it, intelligence never spoils anything. Stendhal, Nietzsche are the type of the intelligent genius. Of course Zarathustra is often an old mountain guide, turned phrasemaker by long Alpine solitude. Nonetheless, his diamond scratches everything else. Nietzsche *informed*, he saw, he foresaw everything. He prophesied the Dionysiac pessimism we are living through now. Who acknowledges it?

*

Disinterestedness, egoism, compassion, cruelty, a craving and a revulsion for the pleasures of the earth, a naïve amorality— make no mistake, these are the signs of what is called *angelism*, characteristic of every true poet, whether he writes, paints, sculpts, or sings. Few persons admit it, for few persons experience poetry.

Until further notice, Arthur Rimbaud remains the type of an angel on earth. Consider his photograph. We see him full-face, in a schoolboy jacket and skimpy tie. Time has erased the main features. What is left is a phosphorescent face. If you look hard at this portrait, if you turn it over, hold it at arm's length, bring it closer, it soon comes to resemble a kind of meteor, a milky way.

One day, when I happened to refer to Verlaine's angelism, an eminent critic burst out laughing and said, "It's obvious you never knew him." He remembered the faun, the Russian coachman, the drunkard, nothing else. And yet, aside from his work and his life, another photograph—one I own—gives Verlaine away: standing, wearing a velvet top hat brushed against the grain, with a muffler thrown over his shoulder, his eyes starry: adorable.

Another poet who was counseled, aided, teased by the angels, miraculously walking home every night from Montmartre or Montparnasse to Arcueil-Cachan (or did the angels carry him in their arms?), Erik Satie told me of one truly angelic salutation he witnessed. It was at the Auberge du Clou. Mallarmé came in to buy some snails. Verlaine was drinking at a table. They did not know each other. They spoke. Impossible to reproduce the timbre of Satie's voice and the expression on his face when he described this episode.

*

A masterpiece for the critics will be a work that *compares*, that has the look of a masterpiece. Yet a masterpiece cannot look like a masterpiece. It is of necessity lame, lacking, full of faults, for it is the triumph of its errors and the consecration of its faults which will make it into a masterpiece.

*

A true poet rarely bothers about poetry. Does a gardener perfume his roses? He subjects them to a regimen which perfects their complexion, their breath. Paul Valéry boasts of being a versifier, of performing exercises. The better for us, if he is a poet. But this mystery does not concern him.

The story of the tourists in China where the car breaks down in a village, a tiny hole in the gas tank. An artist is discovered who cannot repair the tank but who will copy it in two hours. The tourists set out again with a splendid new tank. In the middle of the night, a new breakdown. The Chinese had also copied the hole.

An Indian chief was recently invited to the White House. At President Wilson's table, his friends suggest that perhaps he is eating and drinking a little too much. "A little too much," he answers, "is just enough for me."

If I were to adopt a motto, I should choose this magnificent reply.

Le Numéro Barbette

> *"The nonchalance which crowns every*
> *true labor deceives the world:*
> *what appears on the surface*
> *is merely the aspect of facility."*

Barbette is a young American of twenty-four who hunches his shoulders like a bird and walks a little unsteadily (doubtless because his feet, like his hands, are so small). A fall from a trapeze has left a scar which curls his upper lip back from an irregular row of teeth. Only the astonishing superciliary arch above his inhuman eyes calls attention to Barbette's person, anonymous as Nijinsky in the city streets.

It is long after six. Suppose we take a sandwich and a hard-boiled egg with our acrobat, then accompany him to the dressing room where he appears at eight (he goes on at eleven), with that conscientiousness unknown to our actors and characteristic of clowns, Annamese mimes, and the Cambodian dancing girls who are sewn each night into their gold costumes.

Barbette substantiates the Greek legends about young men changed into trees, into flowers: an antidote to their easy magic.

We shall follow, in slow motion, brightly lit, some significant phases of a metamorphosis Man Ray agreed to capture for me on film, including the one in which Barbette—his woman's head belied by his naked torso in its leather girdle—looks exactly like the trussmaker's Apollo.

I am not intimidated, at first, by this dressing room where I smoke, gossip with my athletic friend who washes up, then covers his skin with handfuls of cold cream. Some chorus girls stand giggling and squealing at the door until Barbette puts on a terry-cloth robe and goes over to chat with them. Even when he is completely made up, his face as precious as a brand-new box of pastels, his jaws enameled with shimmering gum, his body rubbed with pipe clay until it looks unreal, this strange young Satan, this vision of Saint-Just, this psychopomp will remain a man, tied to his double by a hair. It is only when he pulls on the blond wig, securing it by elastic around his ears, that he assumes—a bouquet of bobby pins in his mouth—every last gesture of a woman doing her hair. He stands up, walks around the room, puts on his rings. The metamorphosis is complete. Jekyll is Hyde. Yes, Hyde! and I am frightened. I look away, stub out my cigarette, take off my hat. It is my turn to be intimidated. The door opens and the chorus girls, as if the place belonged to them now, walk in and out, sit down, powder their faces, talk about clothes.

The dresser helps Barbette into his gown, fluffs the feathers, hooks up the bodice (tulle shoulder straps which do not even conceal the absence of breasts), and as the procession—dresser, visitors, chorus girls—moves downstairs, Barbette turns back into a boy dressed up for a joke, tripping on his skirt and threatening to slide down the banister.

He remains a man once we get to the stage, inspecting his equipment, doing knee bends, squinting under the glare of the spotlights as he tests his rigging and clambers up the ladders. Once the question of danger is disposed of, the woman reappears, a great lady glancing one last time round her salon before the party, plumping cushions, shifting vases and lamps.

The orchestra strikes up. Let us take our seats and, like the other spectators out front, watch *le numéro Barbette*.

The curtain rises on a functional set: a tightrope between two platforms, a trapeze and rings hanging from the proscenium. Upstage, a couch covered with a white bearskin on which, between the tightrope part of the act and the trapeze part, Barbette will remove his cumbersome gown and perform a scabrous little scene, a real masterpiece of pantomime in which, parodying, recapitulating all the women he has studied, he becomes woman herself, eclipsing even the loveliest creatures who precede and follow him on the bill. Do not forget: we are under the theatre's lights, inside that magic box where truth has no currency, where nature has no value, where the short are made tall and the tall can shrink, where the only realities are feats of prestidigitation whose difficulty the public never suspects. Here, just as Guitry used to be The Russian General, Barbette will be The Woman. He proves that it was for more than mere propriety's sake that great nations, great civilizations entrusted women's roles to men. He brings to mind François Fratellini's explanation of why I could not show a British clown how to do the Bookmaker in *Le Boeuf sur le Toit:* an Englishman cannot act an Englishman. And Réjane's remark: "When I play a mother, I have to forget my Jacques. Sometimes I have to imagine I'm a man to get across the footlights." That was detachment, that was diligence—that was an initiation into the art! Listening to them, seeing Nijinsky or Pavlova gasping like winded boxers between rounds, discovering that backstage atmosphere of a ship without a course while the charming ballet continues—I have learned the secrets of the theatre.

When Barbette comes on, he deceives us with one flick of the wrist, allowing him to concentrate entirely on his work as an acrobat. Henceforth his male gestures will serve instead of betraying him. He will seem to be one of those Amazons who dazzle us in the advertisements of American magazines. The scene on the couch, another sleight of hand: for afterwards he will require complete freedom of movement in order to fly over the audience, pretending to fall, hanging by one foot, offering upside down his mad angel's face, linking his twin shadows which enlarge with each backward swing of the trapeze.

When he makes his entrance, and now over our heads, and when he comes back to earth, even when he skips along the tightrope, there is nothing particularly feminine about him. One thinks of those Florentine painters who had young men sit for the women's heads, and of Proust when he scrambles the sexes with a cunning and a clumsiness which give his characters a mysterious glamour.

The reason for Barbette's success is that he appeals to the instinct of several audiences in one, obscurely amalgamating contradictory enthusiasms. For he pleases those who see him as a woman, those who divine the man in him, and those others who are stirred by the supernatural sex of beauty.

Barbette moves in silence. In spite of the orchestra which accompanies the proceedings, underlining his postures, his perilous exploits, we seem to be seeing his act from a great distance, as if it were happening in the streets of a dream, a place where sounds cannot be heard, brought into being by a telescope, or by sleep.

The movie camera has superseded our realistic sculpture. The marble personages of the cinema, its great pale heads, its shadowy volumes with their splendid saliences, all that abstract humanity, that silent inhumanity, replace what the eye once asked of sculpture. Barbette derives from these moving statues. Even when you know him, he cannot lose his mystery. He remains a plaster model, a wax mannequin, the living bust which sang on its velvet-draped pedestal for the conjuror Robert Houdin.

His is the solitude of Oedipus, the loneliness of one of Chirico's eggs in the foreground of a city on the day of an eclipse. Moreover, I leave to poets the responsibility of comparisons, of images. For me, what matters is the technician who searches for the one apparatus that will work, then dismantles it as Poe dismantled Maelzel's chess-playing automaton.

At the end of this unforgettable lie, what a letdown if Barbette merely removed his wig! He does remove it, you will say, after five curtain calls, and the letdown does occur. We even hear murmurs throughout the house. We see embarrassed faces, blushes. Of course. For after having reaped his reward as an acrobat and nearly scared us to death, Barbette must reap his reward as an actor. But consider the final tour de force: to become a man again, to run the film backward, is not enough. The truth, too, must be translated, must be heightened to keep on an equal footing with the lie. That is why Barbette, once his wig is pulled off, *acts the part of a man,* rolls his shoulders, spreads his hands, swells his muscles, exaggerates the casual gait of a golfer.

To perfect this apparatus of enchantments, of emotions, of skills that trick our senses and our souls, what an inspiration! when the curtain rises for the fifteenth time and the ex-Barbette, winking, shifts his weight from one foot to the other, makes an awkward gesture of protest, performs a sort of street urchin's shuffle in order to erase all traces of the dying swan, all vestiges of the fabulous which he knows so well without having to calculate and which seems no more than a lapse of taste in his perfect modesty, the modesty of the craftsman.

Raymond Radiguet

> *"Since he lived in the Parc-Saint-Maur*
> *on the banks of the Marne,*
> *we called him The Miracle of the Marne."*

> *"You know what I mean by 'heaven's gloves':*
> *in order to touch us without defiling itself,*
> *heaven sometimes wears gloves.*
> *Raymond Radiguet was one.*
> *His form fitted heaven like a glove.*
> *When heaven takes out its hand,*
> *that is death."*

From my first meeting with Raymond Radiguet I can say I divined his star. How? I wonder.

He was fourteen when I met him, through Max Jacob. Max lived in the Rue Gabriel—in Montmartre, still, like Juan Gris.

Raymond Radiguet lived in the Parc-Saint-Maur, and when it was too late for him to go home at night, to cross the Bois—besides, he was terrified of the roaring lions in the zoo—he would sleep either at Juan Gris's apartment or at Max Jacob's, but on a table, among the paint pots! He was short, pale, near-sighted; his unruly hair hung over his collar, and he squinted as though at the sun. He skipped when he walked—as if the side-walks were trampolines. Out of his pockets he pulled the pages of a schoolboy notebook which he had crumpled into little balls. He smoothed them out and, awkwardly rolling a cigarette, managed to decipher poems as fresh and tart as currants, almost pasting them against his eyes.

These poems were not like any others being written; in fact, they contradicted the period and relied on no previous work. Let me say, in passing, that Radiguet's supreme tact, the soli-tude of his words, the density of the void around them, and the aeration of each poem as a whole have not yet been understood in France—the numerous pastiches offered for sale today are not even caricatures of the originals.

He rejuvenated the old formulas. He unvarnished the stereo-types. He scoured the clichés. When he touched them, it was as if his clumsy hands were putting some shellfish back into water. That was his privilege, his alone.

"We must be precious," he said, and from his lips the word took its true meaning: exceedingly rare, the meaning of a pre-cious stone.

*

I had immediately seen what he would be. I had sensed what he would become. Not that I was certain, but after all, he was exceptional . . . His silence was demoralizing. He saw noth-ing—when we discovered how nearsighted he was, we bought him glasses: then he found everything horrible, hideous, and he never used them, only one of the lenses as a monocle, making a dreadful grimace with his left eye.

He never opened his mouth except to say: *Don't contradict the ordinary. Contradict the avant-garde.* One day in Montparnasse a group of us—Picasso, Modigliani, Reverdy, and some others—visited a painter who wanted to show us his work, and our silence became oppressive. As he put up the last canvas, he began making excuses, saying, "This one really isn't done, it's not finished." And then we were startled to hear these words come out of Radiguet's mouth: "Wouldn't it be a kindness to put it out of its misery?" That was one of the only times he said something, usually he trailed behind us in silence, but his silence spoke, his presence was not silent. And his rages, his cold rages!

We spent one summer vacation—the Aurics, the Hugos (Jean and Valentine Hugo), Lipschitz, and others—at Le Picaye, on the Bassin d'Arcachon; we all lived together in an uncomfortable, candlelit log cabin we called the Hôtel Chantecler. In those years, the place was really a backwater, and there was no such thing as a barber: we shaved Raymond with an oyster shell, as Lipschitz's bust of him shows. One day we were sitting around the kitchen table—Valentine was knitting, Jean Hugo was drawing, Auric was drumming on the table, and I was reading *Les Stances* by Jean Moréas—when all of a sudden I looked up and remarked, "You know, Moréas isn't so bad." And Radiguet, with a glance like a pistol shot, snatched the book out of my hands, ran down to the beach, and threw Moréas's poems into the Bassin d'Arcachon. And he came back and sat down among us with the expression of a murderer, unforgettable.

*

He was very affected, for he belonged to the most audacious group of the period, but always in a spirit of counter-fashion, moving against the avant-garde, against the vogue. And, as I was saying, he moved toward me. One day my mother's old housemaid said to me, "There's someone waiting to see you—a child with a cane." That was Raymond Radiguet, and he never left me again.

Radiguet was the bad student who jumps out the window in order not to do his homework. He was writing *Le Diable au Corps*, which I had to force him to finish . . . That is why there are manuscripts which arouse the suspicions of bibliophiles, for I copied out passages on them so that he would write more. I locked him in, as I said. He jumped out the window.

He would read nothing but mediocre books, comparing them with masterpieces, returning to them, rating them, annotating them, licking his cigarette papers, and declaring that since the mechanism of a masterpiece was invisible, he could learn only from books which passed for masterpieces and were no such thing. He went on to explain that anti-avant-garde attitude which had led him to write two masterpieces, *Le Diable au Corps* and *Le Bal du Comte d'Orgel*, at a time when it was scandalous to write novels, and which led me to write the strophes of *Plain-chant* at a time when it was scandalous to produce alexandrines, regular verses.

According to his theory, you must put your easel in front of a masterpiece and copy it without your picture coming to resemble it. He had put his easel in front of *La Princesse de Clèves*. The result was *Le Bal du Comte d'Orgel*. I put my easel in front of the first hundred pages of *La Chartreuse de Parme*, and the result was *Thomas l'Imposteur*. We wrote—he *Orgel* and I *Thomas*—at Pramousquier, near Cap Nègre, at the Pension Bessier, where we were staying with Georges Auric.

*

But, alas! Radiguet drank: a bottle of whisky and a bottle of gin every day. He fell ill while he was living in the Hôtel Foyot. I myself was very ill at the time.

I should say that when Radiguet was writing *Le Diable au Corps*, I had started, with Cendrars and M. Laffitte, a publishing house which we called Editions La Sirène . . . Our purpose was to sell the unsalable—i.e., Apollinaire, Max Jacob, Cendrars, myself. It was this house which published *Le Cap de Bonne-Espérance*. And the unsalable sold, and that turned M. Laffitte's head, who wanted to sell the salable. Having asked Galliot, "Is the revolution coming?" he rented a huge apartment, hired secretaries. He went bankrupt. I had the innocence to suppose our enterprise would continue, and I had submitted Radiguet's manuscript to La Sirène. Then I happened to meet Bernard Grasset, who was looking for a best seller to publish after *Maria Chapdelaine* . . . I gave him the manuscript. He went wild over it: Radiguet became his star dancer. At the time, I remember, he called him his Bébé Cadum. Grasset paid a lot of money for the rights, but Radiguet gave none of it to La Sirène. He bought himself a magnificent camel's-hair overcoat and a magnificent pigskin valise and went off with a crowd of American boys and girls to Fontainebleau, where he claimed he would finish his book. I had a bad case of sciatica, I was in bed, and when he came back with the slapdash work of a bad student, I told him so. He flew into one of his icy rages, threw his manuscript into the fire, and the next day admitted that I was right. As soon as I recovered, I took him to Chantilly, where I locked him in a hotel room and made him write the magnificent end of his book.

And then, Le Boeuf sur le Toit bar, over and over, night after night: whisky and gin. He announced his engagement to a young lady who has since become Mme René Clair, and I could say, like Verlaine: *But God came, Who brought upon him the dim death of typhoid.* It was like tossing a match on a haystack doused with gasoline. He was finished. I can see him still, the day I took him to that hospital in the Rue Piccini, paid for by Mlle Chanel among others, for we were all very poor. I can see him still, in that ambulance, with a little cap and a book bag slung over his shoulder, and in that bag the manuscript of *Le Bal du Comte d'Orgel*. I prefer not to speak of his death. It is very painful. I did not want to see him on his deathbed. I stayed at home. Moreover, I was paralyzed with stupor and disgust . . .

*

I believe he had a plan, followed a schedule which accounted for the future. Some day he would have orchestrated his work and even, I am convinced, taken the steps necessary to attract attention to it. He was waiting for his moment. Death took him first.

That is why, since it was from him that I took whatever clear-sightedness I have, his death left me without direction, incapable of managing my affairs, of promoting and providing for my work.

When I met him, at Max Jacob's, he extricated me from a trap: running away as fast as I could, I risked finding myself, some day, God knows where. Radiguet calmed me with his own calm. *He taught me the great method, which is to forget one is a poet and let the phenomenon occur without our knowing it.* But his machine was a new one. Mine was dirty and noisy.

Raymond Radiguet was then fifteen years old. Erik Satie was nearly sixty. These two extremes taught me to speak in order to be understood. The only glory I can boast of is to have submitted to their instruction.

CALENDAR

1923–1929

Having begun as a jongleur for fashionable Parisians, and gone on to serve the postwar avant-garde as poet-chanticleer, Cocteau now became something else: a legend, an emblem, a myth, someone (like Gertrude Stein) about whom others exchanged gossip and invented characteristic jokes and stories. Sometimes the tone was cruel, as when, after Radiguet's death, an epithet punned on the title of one of his ballets, calling Cocteau Le Veuf sur le Toit, the Widower on the Roof. Sometimes it was fondly malicious, as when Bernard Berenson told a visitor that Cocteau "is just a brilliant talker I love listening to, but not half as much as he loves someone to talk to!" More often, it was respectful, as when playwright Fernand Crommelynck visited Cocteau's 1924 adaptation of Romeo and Juliet (in which Cocteau played Mercutio) and reported: "It's a marvelous spectacle, but the house is half empty. Many people go for a lark, to joke and laugh aloud. The costumes are all velvet and painted, even the lace on the sleeves, even the folds in the crinolines. The effect is magnificent. The entire stage is hung with black velvet. It's a sort of tragedy in slow motion. Let me assure you, Cocteau is a genius." And everywhere, in England and America as well as France, the youngest generation was moved and excited by the drama of this vulnerable, narcissistic, unabashed, scandalous, yet superlatively winning man.

The opium-smoking began in 1924, and after a first attempt at

disintoxication the following year, Cocteau went to the South
of France, to convalesce in the little fishing village of Villefranche-sur-Mer, on the coast between Nice and Monaco. Here,
during the summer of 1925, he "finally found my personal
mythology." He also found an important strategy as an artist. In
an open letter to the Catholic philosopher Jacques Maritain, he
described a religious crisis after the despair over Radiguet's
death, thus for the first time directly inviting the public to mix
(or, rather, not to separate) his art and his life, to see his published work as a poet-dramatist in historical terms of his private
suffering as a bereaved lover, and to raise the whole question of
what, in the case of a self-mythologizing writer, is to be believed.
Cocteau's answer came in one of his best poems: "I am a lie
that always tells the truth."

That summer he also finished his most original play, Orphée,
in which Death is an elegant lady wearing rubber surgical gloves
that enable her to pass through mirrors, and Orpheus' guardian
angel speaks the lines for which, in all his writing, Cocteau
became best known:

"I shall tell you the secret of secrets. Mirrors are the doors
by which death comes and goes. Don't tell this to anyone.
Just watch yourself all your life in a mirror and you will
see death at work like bees in a glass hive . . ."

And he wrote poems—"the first, I think, really to come from
inside . . . I will see myself circulating between my room and
those of Glenway Wescott and Monroe Wheeler to read them
poems from my Secret Museum . . ."

It was a summer of hard work. "I correct proofs and more
proofs," he wrote Poulenc. "I see a lot of Igor, and I have visited
the Picassos . . . What a pity you're not living here . . ."
They all lived in the waterfront Hôtel Welcome, with windows
looking out over the harbor. Just down the hall were the English

novelist Mary Butts; Gertrude Stein's future protégé Sir Francis Rose; Christian Bérard, who was to design the sets for many of Cocteau's plays and films; and assorted other young artists who had discovered that Provence was inexpensive in the summertime. Isadora Duncan was living nearby and on one occasion tried to entice Cocteau to bed by pleading, "Mais j'ai encore la peau possible . . . *But my skin is still possible.*" In a corner room, twenty-four-year-old Glenway Wescott was writing The Grandmothers, and in a letter to a friend described Cocteau as "serious, indolent and sound. He has the tiniest boat in the harbor, and in billowy pajama pants of waxed silk which once belonged to Yvonne Georges [who had played Juliet's nurse in Romeo] rows across the sleepy water with a handsome, sturdy boyfriend."

In spite of his cure and his relations with Maritain, Cocteau soon resumed his opium-smoking, and though complications and derèglement ensued, his fertility and production as a writer only increased. In the five years from 1924 to 1929, he published over twenty books and, among other things, appeared as the guardian angel Heurtebise in Orphée, conducted a running scrimmage with André Breton and the Surrealists, illustrated his own and Radiguet's novels, and wrote the text for Stravinsky's oratorio Oedipus Rex, which was first performed in Paris in May 1928. On December 16 of that same year, he undertook a second cure, and this time kept a graphic diary of his experience. In the clinic, he also began and finished a novel in seventeen days, with a currently popular American song, Jerome Kern's "Make Believe," running through his head as he wrote. A friend had told him, "You have Masterpiece Cramp. The sight of white paper paralyzes you. So just begin with whatever comes into your head. Write: 'One winter evening' . . . and keep going." Cocteau offered the manuscript to his publisher apologetically, explaining that he was sure only a few people would want to read it. But he was entirely wrong. Les Enfants Terribles became a best seller at once, and Cocteau, freshly emerged from his hospital room and turned forty years old in July, found himself rewarded with the first large-scale success he had ever known.

Villefranche: A Letter to Jacques Maritain

> "After fifteen days' work, in Rome, on Parade, which left us no time for sightseeing, Picasso and I took a walk.
>   Picasso: Let's go in and look at this church.
>   (The church is full of worshippers, candelabra, music, prayer. Observation impossible.)
>   Cocteau: Let's go look at another one.
>   (Same result. A long walk in silence.)
>   Picasso: We're living like dogs."
>
> *
>
> "I am a lie which always tells the truth."

Radiguet's death had operated on me without chloroform. Hoping to distract me, the Comte de Beaumont had me direct *Roméo et Juliette*, my text for which had existed since 1916. In it I had tried, even before *Antigone*, to effect the rejuvenation of a masterpiece, to reconstitute, to reveal it in a new light by scraping off the dead skin, the patina; or, in the terms of Stravinsky's answer to the accusation of disrespect toward Pergolesi: "You respect him—I love him," I wanted to marry a masterpiece.

What a brilliant nightmare, those performances at La Cigale! In the wings—even during a play which gives the impression of calm—hysteria and madness lurk in the shadows where actors, crew, and dressers scurry about in silence. I was playing Mercutio. My dressing room was just offstage. The bagpipes that emphasize certain passages of the text rang in my ears, filled the air. I wept with fatigue. I slept on my feet. My friends pushed me onstage like an animal.

My dresser had the habit of saying: "Before Monsieur Jean dies," or "After Monsieur Jean dies," and that was the truth: I never played the duel scene without hoping that my pantomime would deceive death into taking me.

All in all, two months of work day and night, depression, pills gulped down pell-mell, turned me into an insect of which Jean Hugo's costume was the carapace. If someone had cut me in two like a wasp, I would have gone on living, worrying my painted collar and waving my legs. The life in me is a tough one, as it must be, to endure such things.

I begged for mercy. It was so easy to beg for mercy. Like those Niçois whose shutters are set inside the huge letters of a sign painted on their houses, I lived inside God, and I had never left the building to see my window from outside.

A wretched strength continued to be my ruin: I saw before me nothing but futility and mementos. I announced my silence *until further orders*, taking the word *orders* in its supernatural sense. In short, mine was the anguish of a runner who gauges his powers poorly and collapses halfway round the track.

*

Here in Villefranche, every evening, I sit alone, facing the harbor. The routine is mild enough: one star appears to the right, another comes out over Saint-Jean. I know by heart the order in which the stars light up. Between the first and the second, an old man passes, leading a goat on a string. The boats knock together, the lighthouse swivels its megaphone over the sea. Fishermen talk to me without seeing the death in which I am enclosed, and I have the illusion of living.

*

The Hôtel Welcome, in Villefranche-sur-Mer, is a source of myths, a site which the young enthusiasts of lyricism should transform into an altar and cover with flowers. Poets of all kinds, speaking every language, lived there and by a simple contact of fluids transformed the extraordinary little town, whose steep chaos ends at the water's edge, into a veritable Lourdes, a center of legends and inventions.

Villefranche was once a royal anchorage. Our ambassadors received one *Princesse lointaine* after another here for Marriages of State. The tiniest of its squares might serve as the setting for a Goldoni imbroglio, a Mozart *opera buffa*, some cruel farce by Molière. But the Hôtel Welcome was simply charming and seemed to have nothing to fear. Its rooms were enameled bright colors, and a coat of yellow paint had been brushed over the Italianate *trompe-l'oeil* of its façade. The bay harbored naval squadrons. The fishermen mended their nets and slept in the sun.

Everything began with Francis Rose. His mother had second sight: in the dining room she would leave her table, approach some lady or gentleman, and announce the future. She wore linen gowns on which Francis had painted flowers. He was going to be seventeen, and it is from his birthday party that I date everything. I was seated at one end of the table, in a red plush armchair, and in front of my place was a bust of Dante. Lady Rose had invited only English officers and their wives. Around eight o'clock, a strange procession appeared on the road that leads down to the harbor. Crowned with roses, Francis Rose supported on his arm Madame Isadora Duncan* in a

---

* Isadora! Let my reverie linger over her a little: an admirable woman, worthy of those epochs and cities which escape, overthrow, and transcend *good taste*. To paraphrase Nietzsche and Wilde, *she lived the best of her dance*. Details meant nothing to her. She would not exchange an artist's wink with the public, she would not keep her distance. What mattered was to live *en masse*, beyond the beautiful and the ugly, to lay hold of life and live it face to face, eye to eye. That was Rodin's school. What did it matter to our dancer if a gown slipped and revealed shapeless shapes, if the flesh trembled, the sweat flowed? Such things were all in the wake of her *élan*.

Greek tunic. She was very fat, slightly drunk, and escorted by an American girl, a pianist, and some people picked up along the way. The astonishment of Lady Rose's guests, her anger, the entrance of the procession, the fishermen pressing their faces against the windows, Isadora kissing me, Francis very proud of his crown—that was how the birthday dinner began. A deathly silence turned the guests to statuary. Isadora laughed, draped herself over Francis. She even stood up and dragged him into the window recess. It was then that Captain Williams, a friend of the family, played his part. He was in the habit of pulling pigeons and rabbits out of his sleeve. He drank a good deal. I suppose he *had* drunk a good deal. He was holding a cane. He strode across the dining room, approached the window, and shouting in a tremendous voice "All right, old lady, let go of that child!" he brought his cane down on the dancer's head. She fainted.

Everything dates from that caning. Our bedrooms became, as in *Le Sang d'un Poète*, stage boxes from which we would watch the fights between French, British, and American sailors on the waterfront. Christian Bérard, Georges Hugnet, Glenway Wescott, Mary Butts, Monroe Wheeler, Philip Lassell lived in the hotel. We drew, we wrote, we visited each other, from room to room. A mythology was created here whose style is epitomized by *Orphée*. Stravinsky was living in Montboron, where he was reorchestrating *Le Sacre* and composing *Oedipus Rex*, whose music he wanted to be curly, like the beard of Zeus.

I brought him the texts as I finished each section. I was young. There was the sun, the fishing boat, the fleet. After our

---

Asking men to give her children, and getting them, and raising them only to lose them in a single cruel disaster, dancing at the Trocadéro accompanied by the Orchestre Colonne or, by a phonograph, on the esplanades of Athens and Moscow—as this Jocasta lived she died, victimized by the complicity between a racing car and a red scarf. A scarf which hated her, threatened, warned; which she defied and insisted on wearing.

work I walked home, at night, without weariness, all the way to Villefranche.

*

When we first met, my reputation—my legend—was exorbitant.* It protected me. Public opinion lacerates the personage it invents. Instead of burning us, it burns us in effigy.

I can tell it is the child in you who has recognized me. One child has seen another: that is how children devour each other with their eyes from opposite ends of a table of grownups.

Yes, my dear Jacques, long afterwards, at my first meal in your dining room in Meudon, I rediscovered the odor of Maisons-Laffitte, where I was born, the same chairs, the *same plates*, which I would obsessively turn until their blue design was aligned with the foot of the glass at my place.

It is under the sign of childhood that we have come to know each other. I must remind myself of this in order to feel I deserve your welcome—you who make us wonder if your body is no more than an example of good manners, a garment thrown over the soul in order to receive your friends.

*

I have lost my seven best friends. Which is to say that God has had mercy on me seven times without my realizing it. He lent me a friendship, took it from me, sent me another, and so on. Seven times He has thrown out his line and pulled it back without catching me: I let go the bait and fell back, stupidly. Don't for a moment believe He was killing the young; He was costuming angels. A sickness or a war afforded them an excuse for undressing.

So I was on my guard. I had seen from the start that

* Because a fashionable restaurant, Le Boeuf sur le Toit, is named after one of my farces, people imagine that I run cabarets, lead a night crawler's life. I am accused of every extravagance, every vice. You know my habits.

Radiguet was on loan, that I would have to give him back. But I deliberately played dumb, hoping at all costs to distract him from his vocation of death.

Pathetic subterfuge! Supposing I could weigh him down by making him write books, I was actually heaving ballast. With each book, I saw him put farther out to sea, rejoining a mystery with which he obviously had a rendezvous.

That summer I took him to the country; the following winter in Paris was a terrible one. Why did I plead with him, change my own life, try to set an example? Debts, alcohol, insomnia, piles of dirty clothes, and flights from hotel to hotel, from one scene of the crime to the next, formed the principle of his metamorphosis. Which occurred in the hospital in the Rue Piccini, December 12, 1923.

*

"Make your confession and take Communion," Max Jacob had advised. "What!" I wrote back to Saint-Benoît, "you prescribe the Host like an aspirin?" "The Host," he answered, "must be taken like an aspirin."

I was being offered the falling snow; altar bread, altered bread. But I, perennially resistant to Orientalism—I chose the Flying Carpet.

Opium must not be confused with drugs. I have never smoked opium with those who compromise it.

Diaghilev had taken me to Monte Carlo for the rehearsals of *Les Fâcheux* and *Les Biches,* and there I met Louis Laloy, author of a famous book, *La Fumée.* Louis Laloy had some official position at the Opéra, and he was there as a critic as well. And he saw me in so lamentable a state that he urged me: "*Mais fumez! fumez! fumez!*"

*

My dear Jacques, there is no end to your indulgence: it acknowledges that a man exhausted by troubles and tasks beyond his strength may fall asleep. For a long time, sleep was my refuge. The prospect of waking kept me from sleeping well and dictated my dreams. In the morning I no longer had the courage to unfold my life. Reality and dream were super-imposed: a bedraggled smear. I would get up, shave, dress, and let whoever was in my room take me . . . anywhere.

Oh, those mornings! When you are thrown into dirty water, you must swim. In a state like mine, reading a newspaper was unendurable. That testimony to universal activity, and to those who record it, liquidates you. My flight into opium was what Freud calls the *Flucht in die Krankheit*.

*

Opium is not something to be tried out. It is not a distrac-tion, an affair: opium marries you. The first contact is disap-pointing. The benefit comes only in the long run, and the beatitude is evident when it is too late to do without it. More will power was necessary to accustom myself to it than to over-come it. The smoke made me ill. It took nearly three months of disgust to get used to the pitching and rolling of the aerial carpet. I persisted; I could no more admit the discredit cast upon opium by literature than the ridicule to which we are exposed by snobs.* I do not regret the experiment, and I claim that opium, if its management were not of such extreme delicacy, would prepare many spirits for an ascension. The difficulty consists in discovering the point at which it ceases to be charitable.

(One of its tricks, which it would be inaccurate to ascribe to anesthesia, is to extend the sense of touch until we are con-vinced that the object touched is part of our own body. A finger

---

* As a true painter no longer carries his apparatus around with him, the true smoker no longer uses fancy pipes. He smokes an old bamboo, with a minimum of utensils. To Benares, which is the luxury tobacco of opiomaniacs, he prefers a mixture which corre-sponds to Caporal.

falling from the smoker's hand would not surprise him more than the cigarette that he drops and that burns his clothes.)

Is it opium which makes us invent specious reasons to defend it, or does it afford us an insight which vanishes in our usual moments?

When its noble rites became indispensable to me, I seemed to understand that the prejudice against opium was a piece of romanticism; the prejudice of discomfort. When a remedy acting on the sympathetic nervous system suppresses moral pain or transfigures it until it becomes pleasure, it does so because there is no such thing as moral pain, there is merely physical pain. Which led me to conclude that it is madness to consult a dentist and to refuse the relief of opium. Why, the Lorelei murmured on, why is it good to suffer? Only mediocre poets profit from suffering; great ones produce in serenity.

You see the trap: opium cushions us, floats us down the river of the dead, disincarnates us until we are transformed into a weightless meadow. The body's night swarms with stars, but our joy is joy in a mirror. We become, from head to foot, a lie. We mummify; the machine stops. The organism refuses to obey; temperatures and irritations find us and leave us insensible; we feel neither cold nor heat.

Neapolitan painters decorate hotel rooms in *trompe-l'oeil*; opium is a painter in *trompe-l'esprit*: it covers the walls of the room where I am smoking, each one to my advantage. Two and two no longer make four; two and two make twenty-two. A disturbing euphoria seizes us. Qualms are the weak point. Opium is quietude. Once anxiety sets in, we are lost.

The Chinese smoke little and move little. They do not ask exceptional services of opium. They respect it, they leave it free to work, to widen its circle. In our coarseness, we Westerners try to draw from opium the resources of a commotion it detests, an agitation it will always punish. China smokes in order to approach her dead. Invisibility results from a motionless speed, from speed-in-itself. Opium is like this velvet speed. If only the dead slow down, a zone of encounter is formed: life and death remain as remote from each other as the heads and tails of a coin, but opium passes through the coin.

*

But, I repeat, in Europe we do not know how to smoke. We no longer admit the distresses a healthy man accepts: we increase the doses. Is waking painful? we smoke in the morning; and if smoking at home is difficult, we eat. To eat opium leaves us far from the mark. It takes twelve pipes to gain the effect of a single pellet, for when we eat opium we absorb the morphine and the dross. The problems begin: hot flashes, cold sweats, uncontrollable yawning, tears, spasms. I confess I know little about such symptoms. My aim was suicide, and I swallowed enormous doses. But suicide is not within everyone's reach. The optimism this very prison affords urged me to escape. Suicide is a prestidigitation, and I am clumsy. I was expelled from the Suicide Club for not knowing how to juggle.

Such was the detour by which I made myself a prisoner, in the Rue de Chateaubriand, at the Thermes Urbains, where you were the first visitor I had after sixty days of tête-à-tête with my nurse.

*

Opium resembles religion to the same degree that an illusionist resembles Jesus. It conjures away sufferings. Which wait—in the wings. You can imagine the chaos of the veins and of the soul upon rediscovering, brand-new, these sufferings kept in deep storage for a year. Yet Drs. Capmas, Dereck, and Marion-Landais never persuaded me to vilify opium. I must insist: it was not I who left opium; doubtless, opium no longer wanted me.

*

After my convalescence in Versailles, without baiting the trap, without a shadow of proselytism, you shared with me your friends and your prospects; you were editing a collection of books for Plon that would be a forum for writers of different backgrounds but the same caste. One evening, several of us met at your house to discuss the series. Souls are wretched organizers; we seemed so many children playing grownup.

You had referred to a possible visit from Père Charles. I knew nothing about him, except that he belonged to the same order as Père de Foucauld and that he had lived as a hermit in the African desert. I also knew that he had met Claudel when he landed at Marseilles (Claudel was in Aix for Darius Milhaud's wedding), that he would be spending a week in Paris, a month or two in the Vosges, and would then return to his prayer outpost, a shack in the sand.

*

Jacques, was that your trap? Were you waiting for that moment? A heart entered the room, a red heart beneath a red cross in the center of a white shape which glided in, bent down, spoke, shook hands. That heart hypnotized me, distracted me from the face, decapitated the cowl. It was the true face of the white shape, and Charles seemed to be holding his head over his breast, like the martyrs. And the sunburned head became a reflection of the heart, a mirage in all that African light. The cheekbones and the chin outlined the upper curves and the point. Then I distinguished a gaze uncertain of short distances, and a blind man's hands—I mean, hands that see.

I shall not labor the point. I am coming to what matters: the ease, the freedom of the man. What was mine in his presence? a strolling player's charm. He smiled, told stories, exchanged reminiscences with Massis. And I watched; stupid, groggy, I watched from behind a thick pane of glass that white shape moving against the sky.

I suppose your wife and your other guests must have realized: room, books, friends, nothing existed any longer.

It was then, Maritain, that you pushed me. Pushed me from

behind, your soul which is an athlete shoving me head first. Everyone saw I was losing my balance. Yet no one helped me, for they knew that to help me now would have been to destroy me. Thus I learned the spirit of that family which Faith instantaneously affords us and which is not the least of God's mercies.

*

The morning of the Feast of the Sacred Heart, in your chapel, among several intimates, I received Communion from Père Charles.

After the ceremony, we resumed our habitual relations. Nothing indicated the difference except an occasional glance you gave me, a sounding, what cod fishermen call "making the blue pigeon fly."

What did you see?

*

Eager young men, believe me. There are only two ways of winning: to play hearts or to cheat. To cheat is hard. Once caught, the cheat is lost. The great race of crooks is never caught; they are the men in power, cabinet ministers, famous painters, poets, novelists, musicians, actors. I admire them. How could I admire a cheat caught and clapped in jail? He has missed his calling.

To play hearts is simple. A man must have one, that is all. You believe yourselves to be heartless. You do not look at your cards properly. Your heart is hidden in dread of ridicule, in obedience to an old criminal code: "*Voici venir le temps des assassins.*" Show your heart and you will win. *Voici venir le temps de l'amour.*

*

Heaven would shock the earth. Merely consider Jesus' manners and you will realize that heaven cannot be official. Jesus refuses to arrive: he seeks to be born and to die at every moment. Our crusade will be to scandalize by love.

*

Art for God's Sake

A phrase of Père Charles strikes me: "Keep free." Indeed, why strain my voice? Since *Le Potomak*, I have demonstrated my desire to set in order a mad disorder, to caulk romanticism, to kill the virtuoso—to make of my weakness an instrument like the pressurized steam with which the Americans cut granite. It is not for me to complain of this search for a straight line if it leads me to the line of lines, to the melody of silence which is the Holy Virgin and to the classicism of mystery which is God. Some will ask: "And mysticism?" Of course: religion includes all experience. But that side of it too dangerously resembles the devils who seek my destruction.

Since 1913 I have lived and died of a disordered mystery. *Le Potomak* proves that. During this period I trained myself on dreams. I read that sugar makes you dream, and swallowed boxes of it. I went to bed, fully dressed, twice a day. I plugged my ears with wax so that my dreams would take root more deeply than in the sounds around my body.

*

Literature is impossible. We must leave it behind. There is no use trying to leave it behind by literature; only love and Faith allow us to leave ourselves behind. To resort to dreaming is not to leave the house; it is to explore the attic, where our childhood made contact with poetry.

Art for art's sake, art for the people's sake are equally absurd. I propose art for God's sake.

*

Rien ne va plus

My dear Maritain, it is hard for me to say what I mean. Transitions are beyond me. Apparent incoherence suits me better

than a graded spectrum of colors. Books like *Le Coq et l'Arlequin, Visites à Barres, Le Secret professionel*, or this letter are
only the pyrotechnist's wick. I walk underneath a nocturnal
scaffolding. Unknown young friends are somberly stuffing fire-
crackers they dare not light; and how joyously I now strike the
match, for you know as well as I the name the rockets will
form.

That is my role. I abide by its limits, and I make your motto
my own: "I am the ass, and I bear the Lord." For God tolerates
no adroitness. In praising Him, may I keep my way, keep free,
as Charles advised, nor fear stumbling.

*

I say no more: I fear betraying myself, compromising you.
People will invoke caprice, of course, and my whims, and my
dance. The chorus grows louder with the grandeurs I approach.
They will act out for me Michael's reproach to David: "Dancing
before the Ark—at your age! And on the sidewalks!"

*

Our age is infested with fools in horn-rimmed glasses who
stand in the wings of audacity, talking loud and judging everything. Already I hear them saying: "What good does this letter
do?"

Make way for the marvelous, young fools! It is a love letter.
Le Coq et l'Arlequin was a book of love, created by the fatigue
of my ears as this letter is created by a fatigue of my soul. It
could have succeeded, or failed. To make the music it speaks of
depended on the musicians; they made it. To initiate the heart
is a matter for poets. To sustain them is your role, my dear
Jacques. I have only the strength to call out, with the croupier,
"Rien ne va plus."

Le Livre Blanc: Notes on Homosexuality

"Every morning, I tell myself,
'You can do nothing about it:
submit.' "

Homosexuals recognize each other—the way Jews do. The mask dissolves, and I would venture to discover my kind between the lines of the most innocent book. This passion is not so simple as our moralists assume. For just as there exist homosexual women, women who look like Lesbians but seek out men responsive to their particular style, so there exist unconscious homosexuals who spend their lives in a malaise they attribute to poor health, to nerves.

I have always thought my father was too much like me to differ on this crucial point. Doubtless he was unaware of his inclination and, instead of yielding to it, laboriously pursued another, without knowing what it was that so burdened his life. Had he discovered the tastes he never found occasion to express—tastes revealed to me by certain phrases, movements, a thousand details of his person—he would have collapsed. In his day, a man killed himself for less. But such was not the case; he lived in ignorance of himself, and accepted his burden.

Perhaps it is to such blindness that I owe my existence. I deplore the fact, for justice would be done had my father known the joys which would have spared my misfortunes.

*

As far back as I can remember, even at the age when the mind does not yet influence the senses, I find traces of my love for boys.

I have always loved the stronger sex, which I consider it

legitimate to call the fair one as well. My misfortunes result from a society which condemns the exception as a crime and obliges us to alter our inclinations.

Three decisive occasions come to mind.

Beyond my father's country estate was a farmhouse and a horse pond—there were no fences, and my father allowed the cattle to graze on our property in return for the milk and eggs the farmer brought to the house every day.

One August morning I was prowling through the grounds with my toy rifle, waiting behind a hedge for some animal to pass, when I saw from my ambush a farm boy leading a plow horse down to the pond. In order to get into the water, and knowing that no one ever visited this part of the property, he was riding the animal naked, and guided the horse into the water a few yards away from me. The tanned skin on his face, neck, arms, and feet contrasting with the white skin elsewhere reminded me of Indian chestnuts bursting out of their hulls, but these dark patches were not the only ones. Another drew my gaze, in the center of which an enigma was presented down to its last details.

My ears buzzed. The blood ran to my head, and the strength out of my legs. My heart was pounding like a murderer's. I must have fainted dead away, for I was found only after a four-hour search. Once back on my feet, I instinctively avoided disclosing the reason for my weakness, and insisted, at the risk of making myself ridiculous, that a hare bolting out of the underbrush had startled me.

The second incident occurred the following year. My father had permitted some gypsies to camp in the same part of the grounds where I had fainted. I was walking there with my nursemaid. Suddenly, bursting into shrieks, she dragged me away, forbidding me to look back. It was a hot, brilliant day. Two young gypsies had stripped off their clothes and were climbing trees: a sight which shocked my nurse and which my disobedience preserved in an unforgettable frame. If I live to be a hundred, because of that shriek and that flight, I shall always see a gypsy caravan, a woman rocking a baby, a smoking camp-fire, a white horse cropping the grass, and, shinnying up the trees, two bronze bodies thrice dappled with black.

The last incident, if I am not mistaken, involved a young servant named Gustave, who had all he could do to keep a straight face when he waited on table. His giggles delighted me. Having so often pondered my memories of the farm boy and the gypsies, I now reached the point of longing to touch with my hand what I had seen with my eyes.

My scheme could not have been more ingenuous. I would draw a lady, I would take my drawing to Gustave, I would make him laugh, encourage him, and ask him to let me touch the mystery I divined at dinnertime under a suggestive bulge of his trousers. Now, as for a naked woman, I had seen only my nurse, concluding that artists had invented the firm breasts they be-stowed on their subjects and that in reality all women were as flabby as the one I had seen: my drawing was a realistic one. Gustave burst out laughing, asked me who my model was, and when I took advantage of his fit of laughter to make for my target with inconceivable boldness, he turned beet-red, pushed me away and pinched my ear, claiming that he was ticklish, and, deathly afraid of losing his job, sent me out of the room.

A few days later he stole some wine. My father fired him. I interceded, I wept—to no avail. I accompanied Gustave to the station, carrying the checkerboard I had given him for his little boy, whose photograph he had often shown me.

*

From all over the world, men who have lost their hearts to masculine beauty come to Toulon to marvel at the sailors lounging around the town alone or in groups, answering stares with smiles and never refusing propositions. A kind of noc-turnal salt transforms the toughest convict, the crudest Breton, the wildest Corsican into tall, décolleté whores with swinging

hips who love to dance and without the least embarrassment
lead their partners to disreputable harbor hotels.

One of the cafés where you dance is run by a former night-
club entertainer with a woman's voice who used to perform in
drag. Now he wears an Angora sweater and rings. Flanked by
adoring red-pompomed giants whom he mistreats, he scribbles
in huge, childish letters, biting his tongue with the effort, the
orders his wife screams out with naïve asperity.

One evening, as I entered the establishment of this amazing
creature to whom his wife and several husbands so devotedly
defer, I stood rooted to the spot. I had just glimpsed, in profile,
leaning against the player piano, the ghost of Dargelos—Dargelos as a sailor.

Of Dargelos what this facsimile paraded most was the arro-
gance, the casual, insolent temper. *Tapageuse* was lettered in
gold on the cap cocked over his left eyebrow, a black scarf was
knotted around his throat, and he was wearing those bell-
bottoms which once allowed sailors to roll their trousers up over
their thighs (and which the latest regulations forbid, since they
have come to symbolize the procurer).

Anywhere else, I should never have dared submit to that
proud gaze. But Toulon is Toulon; dancing makes it possible to
avoid the discomfort of preambles and flings strangers into each
other's arms, a prelude to love.

To a music full of airs and graces, the men waltz—hips
arched, bodies welded together at the crotch, solemn blind
profiles revolving slower than the stitching feet which stamp
sometimes, like horses' hoofs. A burgeoning exhilaration seizes
the paired bodies. They sprout branches which collide, sweat
mingles with sweat, and one more couple is on its way to the
rooms with dangling lightbulbs and eiderdown quilts.

Stripped of the accessories which intimidate a civilian and of
the style sailors affect to keep up their courage, Tapageuse became a shy animal. A wine carafe had broken his nose in a

brawl. A straight nose might have made him look insipid—that carafe had added the finishing touch to a masterpiece.

On his naked torso, this boy, who to me represented luck itself, had had tattooed the words PAS DE CHANCE. He told me his story. It was short, epitomized by that pathetic tattoo: he was just out of jail; after a mutiny on the *Ernest Renan* he had been mistaken for someone else; that was why his hair had been shaved off—which he lamented, though it was wonderfully becoming. "*Pas de chance,*" he repeated, shaking that little bald head from some ancient bust. "I'll never have any luck."

I slipped my fetish chain around his neck. "I'm not giving it to you," I told him. "That wouldn't do either of us any good. But keep it for tonight." Then, with my fountain pen, I crossed out the ominous tattoo and drew underneath it a star and a heart. He smiled, realizing more by his skin than his brain that he was safe, that our meeting was not like the ones he was used to, those hasty encounters in which only selfishness is satisfied.

No luck! Was it possible? With that mouth, those teeth, those eyes, that belly and those shoulders, the iron muscles of those legs? No luck, with that fabulous little undersea plant, dead, withered, stranded on the moss, which grows smooth as it swells, rises, and flings out its sap once it regains the element of love? I could not get over my amazement; and to solve this problem I let myself sink into a false sleep.

Pas de chance lay motionless beside me. Gradually I felt him performing a delicate maneuver in order to free his arm, on which my elbow was resting. My only thought was that he would now pull some dirty trick . . . which was to misunderstand the ritual of the fleet. "Regulations, the right thing," embellish the sailors' vocabulary.

I watched him through my closed lashes. First, over and over again, he hefted my chain, kissed it, rubbed it on his tattoo. Then, with the terrible deliberation of someone cheating in a game, he tested my sleep, coughed, touched me, listened to my breathing, brought his face close to my open right hand, and gently pressed his cheek against it.

Indiscreet witness of this miserable child's attempt to reach the buoy which had floated within reach on the high sea, I had to exert all my self-control not to lose my head, fake a sudden awakening, and destroy my life.

At dawn I left him. My eyes avoided his, filled with all the hope he felt and could not utter. He gave me back the chain. I kissed him, edged past, and turned out the light.

Returning to my own hotel, I paused downstairs in his to write on a slate the time (5 a.m.) when sailors get up, under a list of countless instructions of the same kind. The moment I picked up the chalk, I realized I had forgotten my gloves. I went back upstairs. There was a light under the door: the lamp must have been turned on again. I could not resist looking through the keyhole, which supplied a baroque frame to a tiny shaved head. *Pas de chance*, his face buried in my gloves, was weeping bitterly.

For ten minutes I hesitated in front of that door. Then I crept downstairs again, hurried out, and slammed the hotel door behind me. Outside, a fountain murmured its gloomy monologue in the empty square. "No," I thought, "we don't belong to the same kingdom. It's enough to move a flower, a tree, an animal. Impossible to live with one."

Day was breaking. Roosters crowed over the sea revealed by a dim coolness. A man came round the corner with a rifle over his shoulder. I returned to my hotel, hauling an enormous weight.

*

Later, at a very different period, I lagged behind my life, sick in body and soul, disgusted by one affair after another, incapable of responding to my own feelings. I longed for the counter-irritant of a secret atmosphere. I found it in a public bath which suggested—the tiny cells, the central court, the

Turkish divans on which young men were playing cards—the *Satyricon*. At a sign from their boss, these young men stood and lined up against the wall. The boss fingered their biceps, patted their thighs, exposed their intimate charms, and parceled them out like a butcher his merchandise.

The clientele was certain of its tastes, discreet, swift. I must have been an enigma to these youths accustomed to specific requirements. They stared at me uncomprehendingly; for I prefer conversation to actions.

In me, heart and senses are so amalgamated that neither can be engaged without the other. Which leads me to overstep the bounds of friendship and makes me dread the fugitive contact by which I risk catching the disease of love. How I came to envy those who, not suffering vaguely from beauty, know what they want, perfect their vice, pay the price, and fulfill it.

One man had to be insulted, another loaded with chains, another (a moralist) obtained his satisfactions only by watching a Hercules killing rats with a red-hot needle.

How many of these sages I saw pass before me who know the exact recipe of their pleasure, whose existence is simplified because they indulge, at a specific date and price, in honest, in bourgeois complications! Most were rich businessmen from the North who came to gratify their senses, then rejoined their wives and children.

In the long run, I curtailed my visits. My presence was becoming suspect. France mistrusts a role which is not all of a piece. The Miser must be always miserly, the Jealous Husband always jealous. That is Molière's triumph. The boss of the baths suspected I worked for the police. He made it clear that a visitor to his establishment was either clientele or merchandise. The two were not to be combined.

This warning shook me out of my lethargy and forced me to break with certain unworthy habits. My only regret was the transparent mirror. You get into a dark booth and shove aside a panel, revealing a metallic sheet through which you can make out a little bathroom. On its other side, the sheet is a mirror so smooth and shiny it is impossible to guess it is full of eyes.

When I could afford it, I would spend my Sunday there; of the twelve mirrors of the twelve bathrooms, this was the only one of its kind. The boss had paid a fortune to import it from Germany. His staff knew nothing about this observatory. Young working-class men provided the show.

All followed the same program. They undressed and carefully hung up their new clothes. Out of their Sunday best, you could guess their jobs from certain attractive vocational distortions. Standing in the tub, they looked at themselves (looked at me) and began with that special Parisian grimace which exposes the gums; then they would rub one shoulder, pick up the soap, and work it into a lather. The soaping turned into a caress. Suddenly their eyes left the world, their heads snapped back, and their bodies spat like furious animals.

Some, exhausted, slid slowly into the steaming water, others began over again; the youngest ones always straddled the tub and with an absent gaze wiped off the tiles the sap which their blind stem had cast toward love.

I remember one Narcissus who lovingly brought his mouth to the mirror, pressed his lips against it, and carried to its frenzied conclusion his adventure with himself. Invisible as the Greek gods, I glued my lips to his and imitated his gestures. He never knew that, instead of reflecting, the mirror had acted, had lived, had loved him.

Opium: Journal of a Disintoxication

"You must pay, pay, pay."

*"Only the aesthetic of failure
is a lasting one. Leave failure
out of the account and you are lost."*

These notes date from the Saint-Cloud Clinic (December 16, 1928–April 1929). They are addressed to opium smokers, to the sick, to the unknown friends whom our books recruit and who are the only excuse for writing.

*

I became an addict a second time in the following circumstances.

First of all, I must have been incompletely disintoxicated the first time. Many brave addicts are unaware of the traps of disintoxication, are content with mere suppression, and emerge ravaged from a useless ordeal, with weakened cells which they keep from recovery by overindulging in alcohol and sport.

I shall explain later that the incredible symptoms of disintoxication—phenomena against which medicine can do no more than make a padded cell look like a luxury suite and which require patience, presence of mind, and flexibility of the physician or nurse—instead of characterizing an organism in decomposition, must be, on the contrary, the uncommunicated symptoms of the suckling child and of budding plants.

So I became an addict again because the doctors who disintoxicate—one should simply say, who purge—do not attempt to cure the initial disturbances which motivate addiction; because I had lapsed back into my nervous imbalance and preferred an artificial equilibrium to none at all. This moral cosmetic disguises more than a ruined countenance: it is hu-man, almost feminine, to resort to it.

I returned to addiction with caution, under medical super-vision. There exist certain doctors accessible to pity. I never exceeded ten pipes. My ration was three in the morning (at nine), four in the afternoon (at five), three at night (at eleven). I thereby supposed I was diminishing the likelihood of addiction.

*

I am writing these lines after twelve days and nights without sleep. . . .

*

Do not expect me to turn traitor. Naturally opium remains unique and its euphoria superior to that of health. To it I owe my perfect hours. It is a pity that medicine, instead of perfect-ing disintoxication, does not try to render opium harmless.

But here we return to the problem of progress. Is suffering a discipline or a lyricism?

It seems to me that on an earth so old, so wrinkled, so patched, where so many compromises and laughable conven-tions prevail, an eliminable opium would refine manners and do more good than the fever of action does harm.

*

Clinics admit few opium addicts. It is rare that an opium addict stops smoking. The nurses know only pseudo-smokers, the fashionable addicts who combine opium, alcohol, and décor (opium and alcohol are mortal enemies), or who switch from pipe to syringe and from morphine to heroin. Of all drugs, opium is the subtlest. The lungs absorb its smoke instantane-ously. The effect of a pipe is immediate. I am speaking of true smokers. Amateurs feel nothing, wait for dreams, and risk sea-sickness, for the effectiveness of opium results from a pact. Once it casts its spell on us, we can never leave it again.

To preach to the opium addict is to tell Tristan: "Kill Iseult. You will feel much better afterwards."

*

Opium does not tolerate impatient adepts, bunglers. It withdraws, leaving them morphine, heroin, suicide, death.

*

Certain organisms are born to become the prey of drugs. They require a corrective without which they cannot make contact with the outside world. They float. They vegetate in no-man's-land. The world remains a phantom until some substance *embodies* it.

In some cases, these unfortunates live without ever finding the slightest remedy. In others, the remedy they find kills them.

It is a piece of luck when opium affords them an equilibrium, grants these cork souls a diver's suit of lead. For the sickness caused by opium will be less severe than that caused by other substances and less severe than the disease they seek to cure.

*

If the nature of disintoxication is a matter of physiology in a man, it produces, in a woman, chiefly moral symptoms. In a man, opium anesthetizes not the heart but sex. In a woman, it awakens sex and anesthetizes the heart. The eighteenth day without opium, a woman becomes tender, whimpers. This is why, in disintoxication clinics, every woman patient seems to be in love with the doctor.

*

I remain convinced, despite my own failures, that opium can be beneficial and that it is our duty to make it so. We must learn how to handle it. At present nothing equals our clumsiness. A severe discipline (laxatives, exercise, sedation, abstentions, liver treatments, schedules which permit a night's sleep) would allow the use of a remedy now compromised by fools.

I will not be told: "Habituation forces the smoker to increase his dosage." One of opium's enigmas is that it permits the smoker never to increase his dosage.

*

Living is a horizontal fall.

Without some fixative, a life perfectly and continually conscious of its speed would become intolerable. With it, a man condemned to death can sleep.

This fixative is what I lack. Some gland, I suppose, is sick. Medicine takes this infirmity for an excess of consciousness, for an intellectual advantage.

Everything suggests, when I look around me, the functioning in *others* of this absurd fixative, as indispensable as the habit which conceals from us the daily horror of having to get up, shave, dress, eat. Even a *photograph album*, that fatuous impulse to turn a collapse into a series of solemn monuments.

Opium granted me this fixative. Without opium, projects— marriages, for example, or trips—seemed to me as insane as someone who has fallen out the window trying to make friends with people in the rooms past which he is falling.

*

Phèdre, or Organic Fidelity. Legally one must be faithful to a person, humanly to a type. Phèdre is faithful to a type. This is not an example of a kind of love, but *the* example of love. Besides, what about that famous incest? Hippolyte is not her son. It is a juridical matter that Phèdre should respect Thésée, that Thésée should love Hippolyte. It is a human matter that Phèdre should love Hippolyte and that Thésée should loathe him.

*

We are no longer, unfortunately, a nation of farmers and shepherds. That we require another therapeutic method for the defense of our overworked nervous system cannot be doubted. We must discover a means of rendering harmless the beneficent substances which the body eliminates so poorly, or of armoring the nerve cells.

Tell any doctor this banal truth, and he will shrug his shoulders. He will dismiss what you say as literature, utopia, addict's babble.

Yet I declare that a day will come when the substances which give us peace will be used without danger, that addiction will be avoided, that the bogy of "drugs" will be an absurdity, and that a tamed opium will assuage the sickness of our cities, where the trees die standing.

*

The poppy's patience. Once you have smoked, you will smoke again. Opium knows how to wait.

*

Nothing more abnormal than a poet who resembles the normal man: Hugo, Goethe . . . A madman on the loose. A madman who is never suspect. When I wrote, once, that Victor Hugo was a madman who believed he was Victor Hugo, I was not joking. It is no accident that in French we say the typical sin against the Spirit is to be *spirituelle*, to be witty. My remark was more than a wisecrack; it was a synthesis, the résumé of a study I refuse to write—which others will write some day. It is not the poet's role to prove but to affirm, without supplying any of the cumbersome proofs he possesses and from which his affirmation results.

*

With proper hygiene, a smoker who inhales his daily dozen pipes all his life would be not only forearmed against grippes, colds, anginas, but even less in danger than a man who drinks a glass of cognac or smokes four cigars. I know individuals who have smoked one, three, seven to twelve pipes a day for forty years.

*

Each of us carries something compressed inside himself, like those Japanese flowers which unfold when immersed in water.

Opium plays the part of the water. None of us carries the same kind of flower. A person who does not smoke never knows the kind of flower opium would have unfolded within him.

*

Picasso once told me: *The odor of opium is the least stupid odor in the world.* It is comparable to the smell of a circus, or of a seaport.

*

When I draw, the nurse tells me: "Your face frightens me, you look like a murderer."

In order not to be caught writing, I have always drawn. To write, for me, is to draw, to knot lines so that they become a calligraphy, or to loosen them so that the writing becomes a drawing. That is where I am. I write, I set precise limits to the profile of an idea, an action. In short, I outline ghosts, I find the contours of the void, I draw.

*

Surprises of God's tribunal

A little girl steals cherries. Her whole life is spent redeeming this sin by prayers. The pious creature dies. GOD: *You are saved because you stole cherries.*

*

Disgusted by literature, I have tried to transcend it, to live my work. The result: my work devours me, begins to live, and it is I who die. Further, the works divide into those which give life, those which kill.

One day, one of our writers—a man I censured for writing successful books and never writing *himself*—led me to a mirror. "I want to be strong," he said. "Look at yourself. I want to eat. I want to travel. *I want to live.* I don't want to become a fountain pen."

A thinking reed! A suffering reed! A bleeding reed! Precisely. Which leads me to this sinister conclusion: by refusing to become a literary man, one has become a fountain pen.

*

The fact is, the poet does not want admiration, he wants to be believed.

*

Children have a magical power to become whatever they want to be. The poets in whom childhood is prolonged suffer greatly from losing this power. That is one of the reasons which impel the poet to take opium.

*

Once a poet *awakens*, he is a fool. I mean intelligent. "Where am I?" he asks, like a lady who has fainted. The notes of an awakened poet are not worth much. I give them only for what they are worth; at my own risk. One more experiment.

*

A writer develops the muscles of his mind. This training has nothing to do with the pleasures of a sport. It requires suffering, falls, indolence, weakness, failure, fatigue, bereavement, insomnia, exercises which are the converse of those to develop the body.

*

I wonder how a man can write the lives of the poets, since the poets themselves could not write their own. There are too many mysteries, too many true lies, too much overlapping.

What can be said of the impassioned friendships which have to be taken for love and which are something else, of the limits of love and friendship, of that zone of the heart in which unknown senses participate and which cannot be understood by those who live seriatim?

Dates intersect, years blur. The snow melts, feet fly; no footprints are left.

*

Les Enfants Terribles was written under the obsession of the song "Make Believe," from *Showboat*; if you like this book, buy the record of the song, and then reread it with the volume turned up high.

*

Cured, I feel empty, poor, sick at heart, sick. I drift. I am to be discharged from the clinic the day after tomorrow. To go where? Three weeks ago, I felt a kind of gaiety, I asked M. . . . about the mountains, about the little hotels above the snow line. I was getting out.

Now it is a book that is getting out. It is a book that gets out, that is coming out, as publishers say. It is not I . . . I can die, the book couldn't care less . . . The same farce begins over and over again, and each time one lets oneself be trapped.

It was difficult to foresee a *book* written in seventeen days. I might have supposed it had something to do with *me*, instead.

The work which exploits me needed opium; it needed me to leave opium; once again I am its dupe. And I was wondering: will I smoke again or not? No use pretending to be casual, dear poet. I shall smoke again, if my work wants me to.

*

And if opium wants me to.

3

Le Sang d'un Poète
1929–1946

*Une oeuvre ne vaut que si elle
s'intègre dans un oeuvre*

A work is worthless unless it
becomes part of a life work

Cocteau directing a scene from La Sang d'un Poète, *1930*

Self-portrait, Villefranche-sur-Mer, 1935

Invitation to a dress rehearsal of La Voix Humaine, *1930*

With *Charlie Chaplin and Paulette Goddard, 1936*

Photograph, by Dora Maar, 1941

Jean Marais as La Bête in La Belle et la Bête, *1945*

CALENDAR

1929–1936

In his diary for 1933, novelist Julien Green tells how Gertrude Stein visited him one day and they discussed Cocteau. "She speaks of him as an important writer of whom something will surely last. But what? She doesn't venture to say . . ." Summing up modern French poetry about the same time, Ezra Pound was as equivocal. He cited "Cocteau's general work," praising it as the best to come out of the twenties, but added vaguely that "the discussion of Cocteau would require a very long essay." So his reputation marked time; assured, it seemed, but not quite defined.

Meantime, Cocteau himself was venturing into a new medium. While still in the clinic, he had said, "My next work will be a film." Now, with a commission from the Vicomte de Noailles, he made Le Sang d'un Poète. He used a crew of professionals, a cast of friends and amateurs, and for inspiration he resuscitated his schoolboy hero Dargelos, who had also appeared in two of his books, Les Enfants Terribles and Le Livre Blanc, and who would haunt others to come. At its première in 1932, the film was found shocking, and as a result it was not shown in France except to private film clubs. But in the United States, thanks to the initiative of Chaplin, it was distributed commercially and ran for years.

In 1930, Cocteau had also produced another play. Called La Voix Humaine, it actually amounted to a long monologue, one

side of the final conversation between a woman and the lover
who is abandoning her. It was accepted by the prestigious
Comédie-Française, and at a special dress rehearsal (for two
thousand of Cocteau's friends!), the performance was broken
up by the Surrealists, in the person of young Paul Eluard, who
had managed to get in by coming with Cocteau's guest, Sergei
Eisenstein. From the balcony, Eluard started to shout that the
play was obscene, that it was actually about Cocteau and his
current boyfriend. The lights came up and Eluard was spotted.
Hustled out into the hall, he was surrounded by a hostile crowd,
and even burned with someone's cigarette, until rescued by
Cocteau himself. Then the play was resumed, making all the
ladies cry and going on to become a film by Roberto Rossellini
in 1947 and an opera by Francis Poulenc in 1959.

The summer of 1931 Cocteau spent in Toulon, where, according to his own cryptic account, he "lived with a monkey and an
Annamese boy." In September he caught the same typhoid fever
which had killed Radiguet. "The boy lost his head, the monkey
began to bite," and Cocteau was asked to leave his hotel. He
was rescued by the playwright Edouard Bourdet and his beautiful wife Denise (for whom Cocteau wrote the last book published in his lifetime, an autobiographical reverie called Le
Cordon Ombilical), who took him to their nearby home. Here,
while recuperating, Cocteau decorated one of the rooms with
murals and read his hosts a play which had been commissioned
by Louis Jouvet, called La Machine Infernale.

Cocteau had twice before treated the Oedipus legend—once
in a terse adaptation of Sophocles' original, then again in the
text for Stravinsky's oratorio. Now he made the material his
own, as he had the story of Orpheus, and for the encounter between Oedipus and the Sphinx he wrote one of the most daz-
zling pieces of lyric prose ever begotten upon the possibilities of
the French language. It was staged in April 1934, with a new
star, Jean-Pierre Aumont, in the lead and with Cocteau himself
reading the offstage narration. Reviewing it, Colette spoke of

Cocteau's "unique privilege": "He has kept what the rest of us have lost: intimate phantasmagoria . . . The French theatre has had little to do with the supernatural, much less with that mixture of the real and the unreal which characterizes Shakespeare and Shaw and which they succeed in bringing together by the use of humor . . . It is impossible not to cite them when evaluating Cocteau . . ."

One of the leading papers in Paris now commissioned a series of autobiographical portraits—"snapshots of my childhood"—which he began to write week by week, illustrating them with his own drawings. Glenway Wescott once described Cocteau's letters as "half telegram, half valentine," which was how his weekend page in Le Figaro came to look. Gathered together as Portraits-Souvenir, they made one of his best books, with a final chapter written from the old Hôtel Welcome, in Villefranche: "I'm closing shop and moving to a new spot. That's the way gypsies relax." But the "new spot" turned out to be the whole globe. Early in 1936, to celebrate the one hundredth anniversary of Jules Verne's Around the World in Eighty Days, another paper challenged him to follow Phileas Fogg's route and write an account of his journey along the way. Cocteau accepted and made a bet with his editor. His traveling expenses would be paid, "but you won't have to pay me for my articles unless I get back in eighty days." With a young Algerian named Marcel Khill as his Passepartout, he left Paris on March 28.

Le Sang d'un Poète

"Poets, to live, must often die,
leaving a trail not only of the heart's
red blood but of the soul's white,
by which they can be traced."

I shall first quote one compliment and one reproach.

The compliment comes from a woman who keeps house for me. She had asked for tickets, and I had been foolish enough to fear her reaction, thinking: "After seeing the film, she won't want to work for me any more." Now, this is how she thanked me: "I saw your film. It was an hour in another world." A compliment indeed.

And now the reproach, leveled by an American critic who accuses me of using film as if it were a sacred substance, as enduring as a painting, a book. Not that he regards the cinema as an inferior art, but he rightly considers that a movie is projected rapidly, that the public primarily seeks entertainment, that film itself is fragile, and that it is pretentious to express all the powers of one's soul by the intermediary of so fugitive and so delicate a substance, the early works of Chaplin and Keaton, for example, now being available only in rare and damaged prints. I shall add that the cinema makes daily progress and that precision and color will cast into oblivion the films which at present seem miraculous to us. All true enough. But, for four weeks now, my film has been shown to capacity audiences so attentive, so alert, and so enthusiastic that I wonder if the cinema, after all, has not formed an anonymous public which seeks something more than entertainment.

*

I want to mention, too, my good fortune. The cinema is unapproachable—it cannot fall into the hands of poets, or if it does, the worst sacrifices are required of them. But in making *Le Sang d'un Poète,* I was left entirely free. This is a unique case, because the film was commissioned (by the Vicomte de Noailles, as was Buñuel's *L'Age d'Or*) and because I knew nothing about the art of the cinema. I invented it as I went along and used it like an artist who dips his finger into India ink for the first time and spatters a sheet of paper. Charles de Noailles had suggested, at first, that I make an animated cartoon. I soon realized that animation required a technique and a staff as yet unknown in France. I therefore suggested that instead I make a film as free as an animated cartoon, choosing faces and locations which corresponded to the freedom of an artist inventing a world of his own. I can even say that chance, or at least what is called chance (for those who immerse themselves in the spell of their work, there is no such thing as an accident), often served me well. Which is not to forget the derision of the studio, where I was regarded as a madman, a derision of which I shall provide one example. I was finishing *Le Sang d'un Poète.* The sweepers were told to clean up the studio during my last shots. As I was about to complain about this, my cameraman (Périnal) told me to do nothing of the kind—he had just realized that the dust raised by the brooms, filtering the light from the arc lamps, would create the beauty of the images; it is this dust which silvers the end of the film, which gives it the style of an apotheosis.

*

In *Le Sang d'un Poète,* I tried to film poetry, as the Williamson brothers film the ocean floor. I had to let down into myself the diving bell they drop deep into the sea. I had to take the poetic state by surprise. Many people suppose that this state does not exist, that it is a kind of voluntary excitation. Yet even those who imagine themselves furthest from the poetic state experience it. Let them merely recall some great grief or great weariness. They sit by the fire, they doze, but they are not really asleep. Immediately certain associations are set up within them, not associations of ideas, or images, or recollections. They are, rather, monsters which couple with each other, secrets which pass into the light, a whole enigmatic, equivocal world, quite capable of suggesting the nightmare in which poets live, which makes their life so moving, and which the public is wrong to identify, more often than not, as an exceptional intoxication.

*

But what chiefly characterizes *Le Sang d'un Poète*, it seems to me, is its complete indifference to what the world finds *poetic*; its concern, instead, to construct a vehicle for poetry, whether utilized or not.

Is not the choice of protagonists a significant one? Amateurs, presences unskilled in their function, their sole responsibility being to play their part. The Statue was Man Ray's friend Lee Miller. She had never worked in films before, has never done so since. We saw her again—in uniform—in 1945. The Poet was Enrico Rivero, a young Chilean chosen for his appearance, which was as "unhaunted" as possible. The Louis XIV Comrade was Jean Desbordes. The black angel, Feral Benga, a jazz dancer. The schoolboys, technical assistants. Barbette, Pauline Carton, Odette Thalazac appeared only in bit parts.

Of course, nothing is more difficult than to approach poetry, which is like wild animals. People say that films of Africa are faked. How could they help being faked? I will not conceal the fact that I used tricks to make poetry visible and audible. Let me tell you some of them.

First of all, you see the Poet enter a mirror. Then he swims about in a world which none of us knows but which I imagine. This mirror leads him down a hallway, and he moves along it as though in a dream. Neither swimming nor flying. It is something else, not like anything we know. Slow-motion is vulgar. So I had the set nailed to the floor and then turned the stage on its side. The character crawls instead of walks, and when the stage is turned right side up on the screen, you see a man walking in a strange, laborious way, the movements of his muscles not corresponding to the effort of his walk.

Miss Miller has pale eyes; yet sometimes, in my film, she has dark eyes. I had painted eyes on her eyelids. Not for an aesthetic purpose, to give her the look of a mask, but because when her eyes are closed and she is blind she walks like a blind person, and since on screen you do not realize that her eyes are artificial, this walk adds to the unreality of her character.

Another trick: I wanted to show the Poet's statue destroyed by the children at play who destroy everything and respect nothing. This stone statue must vanish as if it were snow. So we had to offset this effect with a highly realistic scene to make it stand out. I carried exactitude to the point of replacing real snow with our Parisian slush, that gray mud with which the children of Paris combat each other and which is certainly less photogenic and seductive than the snows of Russia.

*

But *Le Sang d'un Poète* resorts neither to dreams nor to symbols. With regard to dreams, it imitates their mechanism, rather, and by a certain relaxation of mind, like that of sleep, lets memories combine, maneuver, wander at will. As for symbols, the film avoids them, substituting actions or allegories of those actions, out of which the spectator can make up his own symbols, if he wants to.

*

The public often makes the mistake of supposing artists mock their audience. This is impossible. First of all because the artist would gain nothing by doing so; second because the film-

maker's singularly exhausting work is too demanding to permit him to *think*. Thought is replaced by a somnambulist's
mechanism. Do you have any idea of the work involved in
making a film? You arrive at guillotine time. And until midnight you move from one studio to the next. You do everything
possible not to bankrupt the enterprise in which you are engaged. You don't eat. You sleep on your feet. You stumble
through. After four days, unless you have a powerful physique,
you are exhausted. You no longer know where you are. This is
one of the reasons why the cinema is a poetic instrument of the
first order. To sleep on your feet is to speak without realizing it.
It is to make confidences. It is to say things you would tell no
one. You reveal yourself; the shadows cease being shadows. The
diving bell I mentioned begins to move, to descend. And that is
why *Le Sang d'un Poète* is of a confessional nature and as
unclear as possible, in the sense in which audiences understand
clarity.

*

There is no such thing as a synopsis of such a film. I could
merely give my own interpretation of it. I could tell you: the
Poet's solitude is so great, he lives what he creates so intensely,
that the mouth of one of his creations remains in his hand like
a wound, and that he loves this mouth, loves himself really; that
he wakes up one morning with this mouth pressed like a
stranger's against his body, that he tries to get rid of it, and that
he does so by transferring it to a statue, and that this statue
comes alive, takes its revenge, and leads him into terrible adventures. I could tell you that the snowball fight is the Poet's
childhood, and that when he plays a game of cards with his
Fame, or his Fate, he cheats by taking from his childhood what
he should be taking from himself. Then I could tell you that
having tried to create his earthly fame, he falls into that "mortal
weariness of immortality" inspired by every illustrious tomb.
And I would be right to tell you these things, but I would be

wrong too,* for it would be a text written *after the fact,* after the images. Moreover, are these images really images? Life creates great images without knowing it. The drama of Golgotha did not take place for the sake of painters. When I was at work, I repeat, I thought of nothing, and that is why you must let this film function like Auric's noble music which accompanies it, and like all the music in the world. Music supplies an anonymous nutriment to our feelings, to our memories, and if each of us finds in this film a meaning of his own, I consider that I have achieved my purpose.

* Note (1951): Freud is equally right when he writes of *Le Sang d'un Poète* that it is a film about watching a man through a keyhole as he gets up in the morning, washes, etc. . . . There have been countless exegeses of the film, even one that claimed it was the history of Christianity, down to the last detail. When I questioned one of the young philosophers responsible for this interpretation, he told me that only one thing confused him, one of the first lines of the film: "While the cannons of Fontenoy were thundering in the distance . . ." "Heavens!" he suddenly exclaimed. "It's at Fontenoy that the Eucharistic Council was held!" And when I vaguely protested, he flung an irrefutable proof in my face: "You can't deny that the outline of the dead child in the snow is Saint Veronica's Napkin!" Another thing: 300 girls from a Catholic Psychoanalytic Institute regarded the factory chimney which begins to fall in the first frames (to show that the time of the action has the immediacy of a dream) as a phallic symbol. Half the exegetes regard *Le Sang d'un Poète* as an erotic film, and the other half as an icy, abstract work entirely lacking in humanity. It was after these experiences that I declared: "Poetry comes from those who are not concerned with it. We are cabinetmakers. The mediums come afterwards, and it is their business to make the tables talk."

Around the World in Eighty Days

> *"All your old scars*
> *Earth*
> *cast the spell*
> *of your warrior's face."*

My trip around the world was first suggested by Marcel Khill, whom I shall henceforth call Passepartout. We intended to follow in the footsteps of Jules Verne's heroes, to celebrate his centenary by sightseeing for eighty days.

Eighty days! We had imagined that what was a dash into the abyss in 1876 would have become, by 1936, a *largo* promenade with leisurely stopovers in each port of call.

Jean Prouvost, editor of *Paris-Soir*, accepted the project, the wager, though he realized that these famous eighty days were a reality ahead of the fact, a dream of Verne's like his phonographs, his airplanes, his submarines and diving bells. Everyone believed such things because of the persuasive power of masterpieces. Yet by careful scheduling—and barring aviation—we required, in 1936, neither more nor less than eighty days to meet Phileas Fogg's challenge, to follow his ideal route in reality.

The project therefore entirely changed its nature: no longer a promenade in the footsteps of the heroes who once helped us endure measles and scarlatina, it became a record to beat, a performance.

*

So we are under way. We shall no longer use our language, no longer express ourselves except by monosyllables and gestures.

We decided to leave on March 28 and to be back on June 17 before the last stroke of midnight.

The slightest hitch in a steamer schedule, the smallest error in calculating a railroad timetable, and success would be impossible.

To start off, we had decided, God knows why, that the Rome Express left at 10:40 p.m. and had convinced everyone else of the fact. As it turned out, the train left at 10:20, as we were informed at 9:50 by the telephone operator of my hotel, who had wondered at this sudden change in the schedules. The bellhops helped us fling ourselves and our luggage into a taxi, and we reached the station five minutes before the Express pulled out.

Rome: the night of March 29

We preferred a moonlit Rome: at night you see how a city is made. It is empty, human beings do not spoil the scale of its décor; it shrinks, comes closer, and the noblest façades do not hesitate to whisper into your ear. At night, no doubt about it: Rome, the heaviest city in the world, Rome the matron, is gradually sinking under all the weight of her monuments and her statues.

You contemplate her from the waist up, straining to hoist herself on her elbows, swelling her knotted muscles, kneading the flesh of one of Michelangelo's slaves.

*

Athens: March 31

We find a bank and our poor dollars become thousands of drachmas. At the bank door Passepartout, inspired by an innovation which becomes our definitive mode of travel, leaps onto the back of an ancient bus. A tottering rattletrap full of bureaucrats. Passepartout slips to the front, and I cannot follow him through the crowd. The vehicle clatters on, Passepartout standing up front, bent double to look out the windows, I sitting in the back beside four Greeks arguing over a handful of silky seeds, crunching them between their teeth, then thrusting them deep into their pockets, digging them out again, crunching them some more, quarreling, brandishing them, on and on. They interrupt their dispute only to wink at a young secretary standing above me. She is wearing glasses and has one fist on her hip.

Through the triangle formed by her bust and her arm pass what look like the suburbs of Toulouse. I doze, wakened by the jolts.

Suddenly my eyes widen. What do I see? Framed by this girl's body, I see a tiny broken cage, very long and low, the kind children make out of straws for grasshoppers. It hangs high in the air, and the void surrounds it. What? My heart starts pounding. That disemboweled little cage . . . could it be . . . ? Yes, it is, it's the Parthenon!

I want to shout to Passepartout: Look . . . the Parthenon! I don't dare. He must have seen it. Why is everyone so calm? Why are they still sitting down? Why don't they leap up, why don't they shout something like the *Thalassa* of their ancestors?

I was forgetting that the Acropolis affects them no more than the Eiffel Tower astonishes us. And in tense silence I watch it leap past under the girl's elbow: the cage in which the Athenians kept Pallas, grasshopper of the Greek crag.

Rhodes: April 1

Where the feet of the Colossus stood, on each side of the harbor, rise two columns. On one, the Roman wolf suckles Romulus and Remus; on the other, a bronze stag faces this island of venery and roses. Scalloped walls, towers, and crenelated walks enclose the town. You enter it through a portcullis. A breakneck platform, steps, vaults, moats, bridges, loopholes confuse you and quickly bring you back to where you started.

An Italian soldier, silhouetted against the sky, shouts at
Passepartout to put away his Kodak. Passepartout had no in-
tention of photographing the fortress, but rather an old Mos-
lem woman lighting her cigarette as she leans over the rim of a
Byzantine well. It seems like a sacrilege, a holy-water stoop and
a worshipper smoking. But her black veil and the Italian soldier
protect her. The veil is rarely drawn aside. The sea breeze pastes
it against her face. The shadows in their eyes, around their
mouths, make these passing women into death's-heads, lepers.

"Drink once from the springs of Rhodes and you will return." I recite the saying, thinking I will doubtless never see
this island again, where we stop only four hours.

Here I have seen the first turbans of that red the sun fades to
pale mauve. The children chalk their stars of David on the
walls: two interlocking triangles; and the stevedores on the dock
roll a linen rag around their heads, knotting it so that the end
falls over the back of the neck. A first breath of Egypt: the
granite handkerchief which coifs her Gods.

Alexandria: April 3

In Egypt, nothing is concluded, nothing bought, without mysterious glances: the most naïve transaction becomes a kind of
louche trafficking. Every purchase necessitates a scenario of
winks and whispers. We have to follow each other at a distance,
creep along the walls, vanish down an alley, return through an
air shaft, wait for messengers, consult each other by signs, etc.,
etc. A ritual without which commerce is no longer commerce,
and the vendor is ruined. Are you in a hurry? A street vendor
prefers to hurl his merchandise after you rather than wrap it up
in exchange for a fixed price.

You must spend hours reaching a bargain of a few piasters,
and also you must see the sarcophagi piled on top of each other,
in order to understand that Mark Antony's first glimpse of
Cleopatra is no caprice but the true style of Egypt. The queen

is called *Egypt*. She is Egypt. She owes it to herself to invent the most significant means of materialization.

Merchandise is brought to the victor: rugs. One rug, two rugs, three rugs, four rugs, each more precious than the one before; and when the tedium of looking at rugs sets in, the last rug is unrolled. The Queen appears, lying inside it.

Cairo: April 4

On the map of Egypt, Egypt is a funerary stele. Five years ago, I was struck by a newspaper article: an aviation officer described his reconnaissance mission and wondered if the Sphinx, the Pyramids, the obelisks, the Delta were not hieroglyphs, a text for the use of the Gods.

Mena House is an exquisitely elegant hotel. The-Thousand-and-One-Nights in English. The Caliph would run no risk of adventures here. An impeccable staff leads me—what am I saying?—leads Phileas Fogg to his room. Rendezvous with Abdul after dinner to visit the Pyramids and the Sphinx.

We are lucky enough to have a moon: the desert glimmers in the light of an eclipse. Our dinner is soon over. We hurry through the fantastic dining room. English ladies in tulle gowns, escorted by sons in tuxedos, leave a cyclamen wake as they glide to tables where they drink champagne and listen to endless Viennese waltzes.

Abdul is watching for us. In front of the hotel gate, near the camel drivers, wait the camels, lying on their shadows. Abdul rides a donkey. We climb onto the saddles, and the camels stand up. It is the movement of a wall breaking into three pieces, filmed in slow motion and reversed. Our caravan sets off.

The camel is an aquatic animal; the décor it traverses is a submarine décor. Its silhouette is antediluvian. Once, its saurian neck must have thrust above the waves, its legs paddled left and right like fins. The sea has disappeared, the beast has turned into a steed which preserves the waves' rhythm, and it is on a lofty vessel that I imagine I sail to the encounter with Cheops.

The Sphinx

What travelers never tell us (probably they do tell us, but we must experience it for ourselves) is the way beauty materializes, the exact site it occupies.

They separate it from the rest. They observe it as if it revolved on a pedestal, with nothing around it.

That is why I could not understand Abdul when he announced that the Sphinx was in sight. Where was it? Where did he see it? From my camel, I stared over the sands. Gently but excessively, the moon elongated the flat left cheek of the Pyramid of Cheops. Farther off, to the right, on the still-intact revetment at the top of the second Pyramid, it distorted perspectives, and the point seemed put on askew.

A surge of dunes and debris undulates at our feet. Curves and humps, which the camel imitates.

The Sphinx? I make out a ditch, a basin, a hollow in the sand, which our mounts circle and at the bottom of which we divine the contour of a steamer in dry-dock.

Suddenly, like a drawing the eye discovers how to read, I understand—I can no longer not understand. The steamer's prow slowly turns its profile. The Sphinx's head appears, and the rest follows: the hindquarters, the coiled tail, the hind legs, the long straight forepaws between which a marble slab embellishes the chest, and at the ends of which the knuckles are silhouetted, the crests and curves of a sand-cast fresh from its mold.

The camels stop and break apart in three slow jolts. I leap down, I run. A steep wall stops me; the wall of that ditch where the Sphinx has been lying since the discovery of the paws in 1926. It had hidden them for centuries in the sand, as if the desert were the muffs of the Sphinxes at Versailles.

Tutankhamen

It is futile to describe the treasure of Tutankhamen. Since all the descriptions and pictures had given me no idea of it, I should be committing the same errors.

A young Pharaoh of seventeen organizes a posthumous life of luxury and elegance for himself. He endures in the sand, like a brick in the Polar ice. He shows us intact his furniture, his chariots, his jewels, his robes. There has been no time to make him the symbols of what he possessed. He has been buried pell-mell with his properties. The king was the star of a mystery theatre to which the people flocked, bearing his gold. Red-veined gold, gold filigree, gold flatware—the objects in the cases testify to the method.

The chairs, the thrones, the tripods, the ostrich-feather fly whisks, the enemies who serve as stools, the boomerangs, the trumpets, the sandals, the gloves, the flails against evil spirits, the shepherd's crooks, the headdress on which the cobra designates the North, the falcon the South, the series of cases in which the young man lay, inside hollow statues, his beds with their chimera mouths and the hard lapis-lazuli pillows which supported his charming, complicated head—all this panoply of the little Pharaoh is so much theatre, cosmetic, artifice, décor.

The halls of Tutankhamen so astound us that we forget the others: the wooden man who walks, the ochre and plaster couple sitting at the bottom of death with their fixed stare, the green bronze king greaved in his own thighs, the cow painted with the ace of clubs who suckles the Pharaoh in a stable cool as a missal—living portraits, cult objects, or rather objectives, intensities which exist because Egypt never bothered with art for art's sake.

Port Said: April 8

The interminable Suez Canal. The palm trees succeed each other in the porthole, indistinguishable from left to right, each time I open an eye. Like London, which one never escapes, the Suez Canal continually files by. The Red Sea. The special discomfort of a heat not our own. At night, streams of sweat tunnel into the skin, gathering in huge drops. Heat against which we can do nothing—as if it were a fever. The air from the vents merely adds to the discomfort, stokes the furnace.

I visit the stewards' room (you always think it will be better somewhere else), and that is worse still. Poor naked boys, openmouthed, glued in clusters to strips of flypaper. The gasps, the spasms of sleep. The inferno of the engines. The heat grows worse.

Aden: April 12

Aden, vestibule of India, meager site, scorpion, cactus, crucible of enigmatic races, offers no respite of softness or grace. The contrary of Rhodes, it is hopeless, extreme, bitter, planted in the world like a knife.

Aden, valley of lepers. Mine without ore. Heat more lugubrious than any northern cold. This sterile soil mocks the notion of *producing*. The place is an intersection of races and merchandise, a rendezvous of airplanes and warships, a barracks of British sentries.

Just as masterpieces emerge from an agony, a solitude, an insufficient substance, from denials surmounted, so forsaken Aden gives birth to human thoroughbreds of every race.

Broad shoulders, slender necks, narrow hips, fine ankles, hollow bellies, round thighs—everywhere we pass specters of flesh and blood, superb skeletons dressed in dark skin, princes flayed alive, draped in scarves the color of poison: chartreuse, viridian, violet. And the turban's voluminous mass which gives their walk its poise, its nobility . . . Sometimes even garters reach the point of becoming an ornamental motif.

When they sit down, these terrifying dandies, they squat between their own gleaming thighs in the swag of their loincloth, heels against buttocks, knees at shoulder height.

April 16

The first breath of air since the Indian Ocean. The Great Bear completely upside down. Through methylene-blue water calm as any lake, the *Strathmore* glides, never pitches or rolls. The moon has lost its look of an alabaster funerary urn, its black mists, its spectral nimbus.

Bombay: April 17

By its brown-veined eyes, by the way the sole of its foot touches the earth, by its skin which listens and watches, by its moist muzzle scarlet with betel, by its night-black hair, the whole animal betrays itself, still in metamorphosis.

No dogs, no cats, almost no children. Nothing but the disconcerting victims of a magic wand. Vanishing as soon as he has provoked our amazement, this naked skinny stiff solemn boy with his long hank of hair hanging between his shoulder blades seems to have been surprised in transformation from one avatar to the next.

The streets look like bird-sellers' stalls on the Quai du Louvre.

Cages heaped on cages, perches, balconies, swings: a theatre of birds, an opera of birds, and between the cages branches and vines refresh the street flowing like a syrupy river among grandstands, prosceniums, pilings, the beds on which fat merchants lie, dressed in linen, chattering, smoking, outdoing each other in sloth and opulence, fanned by black slaves with eaglet profiles.

A scene out of Kipling: the terrible little battle of a mongoose and a cobra. The fakir and his assistant unpack their suspect baskets. A nasal music begins, some secret refrain. Suddenly the straw basket seems to roil, the lid jerks up and the contents overflow: a disgusting yellow cream, flowing . . . and curdling . . . and escaping over the sidewalk. Then the fakir opens a kind of bingo bag out of which leaps the mongoose. In a second it is on the runaway cream, and the duel begins. A duel of embraces and jerks, of calligraphies, paraphs, and whiplashes. The pink muzzle tries to bite the back of the snake's neck. Three times the cobra pulls itself erect, for its musculature is so distributed that it can support itself on a tiny loop of its tail. It stands up and aims its head at the mongoose like a revolver. The mongoose leaps, and triumphs. The cobra's neck is bleeding. It collapses, suddenly motionless. But a serpent is a procession; the head extinct, the tail trembles still. The news had not had time to reach the end.

I did not know that such heat was possible, that men could survive in this cursed climate. The train trembles, and the arson of India turns its iron, glass, and wood white-hot, covers us with streaming glue, raises the air, now a viscous paste beaten to foam by the ventilators, to the temperature of nausea.

Rangoon: April 22

The Strand Hotel. By day we run from shop to shop. We cross huge depots, the fabric warehouses in which the vendors' families live. After dark the hotel doorman and the bellhops warn us away from the "dangerous" neighborhoods.

"No, no, master. Bad, bad, no good."

Loyal to our method, we spur our long-maned human ponies, the Sikh runners, toward the forbidden districts. From the charming red-lacquer carriage with its iron gingerbread and delicate lanterns, drawn by the tireless trotting coolies almost borne aloft between the shafts, we glimpse avenues where a hodgepodge of races sleeps and swarms and strolls and eats in the open air. On either side, stables of kites, the backstage of a theatre of cooks and barbers, secret sports and incomprehensible professions. Posters, signs, outhouses, sheds, stalls, alleys, streamers, lanterns. Groups part before us, and we pass through crowds of Chinese, Burmese, magnificent Sikhs.

Often some giantess knotting her chignon with a nymph's gesture turns around to reveal the bearded face of a young Sikh.

Formerly warriors, the numberless Sikhs counterbalance the Chinese invasion. Whereas the Chinese surrender even their armpits and chests and legs to the barber, a Sikh is forbidden to cut one hair of his head. Later, on the route which takes us from the Chinese city into the Sikh quarter, the ground is strewn with the corpses of sleep. These male Amazons sleep anywhere, lying in front of the one-story houses, their limbs entangled like sea horses and jackstraws . . . Heads thrown back, one hand flung far from the body, long hair untied, they sleep with their eyes open. The white corneas sparkle in their dark faces, and the red thread of betel juice flows from one corner of their half-open mouths.

Our runners have a terrible time avoiding them, clearing a path for the carriage. Sometimes a wheel passes over an arm, a leg, without wakening the strange cluster pegged to the earth. And everywhere the tortuous poppy emits its deep, forbidden odor. Our pantomime and the pidgin word *chowchow* has made our runners understand that we want to visit an opium den. Opium is forbidden. The entire Chinese city smokes, and the Burmese city too—as a matter of fact, opium is smoked everywhere.

The houses are farther apart now. Fewer sleepers strew the avenues. Our runners turn and set down the shafts opposite a house with scarlet placards. A swinging door. I push it open and we find ourselves standing in a dream barrack, where on berths whose mats are polished to a golden brown, between lamps like stars in the darkness, float bodies inhabited by a cloud. On what river of oblivion do they drift? This visit reminds us of the Pyramids. The same trap doors, the same gleaming surfaces, the same brown patina, the same steep stairs, the same airholes, the same night lights, the same sarcophagi, the same weightless mummies riding the current of eternity.

We go upstairs to visit the compartments of the elegant clientele, and in order not to yield to temptation, to the devil trying to make us lose our wager, we quickly leave the perfumed chambers.

"Passepartout," I say, "if we were to make an accelerated film—the kind they shoot of plants—of Mongol habits, you would see a dance: swimmers, their hair floating like algae on the water of time."

Between Malacca and Singapore

In most cases the picturesque and the fantastic overcome us with fatigue and boredom. Forms, lines, and colors exert a power which the Occidental abuses and out of which the Oriental composes his philters.

A sensitive individual is crushed by the disorder of proportions. An architect's stupidity is more dangerous than any other, for its influence is inescapable. This is not a matter of good taste or bad. It is a matter of a site which exhausts, which envenoms, which debases, which casts its spells and curses in silence, in secret. A hotel, a ship can cause strange ravages. You cannot trace the source of the discomfort which dissipates your resources. Your soul stiffens, loses its adaptability. The malaise is impossible to analyze. At first you laugh at ugliness; it intrigues you, revolts you. Gradually it poisons you; your organism refuses to prosper; it squints, it limps, it dies.

The Orient knows these terrible forces. It uses them to destroy or to enchant. An Indian temple, a Chinese pagoda can hypnotize, bewitch, excite, lull, all by the use of volumes, curves, perspectives.

A monument which *serves*, or which has served, never fatigues us. The Coliseum served, the Acropolis served, the Sphinx served, etc. . . . That is why they delight us. It is not necessary to know what they served *for*, or to take advantage of their services. The fact that they were born of a need, that a purpose directed those who built them and obliged them to submit to certain rules, clears them of all disorder, all frivolity.

Whether they are intended to astound, to thank, to overpower, to assure the survival of the dead by the resemblance of a double, or, by that resemblance, to terrify tomb robbers, the point of departure is not a matter of chance. The great epochs never confront us with works of aesthetes. A scarecrow frightens birds, it does not frighten us; but the mere necessity of achieving a successful result inspires the peasant who devises it, dispenses him from being decorative. That is the beauty of the scarecrow. And of African masks, totems, the Sphinxes of Egypt.

Powerful and almost always secret motives are to be found at the origin of a thousand details which weave the seething beauty of the universe. A singularity may appear gratuitous to us, but its expressive force always conceals roots.

Do you know why China breaks and binds the feet of its women? You will answer: fashion. A long fashion. Moreover fashion itself has unexpected sources. A bald man launches the perruque, a clubfoot the trouser strap, a pimply princess the beauty patch, a pregnant empress the crinoline, etc. . . . Many hidden infirmities were the seed of singular fashions.

The origin of the bound feet of Chinese women is different. A race of executioners does not conceive love without a concomitant suffering. A broken foot remains sensitive where the fracture occurred. This place need merely be touched in order to inflict torture. That is the true motive of this fascinating custom, which, along with other refinements, is coming to an end. The more China imitates us, the more she abandons her mysterious privileges. Eroticism is returning to Europe's barbarism.

Recipes of gastronomy and love are being lost or becoming folklore. Young Chinese brides need no longer dread the conjugal device which wrung from them, at the crucial moment, spasms and shrieks of pain.

What is the source of the etiquette which transposes and inverts, from nation to nation, *what is done* and *what is not done?*

Hindus would rather die than show themselves naked to the doctor. A British colonial officer who undresses on a riverbank to take a swim, should he be seen by a native, loses face and must leave the district. A noise made with the mouth is an Oriental's tribute to his host. A noise of another sort is a mortification after which the only recourse is death.

A young Hindu soldier in Major B.'s troops produces this baleful noise during drill. He is barely heard by one of his comrades. An hour later, with his own rifle, he commits suicide in the jungle.

A father emits this same noise leaning over his son's cradle. His wife calls him a "farter," and he must leave the village. Twenty years pass. He longs to see his son again. He returns to the village in secret. He asks questions. His son has become a soldier in the Indian Army. How proud he is! Now here comes his son, and his old wife is standing at the door to welcome him. The father forgets the past; he approaches. His wife recognizes him. "Look," she cries to their son, "the old farter's come home!" He runs off and never dares appear again.

These two stories are true. Here is a fable.

A princess falls in love with a shoemaker. She is forbidden to marry him. For her health's sake, the doctors oblige the father to consent to the marriage. The shoemaker is given lessons in deportment, and the marriage takes place. During the wedding banquet the shoemaker produces the prohibited noise. He rises from the table, leaves the party, gathers up some clothes, forsakes the palace and the town as fast as he can. He crosses plains, forests, villages, and reaches another town. He sets up in business, opens a stall, marries, and has children.

Grown old, he desires to see the town of his youth again. He leaves his family one night and covers the same route as before, in the opposite direction. He crosses forests and plains. Finally he sees the town, whose new monuments render it almost unrecognizable.

He enters the town, walks to its center. He seems to recognize the site of the palace, but the palace no longer exists—it has been replaced by a park and a post office.

He approaches a beggar woman his own age. "When," he asks her, "when was the palace torn down?"

And with a gesture indicating that the event did not occur yesterday, she answers: "The year of the fart."

A hideous story. In one word we learn that this *criminal noise* has changed the course of events, dividing them into those which occurred before and those which occurred afterwards. It places upon this ancient shoemaker an unwonted crown.

In the West, this indiscretion would have made the princess blush, and her father would have said: "You see!"

In the Orient, walls crumble and a dynasty vanishes.

If China's bound and broken feet have an explanation, it is one which remains an enigma to us. Once we know the source of such nuances, we no longer find them funny. The ignorant tourist who circles the globe by our method must realize that he is passing through a ritual of which he understands nothing. Let this realization make him wary of judging, and strip him once and for all of our European impertinence. Let nothing that disconcerts him make him smile, let him respect signs which lose all their decorative naïveté as soon as our minds penetrate their meaning.

Singapore: Thieves' Alley

"It's all very well being a daredevil and the rest of it, but there are limits. You're making a terrible mistake. Believe an old soldier . . ." How often I've heard those counsels of cowardice, that false wisdom of the fearful who assume knowing looks and brag about their "experience" . . . Ours is now behind us. We have gone around the world. In every city we have unhesitatingly followed our guides down alleys where you stumble along, lighting match after match, up rickety stairways, through muddy courtyards, stinking cellars. It was enough to explain ourselves by gestures. Such places have always been generous to us, welcoming. The sleepers who move aside to make room, their rest disturbed without complaint . . . The heart offered in exchange for a cigarette . . .

That night, in an attic crowded with some twenty comrades around the lamps, a man on the next mat wakens abruptly, staring wide-eyed out of his dream into our pale faces. Behind the partitions, the pipes sing. I supposed I saw us at a distance —in a mirror hanging on the wall; then I realized that the frame of this mirror was a window open on other windows, other lamps, other smokers . . .

May 1

We were almost kept from leaving Sunday. Not knowing English well, not reading the regulations, and not making some direct contact; in short, living like sleepwalkers, we had not registered since our first arrival in Malaya. The mistake must date from Penang. This morning a summons to appear before the magistrate. Luckily Coupeau, from the Messageries Maritimes, who was booking our tickets, had been notified by the Japanese company, and matters were settled before the offices closed. On Saturday and Sunday, England "closes." Not only would this have kept us from leaving and ruined our schedule, but we would have had to pay a fine of 6,000 francs as well.

The French consul, whom we have run into, criticizes my attitude. He does not understand the singularity of this journey, the angle of my vision, and the fact that I must advance over the earth's surface by fits and starts, like those dragonflies which skim the pond and stop an instant at each flower.

If I were to present myself at the consulates, the consuls would invite me, they are obliged to invite me, and I obliged to accept; instead of living one day in each country I pass through, I would be living one day in Europe; indeed, one official day, a day I never live in France, a day wasted!

The China Sea: May 5

We weigh half what we did when we started out. We swim in our clothes, dragging from the bathroom to lunch to dinner to the pool, through the corridors of a nightmare. The consul had told me: "You leave your skin behind."

These disguised jungles take their revenge. They demand a flesh of bronze, the intelligence of insects, the heart of a tiger, a mind which does not think. A single flaw and the black fluids rush in. Wives sob in their hotel rooms, husbands hate their bosses. The bosses torment their employees, etc. You die of bitterness and disgust.

This race around the globe has reinforced our conviction that there are only apparent and transitory injustices. Each of us occupies the place he deserves by virtue of a system of weights and measures which functions more profoundly than our behavior, makes and breaks us, classifies with blind exactitude. Gradually we learn to see rewards and punishments in this system which derives from no morality. You do not say a scale is fair—you say it is correct. Let us testify to the correctness which directs human life and which man persists in taking for justice. When this "justice" disturbs his calculations or disorients him —that is, maneuvers him against his will—he taxes it with injustice. Time, however, restores everything to its rightful place and grants its palm to the slow celerity of the true conquerors. That is the Oriental secret. It is the power of China and Japan. It is the triumph of colonial England; in the colonies, an *arriviste* tears himself to pieces, a dreamer sinks into the quicksand; a man who knows how to breathe properly, to get his second wind, will always succeed.

The Chinese can smile and stroll past a girl having her teeth knocked out, past a man being roasted to death over a slow fire. No one avoids the spectacle, no one rebels, no one dreams of offering help. They do not protest against misfortune—they laugh at it. Their sensibility does not function erratically. They have no sentimentality.

(A Malay or a Chinese announces to his employer: "My son was killed yesterday." The announcement is made with a smile, out of politeness, in order to attenuate the news.)

Hong Kong: May 9

Tonight it was an unknown Chinese who piloted us from one watchmaker to the next to have Passepartout's watch repaired (the Chinese adore burdening themselves with your packages and escorting you), and who then suggests taking us to an opium den.

We arrive between two walls of lilies and gardenias—Flower Street—where florists sitting on the ground are manufacturing crowns and crosses of carnations, gladiolas, dahlias, gardenias, lilies: all the white flowers. The street climbs uphill, hung five stories high with dirty linen, crowded with mothers cooling their behinds, with children playing.

We turn left into a plank shed. Here, forming a stall, the high room displays its shelves of smokers, faces gently illuminated by the night lights. Always the brown patina, the golden filth, the interlacing signs of the ship's serpentine wake . . . Always the silence broken by children crying and the opium cooking by fits and starts. The lower levels are architect's tables on iron X's. The smokers climb onto these, or slide underneath, separated by a board.

A fat woman, who blows her nose into her fingers, weighs out opium on a tiny scale. Her husband floats from smoker to smoker, trims a wick, changes a stove, administers the doses.

The Chinese people has been victimized by a new fashion which I attribute to some enemy. This fashion is four years old. It is the opium gumdrop, a perforated sugar bead, candle-pink in color, which is replacing the opium from Macao, that Monte Carlo built on a crag three hours from Hong Kong, where rich and poor Chinese can slake their passion for gambling. This artificial opium costs less than opium. It is pasted over the aperture of a stove four times larger than an ordinary stove, a kind of converted flower vase with a hole in one side. The spout, provided with a brass screw, is fastened to the end of a pipe. The opium lamp burns in a glass basin which smothers the draft. It is sweetish, subtle, deadly, for you can be sure the worst ingredients are concealed in this harmless-looking paste.

The smoke stinks of the milk caramels we used to make as children on rainy days in the country. It is that country house, my bedroom, my cousins who made me taste their efforts that I see again now, eyes closed, the back of my neck resting on the porcelain cube.

Alas, the perfumes of this new vice disgust me, keep me from relaxing, and we have sworn not to touch the pipe.

Between Hong Kong and Shanghai: May 11

Charlie Chaplin is on board. The news astounds me. Later Chaplin was to tell me: "The real role of creation is to permit friends like ourselves to take shortcuts. We've known each other forever." But at that moment I had no idea that the desire for this encounter was reciprocal. Moreover, our journey had taught me how capricious fame is. Of course I had been happy to find my works translated into most languages, but at certain points where I expected friendship I had met with a vacuum; at others I expected nothing and had been overwhelmed with friendship.

I decided to write Chaplin a note. I indicated my presence on board and my admiration for his person. At dinner he came to table with Paulette Goddard. His attitude made it clear that he wished to keep his incognito. As it happened, my note had not been delivered. Chaplin did not realize I was on board the *Karoa* and made no connection between me and the fellow passenger whom he had glimpsed only in profile. After dinner I returned to my cabin. I was undressing, when there came a knock at the door: it was Charlie and Paulette! They had just been handed my note. Chaplin had suspected a trick, a trap, had rushed to the steward's office for the passenger list, and once he was sure of the facts, had insisted on delivering his answer in person.

Nothing simpler, nothing younger than this man. I was moved. I asked them to wait for me in their stateroom, the time it would take to put on a robe and to tell Passepartout, who was in the ship's library, writing letters.

You cannot imagine the purity, the violence, the freshness of this extraordinary meeting, prepared by nothing but our horoscopes. I was touching a myth in flesh and blood. Passepartout could not take his eyes off the idol of his childhood. Chaplin shook his white curls, took off his glasses, put them on again, grasped me by the shoulders, burst out laughing, turned to Paulette, and kept asking, "Isn't this marvelous? Isn't this marvelous?"

I don't speak English. Chaplin doesn't speak French. And we spoke without the slightest effort. What happened? What language was it? The language of life, more alive than any other, the language born from the desire to communicate at any cost, the language of mimes, of poets, of the heart. Chaplin detached each word, set it down on the table, on a pedestal, stepped back, turned it to the angle where it had the best light. The words he used for me are easy to shift from one language to another. Sometimes a gesture preceded the word, escorted it. Beforehand, it announced the word was coming, then commented on it after it had been spoken. No slowness—or, rather, the false slowness of a juggler's rings that you can follow as they float through the air.

It was certainly a new language we were speaking, perfecting, a language we insisted on speaking, to everyone's great surprise.

This language was understood only by the four of us, and when Paulette was later asked why she hadn't come to our assistance, since she speaks French well, she answered, "If I had helped them, they'd have wasted time on details. Left to them-selves, they said only the things that really mattered." The remark is characteristic of her penetration.

Chaplin spoke of filming a Crucifixion in a dance hall, where no one would notice it. And of a fantasy about Napoleon on Elba (Napoleon disguised as a gendarme). He was abandoning the *persona* we French call Charlot. "I am *overexposed*," he said. "I work in the streets. My aesthetic is the aesthetic of the kick in the behind . . . And I'm beginning to receive it." A remark which illuminates a dim corner of his soul. To use the modern jargon, his inferiority complex is enormous, equaled only by his justifiable pride and a system of reflexes capable of protecting his solitude (from which he suffers) and preserving his prerogatives.

Even friendship is suspect, for the duties and disorders it imposes. Chaplin's confiding impulse was, it appears, unique, and indeed it caused him a kind of dread. I sensed him catch up with himself and, so to speak, pull himself back after being so expansive.

His next film, in which he would not appear, was to be for Paulette. He would shoot three episodes of it in Bali. He was composing the text now, writing all the time. He recited the dialogue. This film seemed to mark the transition to a new cycle. Would he then be able to escape from the "laugh, clown, laugh" theme his genius had redeemed from vulgarity? His next role would be that of a clown torn between the conflicting claims of life and the stage. With what care Chaplin confined himself to the conventions of this facile romance, reworking every detail so that he could be followed on the tightrope by the clumsiest, the heaviest public in the world.

I should have guessed *Modern Times* was a terminal work, from this sign: for the first time, at the end, on the road, Charlie *does not leave alone.*

Moreover, the *type* was gradually being reduced, coinciding with the *man*—mustache and shoes shrinking, etc.

If he interprets *roles*, let us hope that some day Chaplin will give us Dostoevsky's *Idiot*. Is not Prince Mishkin a hero of his race?

Paulette vanishes for five minutes, and Charlie leans forward, whispering conspiratorially: "Besides, I feel so sorry for her." What? Pity for this little cactus with a thousand spines, for this little lioness with her splendid mane and claws, for this Rolls-Royce coupé gleaming with leather and chrome? That is typically Chaplin, the style of his heart.

Pity for Charlie the tramp, pity for us, pity for her . . . The poor little girl whom he drags with him, feeding her when she is hungry, putting her to bed when she is sleepy, rescuing her purity from the wicked cities; and suddenly I no longer see a Hollywood star in her silver satin lounging pajamas, or the rich, white-haired director in his mustard tweeds, but a pale, short man with black curls and a debonair cane, limping across the world with his beloved, fleeing together the snares of the cities and the wiles of the police.

Chaplin, whether he locks himself in his stateroom or races around his studio, is dedicated to his art. Terrified of distraction, he wards off life and limits himself to a few simple problems whose combinations he exhausts. An old man's smile, a Chinese mother nursing her newborn baby, details from the life of the poor—fertilize him. That is all he wants, and cloisters himself with his beloved work.

"I don't like work," Paulette says.

Chaplin does; he loves work, and since he loves Paulette he makes her his work. The rest bores him to death. The minute he is distracted from his work, he yawns, his shoulders sag, his eyes dim. He subsides into a minor death.

Japan: May 16

I am taking away from Japan a very different image from the one I had formed before coming here. Granted, our Mass may be decorative, and priests and worshippers may participate in it without belief. But suicide—I mean the sacrifice of the individual to society or to the Emperor who represents it—forms the basis of all these smiles and all these bows. The flowers of the prints send down into the soil dark and twisted roots. This people, doomed to ruin every sixty years by earthquakes and typhoons, consents to rebuild on the ashes. Death is at the end of its actions. It bows with patience to this harsh fate, and beforehand offers in a holocaust its homes of precious wood, straw, and rice paper.

At Kobe, the first sight which catches my eye is a little girl playing hopscotch. This five-year-old chalks on the sidewalk the perfect circle with which Hokusai signed his letters. Having completed this masterpiece, she hops off, sticking out her tongue.

I should like to take away that circle. It yields up, at our first step, the secret of the Nipponese soul. That calm like the solemn silence of the Meiji temple park, that laborious patience, that sureness of eye and hand, that clarity and cleanliness grant us either this miraculous woodwork or all the junk flooding the European market. Here labor is paid less than anywhere in the world, and the soldier who was once content with a bowl of rice a day now eats four. That is his pay, on land and sea. No possible competition. If a leader disobeys or tries to follow the example of Europe's bulky vegetables, he soon puts a sword in his guts.

In Tokyo, the geishas, high priestesses of good manners, serve us food on their knees, bursting into laughter and drinking out of our cups. The geishas come from poor families. At the age of twelve, they begin their studies. They become geishas when their education permits them to charm the guests, to play certain stringed instruments, to sing, to dance, to converse with men. They are not to be confused with courtesans. Their role is confined to making the atmosphere agreeable. They are bouquets, fragrances . . . This discrimination is honored, and the rules of the game consist in never transgressing certain limits. A central geisha bureau keeps their addresses and sends the girls out on call. Made up chalk-white, pupils sliding behind almond-shaped slits made with a penknife in the perfect mask, mitered with the shells, coils, and scrolls of a monumental black coiffure: how long will they endure their slavish existence, the long evenings of decorative charm?

Exquisite actresses, automata whose liquid white make-up stops at shoulders and elbows, whose mechanism executes a series of movements programed in advance, whose gold-toothed smile is concealed like a yawn behind the fan—what a surprise when one of them slips on a pair of scholarly horn-rimmed spectacles!

On cards, or rather on paper streamers, they hand us their names and addresses: *April Rain. Dynasty of Light. Gay Spring.*

Dynasty of Light is the Utamaro model, the girl one imagines out of books. Her head is a nodding egg surmounted by a black iris of hair. Her body is a chrysalis, a larva in mid-metamorphosis, for motley wings sprout from her round back. April Rain is less oval. Her face, a tiny sphere of ivory, sugar, and India ink. Her mouth bleeds. Her coiffure is the one "modern" ladies adopted in 1870. The scallops and spirals give way to braids and points.

Gay Spring presents the disconcerting spectacle of a rebellious geisha. The geisha who resists being a geisha, who dreams of Hollywood. Gay Spring, victim of the movies, is no longer Kagami-jishi's "maiden driven mad by the lion"; she is the maiden driven mad by the lion of M.G.M. She is ambitious. She does her hair like our Parisiennes. She talks in a loud voice and sways her hips. She is suffering. Her restrictions are extreme, and her suffering only torments her the more because of them. She clings to what she senses is free and *gallant* in us. The task of charming this nation of impeccable cold insects, for whom a woman is a vase of flowers, gives her the eyes of a crazed hen, a grimace in place of a smile. "Oh, Mr. Cocteau! Mr. Cocteau!" She longs to speak up, to explain, to explode, despite several glances from the others which abash her. "Mr. Cocteau! Mr. Cocteau!" She seizes my hand, kisses it, presses it to her breast in an agonized appeal. In wretched English she hurries on: "Ever since I saw your picture in the newspaper, to speak to you." We are stranded. What can she do? What can I do to rescue a poor fly struggling in this spider web? The gramophone replaces the plucked strings and the singsong chanting, the voice that sticks in the throat, stylizing cries and tears. Mistinguett sings. I dance with Gay Spring. That is, I transport around her paper prison a drowned girl who clings to the wreckage, cheek glued to my shoulder, hand clutching mine. "Oh! Oh, Mr. Cocteau!" This plaint rends my soul. Severe eyes follow, inspect, judge us. The deeper she sinks, the wilder she grows, and the more I realize my impotence to help her.

Two geishas fight over Passepartout. They cast lots for the next dance. How far we are from the Parisiennes, for whom the female entity is sufficient, the weaker sex transformed into the stronger. Women who eat or are eaten. Here, the women make us eat, and quarrel over the privilege of dancing with a young man. Mistinguett sings. Her touching voice reminds me of my city where women triumph. Poor Gay Spring! She grows heavier and heavier. When the record stops, she presses my hand to her lips and says, "Thankou." How much training she would need to lose that submissive attitude. Literally before our eyes she is drowning, sinking.

Lafontaine would say, "I am not one of those who say: 'It is nothing.' It is a woman drowning." Our hosts think: "It is nothing. It is a woman drowning." And Gay Spring, with all the strength she has left, reaches for the life buoy I want to throw her. But why throw a fake buoy? I am leaving Japan tomorrow, and in nineteen days I shall have finished my trip around the world. I must return to my place on the matting between my hosts, eat a raspberry from the end of a chopstick, watch Gay Spring under water.

"Oh! Mr. Cocteau!" The tiny plaint, incessantly repeated, fills my ears. This morning a folding mirror was left for me at the hotel—a present from Gay Spring. Leaving, I hoist a fish net over my shoulder, and in that net, Gay Spring, dead. At the door she no longer speaks; she stares, stupefied, at the shoes I am putting on which will take me far from her island. Passepartout whispers, "There's nothing you can do about it." And if he is plotting to kidnap her like Aouda, he abandons the idea, for he meets the gaze of the priests of national duty whom the geishas, too, must obey.

We get into our car. A face less painted than the rest, the face of Gay Spring, is pasted against the glass. A moment ago she was criticizing the Japanese dancers for never smiling, for dancing masked. Now it is an unsmiling mask which is pressed against the window, a mask which the jolt of departure tears away, and which is left behind, forlorn, amid the lanterns and the streamers.

I turn back to look. The rear window frames a dreadful scene. Hands outstretched, caught in the folds of her kimono, staggering on her clogs, Gay Spring, mouth wide in a cry, is trying to run after us.

At the Kabuki-za

The doors slide open on the left, and Kikuguro enters, applauded by the public. He plays the heroine, a young girl. The ladies-in-waiting push him on, despite his resistance, to the center of the stage. His timidity is too much for him. He pulls them offstage, is led on again and entreated to dance. He or she? One has to say *she*. Of this slightly overweight man of fifty, nothing remains but a delicate young creature whose neck is too slender to support her head, whose gestures shift the décor of her stiff mauve and sky-blue robes that end in a long, scarlet-lined train.

This dance, so long, yet without *longueurs*, is worth the whole trip. I would have come just for this. Two kneeling acolytes, dressed in dull gowns, turn their backs to us and hand the mime fans which become, in his hands, razors to cut throats, swords to sever heads, falling leaves, trays loaded with criminal philters, airplane propellers, regal scepters. When he is through with them, he flings them over his shoulder with a dry snap, and the acolytes receive them like arrows.

He approaches the altar and picks up a lion mask, to which is attached a yellow silk scarf. No sooner is the mask in his hand than it comes alive. The jaws clack, the scarf floats, coils around him. The young girl dances. And here are two butterflies. The acolytes flutter them on the ends of wands. The lion leaps. The girl grows more and more exhausted. The mask subjugates and hypnotizes her. Finally the acolytes withdraw and the maiden, beside herself, forced to follow the lion mask, is dragged to the left of the stage.

Here Kikuguro achieves the sublime. He tries to overcome the spell. His head swims. His hand makes the jaws snap and seems to be pulling itself away from him. He gasps, stumbles, falls, gets up, and by a series of spasms crosses the theatre and vanishes in a thunder of applause.

The orchestra parts to make room for a runway between two peony bushes, one red and one white. In Japanese symbolism, butterflies and peonies always escort the lion. The orchestra closes up again and accompanies the butterfly dance: two dancers in scarlet kimonos with sky-blue sashes, in female wigs, wearing tiny gold drums around their necks and waving slender wands. They perform symmetrical dance figures, striking their drums in alternation and hopping in front of the stage.

A roar is heard, repeated by the audience. The butterflies vanish. The music is amplified by musicians who beat the floor with sticks on each side of the proscenium. And suddenly, with tiny swift steps, arms stiff under the gold sleeves, Kikuguro crosses the wicked bridge to the stage. A white mane bristles around his head and trails some five yards behind him. Red make-up torments his eyelids and mouth. His feet prance, his arms are held straight out at his sides. The mane flies up and seems to write the wordless text of the play with an enormous paintbrush. The young girl has become a lion.

Intoxicated with fury and fatigue, the lion falls asleep between the peonies. The butterflies return and tease him. He wakes, and the curtain closes on his anger, his stupefaction.

Kikuguro is not only a mime, he is a priest. The spectacle is liturgical, not in the sense of our medieval mystery plays, but in the religious sense. I am not speaking of a religious theatre, but of the religion of the theatre. Kikuguro and his orchestra are celebrating its rites.

We are taken to his dressing room. We cross vestibules, courtyards, anterooms where we glimpse the machinery of a revolving stage, bridges, platforms. We catch sight of white rooms where kneeling musicians congratulate each other. Stairs lead up, down, up again, and finally we reach Kikuguro's dressing room. We remove our shoes. We find ourselves face to face with the idol, a robust little man in the costume of a Samurai page, who shows us the muscles the mask dance has developed in his arm, and complains that they make it hard for him to perform the female roles.

When the photographers ask me to shake his hand, I realize that Kikuguro is afraid my hand will spoil his make-up. I immediately *pretend* to shake his hand, keeping mine an inch from his. He gives me an inimitable glance, a glance between colleagues who *know*, who understand the stage.

The Brothels

On either side, four steps where the clientele remove their shoes. At the top of the steps, an embroidered silk curtain parts, and we glimpse a white face, watching. Between the strange money-changers who smile and call out to us as we pass, a glass case contains portraits of the courtesans and a niche with ebony sculptures, bronze goddesses, sexual seashells. Lanterns, dwarf cedars, black-lacquer placards daubed with heavy white characters, gold-dusted screens, violet silk braids, moonlight views of riverbanks lined with houses, conscientiously painted in rustic style. Luxury is rivaled only by mystery in the brothels!

Passepartout, lured by the crapulous bronzes, fascinated by the slits in the crimson curtain and the silhouettes behind the paper screens, declares that we must conquer our European timidity and witness the rites of the Shogi, priestesses of the cult. He rushes off and vanishes up the stairs into one of the doorways. I walk up and down, and since I am afraid of losing my way in the labyrinth of alleys, I follow him in and decide to wait for him on the first floor, over a cup of tea. A motherly ancient settles me on some mats, and goes to find some courtesans to keep me company. These girls of seventeen or eighteen live without pimps, sold and exploited by their families. They sign contracts of three, five, and seven years, and earn about fifty yen a year (250 francs: 1936). Passepartout's partner is amazed by a tip higher than three yen and paid in advance. She sends the matron to ask if this tip is really for her, and she cannot believe her eyes.

When Passepartout returns, he is still blushing. It is unbelievable, he says, criminal. All this ritual—the tea poured, the mattresses unrolled, kimonos slid on and off, lamps veiled, to end up with a pale baby giggling in the shadows among the eiderdowns and swaddling clothes, without whose padding nothing more is left than the volume of a Persian cat coming out of a pond.

And Passepartout, crestfallen, lugubrious, congratulates himself on his heroism and regrets his experiment. He accuses me of cowardice, and I confess I could never have managed to conquer my timidity. *Omne animalia, post coitu et sans coitu . . .*

The President Coolidge: *May 26*

In Tokyo, an American lady had given me a cricket in a cage. Passepartout baptizes it Microbus. At night, Microbus leaves his cage. He sleeps on top of the thermos bottle and plays ravishingly on a long green guitar attached to his body.

Tonight I waken with a start. What is it—has there been an alarm signal? The cabin is full of noise. Passepartout, who would not be awakened by thunder, awakens, turns on the light. The noise is our Japanese cricket, that fake leaf the size of a green bean, singing. His song is a phenomenon that risks wakening the *Coolidge*, keeps us from talking, drowns out the murmur of the waves. It sounds like a sawmill in furious activity; a thousand rattles whirling. And when it stops, it does so only with the deafening backfire, the gasps of a motorboat. Then it stammers, rises, finds its range again and continues singing louder than ever. This unheard-of tumult from a tiny insect has something supernatural about it. Passepartout wonders if this is its last moment: perhaps a Japanese cricket dies in the exhaustion of its song, like the swan.

Passepartout unhooks the cage from the thermos handle and sets it on a table between our berths. I go to look for Chaplin. On his shoulder, Microbus is not disturbed—he sings on. Without weakening for a second, he grinds out his high and endless roulade. Will he give up the ghost? Is he summoning his beloved? Is it a love song, a war chant, a death rattle? The infinity of kingdoms separates us. We shall never know what motivates this song. After an hour, the mysterious spring jams, and Microbus falls silent. We all exchange looks. He is not dead. He is perfectly fine. His death would have left a void. We shall never forget this shrieking leaf, this Japanese tenor in the night.

*

Perhaps this is the place to say that, after a whirlwind trip around the world, the notion of *vice* no longer exists.

Europe has its intensity only in vice, in crime. Alas, its virtue is in platitude. Intense virtues are rare. They are the true sanctity: the sanctity of the poet, the Oriental.

The strength of vice is that it does not tolerate mediocrity. The weakness of our virtue is that it does, that it condemns itself to mediocrity, its goal. Marriage, etc. . . .

One of the wonders of the East is its virtuous vice; the nobility of vice; its naturalness. An intense virtue? On every street-corner. This explains the respect for the poet. The poet: *Number One.*

How could they fear the poet's exactitude in a world where the slightest detail of clothing, of personal hygiene, of hairdressing and cosmetics derives from a syntax? A poet breathes, at last, in an Oriental city. Everything here is a procession; orderly and insane.

New York

The Ambassador Hotel. From our window, Park Avenue is Venice, the Grand Canal lined with palaces past which the infrequent Sunday cars glide like gondolas.

On first contact, New York ceases to be the overpowering metropolis I had feared. The skyscrapers have the delicate stiffness of tulle curtains. A brisk air passes through them, surrounds and circulates between the façades.

I think I told the reporters that New York was a tulle city, that here you inhale no moral dust. They understand me halfway, and translate: "The poet discovers that New York is wearing a woman's dress." I never uttered this absurd sentence, but if I had I would go farther and say: "Since your city is a victim of the fashion for undressing, after four days the gown falls and there remains a Rubens, a Statue of Liberty—only naked, young, opulent."

The visit to Radio City flings us up to the top of the building, where we have lunch in the Rainbow Room. From the terrace we overlook the park, the skyscrapers, and the Hudson.

New York is a stone garden. Stone plants send up stems of varying height, and at the top these stems bloom. Lawns, flower beds, tennis courts, chaise longues, gaudy parasols crown these gray towers that are forced, watered, sunned in a jungle where cathedrals and Greek temples balance on stilts.

I want to be fair. These functional forms, these serviceable substances and styles release a genuine beauty—a beauty which relates Rockefeller Center to the Pyramids, to the Towers of Silence, to the Acropolis. Except for a few crude decorations which betray its authentic impulse, Radio City is a masterpiece of those *Modern Times* Chaplin has mocked. In the street I think of his tiny figure and the disorder it opposes to this icy, clean, and sovereign order.

I cherish the dung heap of cities. The dung heap of Paris attracts a Picasso, a Stravinsky, all those who know that the flowers of art cannot grow in crystal and chromium. I look for the dung heap of New York, and soon I shall find it, that gold dung heap without which the skyscrapers would not offer to the sun the lawns and parasols of their peaks. A clean city hangs in the air; down below, a sewer, garbage cans, and filthy cellars nourish that geometric charm and save it from death.

The lindy hop, which has reigned supreme for five years, is a Negro gavotte. They dance it at the Savoy, a dance hall in Harlem.

A long, low room. In the center, surrounded by a railing, the floor and the band. Around it, booths and tables where dancers and onlookers drink their strange cocktails. When we came in, the band was playing a waltz, or rather the shadow of a waltz, or rather the ghost of the shadow of a waltz, a zombie waltz, a waltz motif murmured by a sentimental drunk, and to this dead waltz the couples, as though dangling from the ceiling, drag their legs and limp skirts, stop, lean to the ground, the lady lying on her partner, slowly straightening up and resuming their promenade, side by side, hand in hand or face to face, never smiling. Waltzes and tangos are the only rest these black bodies, these white souls allow each other, somnambulists gripped by the candid eroticism of a ritual intoxication. Suddenly the band comes to life again, the dancing dead waken from their trance, and the lindy churns them once more.

On what grass have they walked? On marijuana, the grass that you smoke, that turns you on. These fat Negresses in wigs, these girls in hats cocked like a slap who thrust out their breasts and point their rumps, turn into lassos which their partners uncoil at the end of one arm, boomerangs which strike them through the heart after circling the void. Severe, ecstatic, a Negress will occasionally duck under her partner's arm, free herself, move away, execute a few steps alone, then take him by assault, like a wave. Sometimes couples separate from the crowd, working out the figures of a quadrille graver than a chess match . . .

*

"Strip tease." Minsky's stars earn up to $2,500 a week and fill his theatres with a mob of men thirsting for an ideal, an abstract eroticism whose mere delirium is enough for them. Desire reaches its peak and breaks off short. The lights come up, enthusiasm dims, the mob disperses, and no one knows where these repressions find their outlet. I suppose some thrifty housewives reap the benefit, for it is impossible to imagine, in New York, a private place where the spectator of *burlesque,* as it is called here, remembers and dreams. Idleness, leisure, reverie do not exist in New York. The city has lost that luxury. It makes the mind's work difficult, except in the theatre, where work demands action. Frenzied action. Even sleepers scarcely sleep in New York. They doze, and the telephone wakens them at dawn.

Miss Lillian Murray, of all the strip-tease artists I have seen, is the one who knows best how to drive her public wild. Her décor is a flamboyant one: behind transparent draperies, their hands in ermine muffs with bunches of violets pinned to them,

stand a row of nudes, motionless around the fan-shaped platform.

Miss Murray crosses the stage, her movements modeled on
those of fashion mannequins. The gown she is showing will
gradually lose a sleeve, a fringe, a scarf, a belt—its blouse, its
skirt, everything. Each forfeiture demands a brief exit into the
wings, and a subtle change in the lighting. A hummed refrain
accompanies the reappearance of her Mexican idol's face, her
hair which falls to her shoulders, her enormous breasts, her pink
rump, her sturdy legs. The audience is stamping. For the
seventh time she returns to the stage, and nothing is left of her
gown. Entering stage-right, she progresses crab-fashion to the
opposite proscenium, modestly averts her face, coils up in the
curtain, and disappears.

After her, a very slender girl walks on in a long white gown
and dances an acrobatic number with exquisite tact. The billing
does not reveal her name, nor do the ushers know who she is.
Doubtless a debut, an astonishingly successful trial run in this
spectacle whose indecency is what a man from Marseilles
imagines the Folies-Bergères to be like. Poor Folies-Bergères!
Your nudes are so timid. But in Paris this girl would stupefy us
more than all the rest—we would wonder what this gardenia
was doing on a garbage dump. In New York her presence
doesn't embarrass us. It is because the power, the violence, the
infernal effrontery of the spectacle cancel out any notion of
corruption. It is not onto a garbage dump that this gardenia
falls: the flower is shown with the same candor as meat and
vegetables, the first fruit of the season, fresh and heavy.

The ambiguous type of the sportswoman, the ephebe, the so-
called *modern girl*, is a subterfuge of women fighting for their
lives. In Marseilles a woman relies only on what I have called
the feminine entity. She rules as a woman. No matter whether
she is ugly, shapeless, old; she does not even try to please. She is
Woman and from that pedestal insults the men who pass by. In

New York the stripper conceals nothing, employs no artifice. Only youth can keep her considerable treasures intact. She deceives no one, and the pride of her sex, The Sex, no longer substitutes for her attractions.

A Lillian Murray exhibits herself without shame on the same level as our lithe acrobat in the white dress. Her youth saves her from absurdity. The Botticelli does not spoil the Rubens. That is why, leaving Minsky's, we take away a memory of joyous flesh. Despite the incredible obscenity of the sketches which punctuate the spectacle, the melancholy of brothels and of their "artistic" groups does not prevail. New York, aerial, fresh, idealistic, mingles in its shop windows the rosy rubber of certain intimate devices, cameras, patent medicines, chewing gum, peanut-butter crackers, perfumes, cakes of soap, and ice-cream sandwiches.

One might compare its riches to the masterpieces of modern horticulture which surrender their savor and smell for the sake of certain shapes and shades.

The Ile de France

I pick up the telephone because I am hungry. A French voice (I suddenly thought I understood foreign languages) tells me that the number of our stateroom does not exist and hangs up. I ring back and ask for some cold sliced meat. After waiting an hour I hear a racket like that of a bowling alley in the corridor, and arguments . . . I open the door. Four waiters are faced with the Freudian problems of trying to construct a table out of a board and the Louis XV legs which screw into it. I leave them to their struggle and look out my porthole. The Great Bear has fallen back on its feet. I recognize the familiar, well-behaved Great Bear of the Seine-et-Oise. I go to bed. I am at peace. We are in France. I have come full circle.

CALENDAR
1936–1940

Eager and tireless as ever, Cocteau continued his personal journalism by writing a column on Paris night life, covering theatres, concert halls, movies, and boîtes. In 1937, he staged Les Chevaliers de la Table Ronde, a play which this time borrowed the legend of King Arthur's court instead of characters from Greek mythology. The role of Sir Galahad was taken by a young actor named Jean Marais, who began at the same time to assume a somewhat analogous place in Cocteau's own life.

It had been in the course of his night-life reporting that Cocteau had encountered Al Brown, the ex-lightweight boxing champion who had lost his title in 1935 and was now taking drugs and conducting an orchestra in a Montmartre dance hall. Under Cocteau's influence, he was disintoxicated and on March 4, 1938, at the Palais des Sports, regained his world title. In November of that year, Jean Marais appeared in Les Parents Terribles, the first of the plays Cocteau wrote especially for him. Banned by the City Council as incestuous, it closed briefly, then reopened, playing to full houses, making Marais a matinee idol, and establishing Cocteau's name in the non-avant-garde theatre.

In the spring of 1939, he began another play for Marais. (Auden: "One has the impression that half his work has been done . . . at the request of his friends.") To work in peace, he moved temporarily to Versailles, where Claude Mauriac visited him in his hotel room: ". . . Beyond the open door, Cocteau's profile appears against a background of smoke . . . The odor is strange, very sweet. We are suffocating. Cocteau says, 'I've just smoked my sixteenth cigarette,' and opens the window to let in a bit of pure night air . . . Impeccable gray trousers, half unbuttoned; a belt buckle hanging loose; shirt-sleeves; a sweater that is too small. His untidiness is as surprising as the disorder of his hair. He begins to talk and will continue until one in the morning, without letting us get a word in edgewise, and with the same verve, the same dashing brio . . . On the table, among the detective novels and paperbacks of Racine and Molière, is the manuscript of his new play, La Machine à Ecrire, which he has written in five days and without a single erasure."

But war was declared in September and production of the new play was postponed. Marais entered the army and Cocteau bided his time by writing two other plays: a comedy about backstage life, called Les Monstres Sacrés; and a curtain-raiser for Edith Piaf called Le Bel Indifférent. He also moved to the Hôtel de Beaujolais, overlooking the gardens of the Palais-Royal. Bérard had a room nearby. Colette was just next door. In June, an autobiographical fantasy called La Fin du Potomak came off the press, and the same month the German Army entered Paris. Cocteau was quoted as saying that "during a war of this gravity the duty of a writer who has no official post is to make himself, until further orders, into the form of a zero and to pass that ring over the finger of France . . ." When he joined the exodus and left Paris, it was to spend several weeks with friends near Perpignan.

Of Criminal Innocence

*"If only you had pleaded guilty! We
can manage the guilty—it is the innocent
who escape us, who cause nothing but
anarchy."*   —Bacchus, Act II

Intimate with Dr. M.'s family (which had given me asylum in
Aix during the exodus of 1940) was a young couple, Dr. F.
and his wife, who lived in a small house, behind which a strip
of orchards and vegetable gardens divided the town from the
countryside. This property had belonged to the young wife's
parents, who had inherited it from theirs, and they in turn . . .
Indeed, so long had the house been lived in by one family that
it provided, in an unstable period, an image of that continuity
of which few examples remain.

The two households often visited each other, exchanged
dinners. Dr. F.'s young wife fascinated me. Her beauty, her
gaiety faded from one breath to the next. And revived as
rapidly. As if she saw a terrible wave approaching, about to
break over her, and mustered all her forces to meet it. Her face
suddenly convulsed, and her very gestures suggested the behavior
of someone menaced by a specific danger. She no longer heard
what was said, no longer answered. She aged so evidently that
her husband's eyes never left her, and we imitated his silence.
The discomfort became unendurable. We had to wait until the
wave rose higher still, claimed its victim, broke, and dis-
persed . . .

An inverse process completed the cycle. The young wife
became enchanting again. Her husband smiled, spoke. The

discomfort gave way to good humor, as if nothing abnormal had occurred.

One day, when I was talking to my host about our young friend's transformations, I asked him if he knew of some incident in her past which might be the cause, or the source, of these symptoms. If, for instance, she had suffered some act of violence—if some buried fear was the basis of her anguish . . .

Dr. M. replied that he believed this was the case, but that the only incident he knew about seemed quite remote and inconclusive. Of course, he added, anything is possible. We doctors don't know that much about what goes on in the catacombs of the human body. And for reasons you will appreciate after what I'm going to tell you, Mme F. refuses to be analyzed. And her condition is complicated by the fact that she has no children, that there have been two miscarriages, and that the mere mention of another pregnancy brings on anxiety attacks which certainly don't improve her health . . .

This is the incident the doctor recounted.

Dr. F.'s young wife was an only child, utterly adored and indulged by her parents. She had just turned five when her mother became pregnant. As the delivery date approached, the parents grew apprehensive about preparing a child so jealous of her prerogatives for the sudden arrival of an intruder and the obligation of sharing a universe in which she had reigned supreme, even refusing to have a pet because she suspected her mother and father might grow attached to the animal and thereby deprive her of some of their love.

With infinite precautions they told their daughter that heaven was sending her a little brother or sister, they weren't sure which, though they were sure when, and that they wanted her to be as happy as they themselves were about this celestial gift, which would be coming quite soon.

They had dreaded her tears, her scenes, but they were mistaken: the child did not cry. Her eyes turned to ice. Instead of protesting, she alarmed them by the silence of a man whose lawyer has just notified him of his bankruptcy.

Nothing is more incorruptible than the gravity of childhood when it has come to a decision. For all the parents' blandishments and cajolery, their efforts to wrap the news in smiling words, their smiles were met by a wall of silence. For weeks the child repulsed every effort. Finally the imminent birth occupied the minds of the couple, leaving their daughter free to shut herself up in her room, to brood over her bitterness.

The baby was stillborn. The father consoled his wife by the thought of their daughter's happiness; she would regain her spirits now, if she was told that the gift had been refused because it had made her suffer. This maneuver was a failure. Not only did the girl not change her attitude, she actually fell ill. Fever and delirium presented the symptoms of an inflammation of the lungs. Dr. M. wondered if some mistake hadn't been made: Dr. F. could discover none, merely commenting on the girl's distressed state of mind. Dr. M. admitted that this distress could have produced a nervous crisis, but it did not explain the inflammation of the lungs, for which the patient would have to be treated according to general medical procedures. The girl was treated and cured. Once she was out of danger, matters became inexplicable—no show of affection could melt the ice. The convalescent child was destroying herself; a mysterious sickness had replaced the known one and continued its work.

It was at this point that Dr. M., not knowing what else to do, suggested psychoanalysis. "A psychoanalyst," he said, "can venture into realms where merely medical knowledge lays down its arms. Professor H. is my nephew. Let him become yours, at least let the child believe he is—let him live in your house. I know him well enough to be sure he'll agree to the experiment."

The analyst was about to go on his vacation. He was persuaded to spend it in Aix, at the house of his "uncle." He soon became a part of the family, an intimate. The child was suspicious but gradually grew accustomed to him and seemed actually flattered by the attentions of a grownup who took her seriously and treated her as an equal. She called Professor H. her uncle.

After four weeks of this arrangement, she became talkative again, and the false uncle was able to draw her out.

One day, when they were sitting together at the far end of the garden, away from the other members of the family and the servants, the child, quite abruptly, with the calm of a prisoner accusing himself before the judge, delivered herself of the secret which must have been smothering her and struggling to emerge from the darkness.

*

The night before the baby was born, it had been snowing. The girl had not gone to sleep. She watched, waited, realizing that in the morning, at dawn perhaps, the gift would arrive at her house. She knew that this kind of gift required a family ritual, surrounded by mysteries. There was not a minute to lose.

Strong in her conviction, her *knowledge*, she got up without lighting the lamp, left her room on the second floor, and, holding up her nightgown, crept downstairs. When one of the steps creaked, she froze, waiting for her heart to stop pounding. A door opened. She shrank back against the rope banister, feeling the hemp prickle against the back of her neck.

An unknown woman in a white dress and cap crossed the oblong of light cast on the vestibule tiles by the open door. The stranger went into the dressing room adjoining her parents' room and closed the door behind her. The other door remained open—the door to a lavatory where her mother always put the last touches to her hair, her powder, arranged her hats and veils before going out.

The child continued downstairs, crossed the vestibule,

slipped into the lavatory the unknown woman had just left, terrified she might return at any moment.

On the dressing table was a pincushion bristling with the long hatpins women wore at the time. She pulled out one with a baroque pearl for a head, then crept to the glass-and-wrought-iron front door, which was kept locked. To open this door she had to get a chair, climb up on it, turn the lock, get down again, put the chair back.

On the steps outside, she pulled the door shut behind her without a sound and looked back through the lowest panes of glass, at the height of her eyes. Just in time: the woman in white was crossing the vestibule. A man in a frock coat accompanied her, gesticulating. They disappeared into the lavatory.

The child did not feel the cold. She walked around the house. In her nightgown, barefoot, she ran across the flower beds, over the hard ground. The moon anesthetized the garden, which was literally sleeping on its feet. Everything familiar and simple about the garden turned to a wicked stupor, the immobility of an armed sentry, of a man hidden behind a tree.

From the look of this garden, something bad was about to happen.

Naturally the child did not account for this metamorphosis; what she said was that she no longer recognized her garden.

She ran on, holding up her nightgown and clutching the hatpin. She thought she would never reach her goal—the far end of the garden, the very place where she was telling the professor, in her own words, the story whose details we learned later.

She stopped, recognizing the cabbage patch. She was burning up, and shivering. The moon did not turn the cabbages into anything very terrible. For the little girl, the terrible thing was that they were cabbages. It was easy to see what they were, sculptured and magnified by the moonlight. She leaned down and without a moment's hesitation, sticking out her tongue the way careful schoolchildren do, she thrust her pin into the first cabbage. The cabbage resisted, the leaves squeaked. She wrenched free the pin, grasped the baroque pearl more tightly, and thrust into the heart of the cabbage. Relentlessly, she stabbed one cabbage after the next, until the pin began to bend. She was calmer now, and slowly, methodically, perfected her technique.

She aimed the point of the pin against the center of the leaves, where the heart begins to form. She pressed down with all her might, thrusting her weapon in up to the pearl head. Sometimes the pin refused to leave the wound. Then she tugged at it with both hands, more than once falling over backwards. Nothing discouraged her. The only thing she feared was overlooking one of the cabbages.

Her task completed, the murderess, like Ali Baba's slave girl inspecting the jars of oil, examined her victims and made certain that none had escaped her massacre.

When she returned to the house, she no longer ran. She no longer feared the garden. It had become her accomplice. Without her realizing it, the criminal aspect of the place reassured her, exalted her. She walked on, in ecstasy.

The dangers of the return were not even apparent to her. She walked up the steps to the front door, pushed it open, closed it, brought the chair, turned the lock, took the chair back, crossed the vestibule after thrusting the hatpin back into its pincushion, crept upstairs, returned to her room, and went to bed. And so absolute was her serenity that she fell asleep at once.

*

Professor H. gazed at the cabbage patch, imagining the scene. *I stabbed them all*, the child said. *I stabbed them all to the heart, and then I went back into the house.* The professor imagined the crime as I have just described it. *I went back to the house. I felt very happy. I slept well.*

She had slept well, and awakened with a high fever.

*

Afterwards, Professor H. explained to the parents, you told her it was better, having just one little girl. She didn't believe you. She considered herself responsible, guilty. She had committed murder—of that she was certain.

She is being devoured by remorse. You must give her some proof—I have taken no initiative here—that babies don't come inside cabbages. I suppose you realize by now what the consequences of such imbecilities can be.

*

Dr. M. added that the parents were reluctant to follow this advice, which they regarded as a sacrilege, a slur on their own childhood. They live in Marseilles, and when they visit Aix, they wonder what causes their daughter's nervous disturbances, her anxiety about her miscarriages.

"Do you think," I asked Dr. M., "that this incident is the cause?"

"I'm not saying it is," he answered, "but I remember that the child was fifteen when her parents took a trip and left her with us. My nephew came to spend a week with us. By that time the girl had learned not only that babies don't grow inside cabbages but that Professor H. was a member of my family, not hers. It had all been so long ago, after all. One evening Professor H. was indiscreet enough to reminisce with my wife and me about those days. 'Do you know,' he asked, 'the real drama of the cabbage story? The real drama is that the child actually *did* kill that baby. By instinct she used all the methods of witchcraft, and witchcraft is no joke.' We went on to discuss witchcraft, agreeing that there was indeed some evidence for its effectiveness."

"It's not impossible," I concluded. "Maybe she did kill the baby. The important thing is that she must never suspect it."

"Only," Dr. M. added, "my wife and I discovered that the girl was in the habit of listening at keyholes."

CALENDAR

1940–1946

The next four years were hard for all Frenchmen worthy of the name. Like Colette, Cocteau returned as soon as possible to the city he loved and resumed his work. Meeting him at a luncheon given by diplomat Paul Morand, the German novelist Ernst Jünger found him "sympathetic, and at the same time tormented, like a man spending time in a private, though not uncomfortable, hell . . ."

With Marais out of uniform, there was the première of La Machine à Ecrire, as well as a revival of Les Parents Terribles. But both provoked right-wing riots and were closed by the German police. Marais and Cocteau were thereafter hounded in the collaborationist press, accused of being Communists (because Cocteau had written for Louis Aragon's newspaper), and on one occasion Cocteau was even attacked "on the Champs-Elysées by members of the L.V.F. because he refused to salute their flag."

But he remained obstinately fixed in the tunnel-like apartment which he had now rented under the beetling arcades of the Palais-Royal and where Colette could see him on her morning walk: ". . . He lives in one of those mezzanine apartments with windows like moleholes . . . but it's just right for a man of the theatre, since in order to reach his room, the daylight has to touch the pavement below and reflect back up under the arches, like footlights. If you happen to glance up as you pass by, you may see a heroic torso chalked on the blackboard, or the portrait of a horse, or a miniature set for a play, or even the author himself, with his tuft of frizzled hair, his greyhound leanness, his shirtsleeves rolled back from hands with veins like branching vines . . ."

He finished a long poem called Léone. He wrote a verse tragedy, Renaud et Armide, in classical rhymed couplets. He illustrated books. At a dinner of close friends, one night in 1943, the novelist Lise Deharme heard him "speak with passion about someone named Genet, author of a prodigious book," which turned out to be Notre-Dame des Fleurs. Most important of all, he began to apprentice himself seriously to the film medium. To learn the ropes, he wrote the dialogue for Le Baron Fantôme (in which he also played a small role); then, in 1943, his original screenplay, based on the Tristan legend and called L'Éternel Retour, was filmed under the direction of Jean Delannoy, with Jean Marais as the star. "We should have filmed it in Brittany, but the Germans believed that the Tristan myth—actually borrowed by Wagner from France—belonged to them, and they forbade us the use of it. So we made our location shots on the south shore of Lake Geneva, which was occupied by the Italians, who looked the other way."

In August 1944, Paris was liberated, legend having it that Cocteau was seen riding into the city on the front of an American jeep. But at the British embassy early the next year, his old friend Harold Nicolson found him worn out and looking "like an aged cockatoo. He came up to my room while I washed. He described how he had felt that he owed it to his art not to join Aragon and others in open resistance. He explained how the milices had beaten him up and nearly knocked out his eye . . ." What he did not mention, apparently, was that he was already preparing to make a film based on Madame Leprince de Beaumont's eighteenth-century fairy tale, La Belle et la Bête, a parable about a beautiful prince who, like France and her heroes and poets, had had to live for years under a wicked spell which made him seem unlovable. In August 1945, the work began.

Making La Belle et la Bête

Diary of a film based on the fairy tale by
Mme Leprince de Beaumont

"Every poem is a coat of arms; the
bearings must be deciphered."

The famous tale of *Beauty and the Beast* is British in origin. Mme Leprince de Beaumont (1711–1780) lived in England for a while and must have heard ghost stories there, as well as rumors of those sons of certain great families who were hidden away because of some birthmark or blemish that might frighten society and dishonor a noble name.

Possibly one of these monsters, shut up in some Scottish castle, gave her the idea of a human beast who bears a noble heart under a frightening appearance and suffers the pangs of hopeless love.

*

In a country which is none other than the vague realm of fairy tales, a rich merchant, ruined by a storm in which his returning ships are lost at sea, lives with his three daughters and his son Ludovic, a charming rascal, whose friend Avenant accompanies him in all his escapades. Two of the daughters, Félicie and Adelaïde, are wicked creatures who reduce their sister Belle, or Beauty, the family Cinderella, to a state of virtual bondage.

In this household of quarrels and shrieks, Beauty waits

on table and scrubs the floors. Avenant loves her and asks her to marry him, but Beauty refuses: she prefers to remain her father's daughter and live in his house.

This father, a good man but a weak one, has just received great news. One of his ships has reached safe harbor. The worthies who had avoided the house now return to it. The wicked sisters demand new dresses, jewels. Ludovic borrows from a usurer. Beauty, when her father sets out for the seaport, asks him to bring her a rose, "for none grow hereabouts."

Now the drama begins: Beauty's request, which she has made so that she, too, will appear to be requesting something, provokes her sisters' derision. And the merchant mounts his horse and sets out.

At the seaport, he discovers that his creditors have preceded him and that, of all his wealth, nothing remains, not even enough to pay for a room at an inn. He decides to return home that very night, though he must ride through a great forest and though the fog is closing in.

As we might expect, the poor man loses his way. He gropes on, leading his horse by the bridle, and glimpses a light. The branches part before him; he enters a lane; the branches close behind him. Gradually he makes out an enormous castle, apparently empty though bristling with mysteries—candelabra which light up of their own accord, statues which appear to be alive. He falls asleep in the strange place, overcome by fatigue, at a table which is anything but reassuring, for all the fruit and wine set out upon it. A distant roaring wakens him, and the mortal scream of some animal. He makes his escape and at once loses his way. Noticing a rose arbor, he recalls Beauty's request. A rose is the only present he can bring home. He picks one. At this moment, the echo of his shouts of "Holla!" becomes a terrible voice, crying "Alas!"

The merchant turns around and sees the Beast, in appearance a nobleman whose face and hands are those of a wild animal. And this creature sets forth the mysterious postulate of the tale: "You have pillaged my roses, you must die. Unless one of your daughters consents to die in your place."

It is very likely that this rose is the first bait of a trap in which Beauty is to be caught, for all eternity.

The father returns home on a magic horse named Magnifique which can be directed by whispering into its ear: "Go where I go, Magnifique, go, go, go!" And this horse is doubtless the trap's second bait.

The sisters fume, Beauty offers to go to the Beast's castle, her father refuses, Avenant protests, but a terrible scene breaks the old man's spirit, and Beauty takes advantage of the confusion to escape during the night, mounting Magnifique, murmuring the magic words into his ear, and galloping toward her doom.

At the Beast's castle, Beauty does not meet the fate she expected. The trap works wonderfully: the Beast surrounds her with luxury and consideration. For this savage Beast is a kind one as well, victimized by his own pathetic ugliness.

Little by little, Beauty discovers this, but her father falls ill, as she learns from a magic mirror. Beauty falls ill in turn. At last the Beast consents to open the trap. He allows Beauty eight days in which to visit her father, provided she returns when the time is up. Several magical objects remain in the Beast's possession, constituting the last secrets of his power. Trusting in Beauty's good heart, he relinquishes them: a glove which will take her wherever she wishes to go; a gold key which will open the Pavilion of Diana, in which is stored his true wealth and which no one—neither he nor she—must touch until his death.

"I know your soul," he tells Beauty. "This key will be my guarantee of your return."

Back at her father's, Beauty's splendid clothes provoke her sisters' jealousy. They lavish caresses upon her and deceive her by their false tears into staying beyond the stipulated time. Once they have kept her from leaving, they manage to reduce her to bondage once again. Having broken her promise, Beauty no longer dares return to the Beast's castle. Félicie and Adelaïde steal the gold key from her. Magnifique arrives—all the magic the Beast has left: his horse and the mirror it brings. Doubtless this is the supreme appeal of his flouted love.

It is not Beauty who will mount Magnifique but Ludovic and Avenant. Félicie and Adelaïde urge them to kill the Beast and seize his wealth. They entrust the key to the young men.

In the magic mirror, Beauty sees the Beast, mourning and alone. She puts on the glove and is instantly at the castle. Where is the Beast? She calls to him, searches everywhere, and finds him dying at the edge of a spring.

Meanwhile, Ludovic and Avenant have reached the Pavilion of Diana. They dare not use the key, for they fear a trap. They climb onto the roof of the pavilion, and through its windows they see the treasure, a statue of Diana, and snow circling slowly in the air—as in the paperweights of our childhood. Ludovic is frightened, Avenant breaks the windowpanes, undeterred. "It's glass, glass!" he exclaims. Ludovic swings down through the window, leaps into the pavilion, and henceforth shifts for himself. Beauty, at the spring, grieves over the Beast, imploring him to listen to her. The Beast murmurs, "It is too late." Beauty is close to saying, "I love you."

At the pavilion, Avenant swings down through the broken panes. Then the statue of Diana moves, raises its bow, takes aim, and the arrow pierces Avenant's back.

Ludovic, horrified, sees his grimace of agony: Avenant's face becomes that of the Beast. He falls.

At this very moment the Beast is transformed under Beauty's eyes—it is a maiden's love which must break the spell. Beauty starts back, for it is a Prince Charming who rises before her, greets her, and explains the miracle.

This Prince Charming bears a strange resemblance to Avenant, and this resemblance troubles Beauty. She seems almost to regret the kind Beast, to fear this unexpected Avenant. But the end of a fairy tale is the end of a fairy tale. Beauty is won over, and with the triple figure of the Prince she flies off to a realm where, he tells her, "you will be a great queen, you will find your father again, and your sisters will bear the train of your gown."

*

Sunday, August 26, 1945

My method is simple: not to bother about poetry. It must come of its own accord. Merely whispering its name frightens it away. I am trying to make a table. You will decide, afterwards, whether to eat on it, question it, or build a fire with it.

*

We reached Tours yesterday, at five. In Paris the sky had been overcast, but gradually, on the road, the clouds frayed into the puffy wisps of the paintings which provide my inspiration. In Touraine the Loire runs flat, glistening under a pale sky. Rochecorbon. I rediscover this tiny hillside manor I happened to come upon during our search for locations—it was one of fifty suggested by the Office of Domains. The roadside wall did not look promising. We nearly decided not to get out of the car. Yet at the first glance I *recognized*, down to the smallest detail, the décor I feared I would have to build. The man who lives in it looks like the merchant of our fairy tale, and his son told me, "If you had come yesterday, you would have heard

your own voice: I was playing my father some of your record-
ings of your own poems." Moreover, the iron rings to which the
horses are attached represent some fabulous beast. Here are the
wicked sisters' windows, the doors, the staircase, the washhouse,
the orchard, the stable, the kennel and the dog, the watering
cans, the tomatoes ripening on the windowsills, the vegetable
garden, the woodpile, the spring, the fowls, the ladders. Everything is where it belongs. The interior matches the exterior, and
this secret precision radiates through the walls. All we need do
is shift the sun, which means shift ourselves several times a
scene, according to its trajectory.

August 27—7:30 p.m.

The artists, Mila Parely, Nane Germon, Jean Marais, Michel
Auclair, will come at nine. I will make them up, dress them,
dirty them, tear their clothes until they look as they should in a
tale in which the dirty is not dirty—in which, as Goethe says,
truth and reality are contradictory (shadows falling the wrong
way in Rubens's etching).

A hard day's getting underway, starting with splendid
weather which clouded over at five. The air was quite heavy. I
combated the wine the owner forced me to drink with water
from a spring so clear the cattle are deceived into thinking the
tank is empty. There are washhouses, streams, tiny waterfalls
everywhere.

The décor is the kind I must make with my own hands, the
kind no one can help me with. Besides, the laundry poles
sagged, the lines snapped, the sheets were too short, and there
were not enough of them. The wind kept making them billow,
destroying the perspectives. The costumes stand out wonderfully between the walls of linen and cast lovely shadows across
them. But by five the sky, which has turned cloudy and stormy,
forces me to give up all long-shots and to use lights for close-
ups. Mila poses, poses, poses, decomposes. The camera shakes.
The technicians try to fix it, unsuccessfully. We stop. Investiga-

tion helps no one but the insurance company. My work is interrupted in mid-flight. I slacken, lose momentum, and return to Tours broken with fatigue, Vouvray, and disappointment. I had hoped the blue sky would continue. I had hoped to interrupt my habitual rhythm and discover a rhythm of improvisation. How naïve! The same difficulties pursue me and since they come, each time, from a different direction, they take me unawares.

Will we have sunshine? Will we have a camera that works? Will we meet some other kind of obstacle? I shall try to sleep, to wait. Waiting: that is the drama of the cinema.

Had I not been so absorbed by this fairground labor, how delightful I would find the spectacle of this orchard and this perfect little manor embellished by the actors washing and putting on their make-up around the huge kitchen table under the trees, by the technicians standing around a plank on trestles, eating their lunch.

August 28—7 a.m.

I get up to look at the sky. It is overcast. The days of waiting will begin with the actors ready and playing cards. Delannoy told me, "You must always be ready in Touraine, where the weather changes so quickly."

I wonder if this delay is not a piece of luck. I would be shooting with a camera I am unsure of, repaired by makeshift means. Perhaps if this weather holds a little longer, I shall have another camera, and a better arrangement of sheets (and more of them).

What makes the task difficult for me, with uncertain weather, is the angle from which each set-up shot must be taken. A clear sky does not permit me to shoot any scene I like. It depends on where the sun is in that sky. The essential thing is that everyone be ready to act and to shift the equipment either in front of the house or behind it, to the orchard or the barnyard. I have reconstituted the crew of *Le Baron Fantôme:*

good humor and cooperation. Each technician is participating in the film, enjoying it, interested in it, and collaborating with the artists from beginning to end. I can ask, and obtain, anything from these men—just the opposite of the theatre, where the technicians work backstage, in the dark, unconcerned by what we do.

August 28—11 p.m.

Before Clément's arrival—he is finishing a film in Brittany, and has sent me his young brother—I must deal with everything, pin up the sheets, knot the lines to the poles, find the chickens and shoo them onto the set, construct the corridor of sheets, and set up the shots. (Inconceivable in 1945 to rent a dozen extra sheets. Our set director, Roger Rogelys, with enormous difficulty succeeds in finding me nine. I had six already.) The corridors are set up as we need them, which means dismantling others, and prevents me from taking any tracking shots. I prefer it that way: if I had to describe this labyrinth of linen in words, I would do it so that my reader would get lost, which would no longer be the case once I raised the lid and showed the maze from above. Avoid tracking shots. Cut back and forth to the white corridors, without the spectator's being able to discover whether the set is enormous or tiny.

I had forgotten about airplanes. When the lights for Mila's close-up were ready, a plane from the flying school was overheard, doing loop-the-loops, and we could not record. I telephoned the Colonel to ask the students to avoid these ruinous capers. He promised they would be stopped.

August 29—11 p.m.

I am so tired that I must force myself to take these few notes. A day of clouds, a few blue holes, the wrong shadows. I managed about seven takes with incredible difficulty, catching the light by surprise. I had the sky and the ground against me. After the shots of Michel and of Jeannot, which last a second and require

an hour of preparation, I had the shots of Josette-Mila-Nane
and of Marcel André set up behind the house. The sun kept
appearing, disappearing. The planes crossed our shooting area.
The camera shook. (A new camera had been brought from
Paris. It imitated the tricks of the other one.) I became impatient (which is exhausting) and controlled myself to keep from
irritating the others. In Touraine you should shoot early in the
morning or late in the afternoon. But the slack hours of the
middle of the day are the busy hours of the unions. Here time is
transformed into a few minutes. The sun appears without our
expecting it. If you expect it, it never comes. It appears during
the set-ups and disappears when you give orders to shoot. I
return to the hotel at seven. In one room, the dressers from
Paquin, who arrived today from Paris, fit Marais for the Beast
and Prince Charming costumes. The Beast is perfect. The
Prince should be more ornate, despite the Perrault style, which
is impeccable. I have asked the actors to report at seven-thirty
tomorrow.

August 30—7:30 p.m.

The first day I've done what I wanted to do. Splendid sun and
clouds. After lunch we take advantage of the clouds to work
behind the house and to produce evening effects with the
lamps.

In the morning we almost lost our little head start because of
the maneuvers of the flying students. Darbon has gone to the
school to see the directors. They come to pay us a visit at ten.
One of them is Mangin's son. He promises to shift the zone of
maneuvers.

I am almost done with the laundry scene. A little luck and I'll
finish it tomorrow, between nine and one. (Ludovic and his
watering cans. Mila's shadow.) — (Josette's arrival in her
princess's gown in the theatre of sheets devised by Marais, who
tucks up the first sheet like an Italian curtain and reveals the
perspectives behind the bench.)

For the close-up of Mila and Nane laughing (on Josette's phrase: "Bring me a rose . . .") I had asked Aldo to disguise himself as a widow: he had plastered his face under a net framed by blond curls made out of wood shavings. Then he stood beside the camera after the clapper signal. Mila and Nane told me they had laughed because they didn't think he was funny.

Aramis, the horse, arrived from Paris at four with his master. He looks like Rommel's horse ridden by Montgomery. A white Arabian which kneels and rears like a wave crowned with foam. I will leave his circus harness on him—it gives him just the style of horses in children's books. I have asked the owner to send us his artificial tail as well. I've seen the sedan chairs (too heavy, too clean). And the crossbows (which don't work). I don't lose patience any more. When I do, it's by calculation, to sustain a general temperature, a certain electricity.

August 31—8 p.m.

Mila's accident. She insisted on riding Aramis. He reared, or she made him rear. I was setting up one of Josette's shots. Mila was in a bathing suit, taking a sunbath, washing her hair in the stream, walking Aramis in the alfalfa patch. In front of the house, where none of us could catch her at it, she must have tried to make this circus horse rear, and pulled on his bit. The horse rolled over on her. It's a miracle she's still alive.

Tomorrow morning I'd have liked to film the crossbow sequence that opens the film. But the only weapons we've found—in the Tours museum—are very heavy and don't work.

Marais has developed a boil on his thigh.

September 2

When the wrong shadows appear and the clouds move mysteriously so that the camera assistant, watching them through his yellow lens, can never know if his forecasts are exact, I lie down on the grass, I close my eyes, and my poem (*La Crucifixion*) torments me. It carries me so far away, having no contact with what's around me, that I seem—if the sun is coming and the assistant announces the fact—to wake up with a start.

Marais has just come into my room. His boil is enormous, in a bad place on the inside of his thigh. Having just gone through the same thing, I wonder what to do. R. has so prejudiced me against the usual medical procedure in such cases that I am worried about being in Tours without his help.

September 3

A day when the threads of fate tangle and form knots. Mila and Jeannot are, alas, heroic natures, and would perform half-dead. Heavy fog this morning. The cameras are set up behind the sheets at the far end of the orchard. The fog lifts at eleven. We shoot the reverse field shot of their heads above the sheets. Mila cannot get off the bench. Jeannot lifts her down. I add a line: "Leave me alone, you!" as if he were teasing her. The camera and the lights change places. I set up the meeting scene (the necklace). We begin shooting after a thousand problems; Alekan, who has the inhumanity of a surgeon or an astronomer, keeps shifting and correcting his lights without realizing that Mila can scarcely stand.

We have lunch. It clouds over and rains. After lunch, I fall asleep. I open one eye. I realize that the crew is playing "portraits" in the little washhouse where I have stretched out. The sun is shining. I get up. The actors have taken off their make-up and costumes. I question Clément. He says the crew will not shoot after four unless they are paid overtime, according to the union agreement. Darbon refuses to pay these wages, on principle. He is in Paris. Clément argues, makes us promise to pay overtime, and sets everything going again. The cameras and lights are moved onto the set. The actors put on their make-up, wigs, and costumes.

The sun is setting, which forces Alekan to shift the camera angles. Then begins the torture of seeing Mila, very very ill, brazen it out in order to avoid a lawsuit with the other company for which she is making a film; she wants to leave tomorrow evening and be back by Saturday. I imagine that she is worse than she seems, and even that she has no idea how sick she is, that the trip will finish her off, that she will ruin her film in Paris and not come back, amputating ours as well.

These circumstances overwhelm her. Exhaustion, pain, nervous tension are tearing her apart. She stammers, stumbles, grimaces. She is on the verge of collapse. The second take (which would have saved us) is no good. The cloudless sky darkens. The final moments are approaching. The collapse occurs: Mila falls to her knees in the lettuce patch, sobbing. They carry her away.

In Tours, I accompany Jeannot to Dr. Vial's. He keeps us waiting while a butler serves white wine and canapés. Then he arrives, drives us to his clinic on the Rochecorbon road. He anesthetizes Marais's leg, lances the carbuncle. Marais, who is very strong and very brave, seems to suffer horribly. I leave him at the clinic. Tomorrow morning we'll pick him up on the way to the set: I'll skip the scenes with the horse and shoot stationary ones. The doctor will keep Marais immobilized for twenty-four hours.

Inconceivable, the problems of an undertaking of ruinous cost in which the sun is our master, in which we must combine the scenes which free Marcel André and which will not require a great effort from our invalids.

September 4—11 p.m.

At the hotel, Mila's manager, Mme T., arrives with an ambulance to drive her back to Paris—to fulfill her commitments. This is insanity, for Mila, miraculously insured for both films, will not cause any financial catastrophe. The insurance doctor comes to the hotel—it is Vial. He is worried. Mila will be Xrayed tomorrow morning. If there is the slightest crack in her pelvis, she will be put into a cast and our film wrecked.

As for Jeannot, he cannot ride horseback for a week. I will be brave enough to admit the inadmissible. Whatever happens, I'll take care of these two, and I'll shoot my film. I shall add this tour de force to a thousand others. I go to bed, broken with fatigue and so thin that a lady journalist declares, "His face consists of his two profiles stuck together."

September 5—11 a.m.

This morning the fog lifts, but the clouds fill the sky, overlapping in all directions. We have to do the scene with the horse ridden by a local woman who is Josette's stand-in. I shoot without sound in order to shout directions. Clément is hidden in the barn. He pours tetrachloride on Aramis's hoofs and artificial tail.

Technicians, ambushed behind beams and woodpiles, pull the invisible wires that open the barn door. The camera is on a scaffolding six feet high. Aramis is given a touch with the crop. He leaves his stall. I give the signal and the doors open. Aramis hesitates and leaves the barn with that dancing gait of his, which we shoot a little too fast in order to slow it down on the screen. Three blue holes in the sky permit us to put this image in the can.

The car brings news of Mila. Nothing broken. A month of rest. I am authorized to let her work tomorrow. So I'll have tomorrow and the next day. The "petits valets" are in Tours. With sun(?) I'll be through with Mila and she can rest.

Marais, wracked by pain, is in very bad shape. He returns to the clinic. He will be operated on tomorrow morning, which means two days without him for us. I'll use them to shoot Mila's scene in the sedan chair.

With the help of Clément and Alekan, I age the sedan chair and set up my shots so that Mila can move as little as possible.

I wonder if these arduous days are not the happiest of all my life. Full of friendship, affectionate dispute, laughter, affording a hold over time as it passes.

I saw some rushes last night. Jeannot chopping wood. Michel filling the watering cans. The sisters on the doorstep, and the father. It is terrible to see so little. I must wait for more footage. But I realize the difficulty presented by a film in which each shot involves only one phrase or a few lines. The rhythm will come from the whole, and the actors cannot understand what they are doing. It is my responsibility to follow the thread that escapes them and to keep them on the right track. That is the problem of film acting. If the actor lacks absolute confidence in his director, he assumes, each time, that he is merely speaking a line of no consequence, he is tempted to speak it without *thinking*, and the whole will suffer from this slackening. Another problem is to find a style that is true without realism, that maintains an equilibrium between the costumes and the strangeness of the story. Be careful not to make the actors speak too loud, but preserve the texture of the language.

September 8

The doctor says that with a special bandage Marais can work the day after tomorrow on horseback. I will use the interim to retake the scene when he sees Magnifique. It is too short, and taken from too far away. Impossible to see the expression on his face.

First feature story on our work, in *Le Monde Illustré*. My photograph, taken during our set-ups, on the cover. A sad old gentleman staring into the blue. Me. I must get used to it. Work so absorbs me that I forget I exist, forget I am changing. All at once I find myself face to face with someone I didn't know, someone *others* know. We are having lunch Sunday at my brother's.

I suppose that the reason Christian Bérard can go around dressed in rags and I, unshaven, in a dirty old hat too small for me is that our passion for each moment's spectacle makes us believe that we are invisible and that others see us no better than we see ourselves. Unfortunately, the photographers inform us otherwise, but do not cure us of this error of taking our conception for our appearance.

The uglier we grow with age, the more beautiful our work must become, reflecting us like a child that takes after its parents.

September 9—11 a.m.

The cloudy weather is consolation for a day off, which to me means nothing but imprisonment. I never work enough. Work keeps me from feeling tired. It is afterwards that I fall into a black hole.

September 11

This morning we shot the sequence which opens the film: the target and the arrows. We recorded the sound of the arrows. As always, the real sound is false. We have to translate it, to invent a sound more exact than the sound itself. Clément comes up with a switch that lashes the empty air. The sun refused to appear. "I'm going to the clinic. As soon as my back is turned, the sun will come out." At the clinic: sunshine.

September 12

Seven o'clock. Nothing of our gypsy camp remains at Rochecorbon. Sad. I had grown used to living here, to inventing our life. A golden wine characterized the region—our technicians consumed an incredible number of bottles. Aldo would invite me to special haunts. He preferred an old bottle, something very rare, which he would share with his favorites. Our last work was done under a radiant, cloudless sky. I am lucky to have had clouds. They are the glory of the sky of Touraine. Even if the sun evades them, they give its light a pearly elegance. Without them, everything would have been too raw.

Too raw and too easy. Each shot was gained by force. And I
would go so far as to say that what I wanted to do I did. No
shot leaves me with that little pang for the gap between what is
and what should be. If there are faults, they are mine, and I can
blame no one else for them.

September 13

Left by car at nine this morning. Out of superstition, I ask the
driver to stop at the bistro where we first drank some Vouvray
on reaching Tours.

Back in Paris. Palais-Royal. A mountain of letters. Sleep.

September 15

At Paulvé's, I show Claude what I have brought back from
Rochecorbon. The laboratories develop chaotically: some takes
are not synchronized, others are missing. On Monday she will
check the film and prepare a suitable projection; then I can
choose.

Now I can see that the film's rhythm is a narrative one. I am
telling a story. I seem to be hidden behind the screen, saying:
first this happened, and then this happened. The characters
don't seem to live—they seem to be living a *narrated* life. Perhaps this was necessary for a fairy tale.

September 18

A bad night. These workless days leave me in a void of boring
appointments with the doctor, the barber. I sleep badly. The
film runs through my mind. I edit it, shift the text, add, cut,
and all without material since my editor is putting everything
together and must get hold of the takes I haven't seen.

September 20

Jeannot's diagnosis is bad. I am very worried about his doing
the Beast in all that hair and glue. He would never dream of

complaining. I have seen him act in *Les Parents Terribles* with double otitis. The blood gushed from his nostrils and people in the first row tossed him handkerchiefs. The joy of my work is spoiled by our invalids. Mila leaves the Tours clinic this week. Nane has to have another stomach operation and wait for the end of the film. I myself . . .

A whole world is involved in a film, and the meaning of responsibility becomes visible, implacable, forces the director to triumph over every doubt and weakness. The slightest sign of discouragement would demoralize everyone. I suppose it is the obligation to seem self-confident which eventually gives directors so much assurance.

September 22

After lunch we join Bérard, back from Saint-Maurice. He doesn't seem pleased with what is being done. Too bad Moulaert is handling two films at once. Ours demands an enormous amount of work. One tooth is bothering me terribly. I consult a dentist, who tells me an abscess is developing. He lances the gum and gives me instructions. A red rash appears on my hands and cheeks. "To make bad blood"—there's truth in the expression. I'm paying for five years of bad blood. Jeannot has the same rash on his hip.

Rain. We leave tomorrow afternoon for Senlis.

September 23

Left Paris for Senlis at five-thirty: Josette, Jeannot, Emile Darbon, and I. On the road, something falls out of the car—the carburetor. After a search we find it, put it back, start again.

Darbon announces we will be living in an abandoned château. As a precaution I reserve rooms—very ordinary ones—at the Grand Cerf. We leave our bags, and the car takes us to Raray under an equinoctial sky, filled with towers of slate, lakes of sulfur, pink forests. Under this sky, the spectacle of Raray's walls is sublime. It is raining.

September 24

Dreadful night. Itching cheeks, right hand. Gums. Eye. Rain. Worrying I will be forced by microbes to interrupt my work.

The doctor comes for Marais's blood test. A new boil is forming near one ear. Despite his courage, Marais is evidently affected by this persecution of fate. The doctor suggests a remedy for the itch in my hand. But the cream he prescribes for my face cannot be obtained. I must endure this absurd torment. It rains, rains. Will it be raining tomorrow morning?

September 25

We reach Raray in a chaos of electrical installations, the mystery of cables and amperages. It is very cold. We dress the actors in the great hall of the château. There is a ping-pong table in the middle of the room; the sound engineer, Jacques Lebreton, and the children of the family are playing. We will set up the trestle table here and lunch on a dreadful *ratatouille*. I shoot Marcel André's scene on the top of the wall with the row of stone dogs. Then down below, between the vase and the pilaster. Then I record his shouts and the echo between the wall and the façade. Marcel takes off his costume, his make-up, eats lunch, and Darbon drives him back to Paris.

After lunch, during which Jeannot, made up as a wild beast, eats only buttered toast, we retake the scene of the wall of busts. It is raining. Umbrellas. The Labédoyère family and their friends come to watch, take pictures. Antoine de Labédoyère, learning that we are on a special diet, invites Marais and me to lunch tomorrow and the day after.

September 26

My face has become an itching carapace of cracks, scabs, gulleys. I must forget this mask and live underneath it with all my strength. This morning it rained, but the barometer was rising. While the actors are being made up and dressed, we build the platforms for the lights. We shoot, at eleven, the two sequences missing from yesterday's takes. The last one is very difficult because of the smoke producers. Marais did not use his stand-in: he insisted on jumping down from the arcade with the help of a springboard. After the takes we realize, too late, that yesterday he had his hat in his right hand. Not today.

Marais and I have lunch at Mme de Labédoyère's. A strange meal. I sit on the right side of this ancient lady in black, Marais on her left, made up as a beast. Obviously the little girls will talk about it the rest of their lives.

September 27—11 p.m.

I shoot the close-up of Jeannot getting the scent of the deer.

Clément, hidden behind his robe, moves the Beast's ears with a forked stick: they stand up. The effect is striking . . .

The crew has lunch. Then we shoot the close-up of the Beast's eyes. I see the rushes of the close-up of the ears: too diffuse, too vague. We retake it, which sets back our schedule.

Escoffier confesses that the pearl necklace for Josette's silver dress has been forgotten. My face and hands are hurting, and I lose my temper. Escoffier bursts into tears.

A dark sky. Black trees. I'd like to take the scene of the deer (which has been brought in a truck, lying hobbled on the floor, fabulous in its elegance, its rebellion), but two strong men cannot manage to keep the animal where I want it on the lawn in front of the château. Despite its hobbles it rolls over, convulses. I give up. I will shoot this scene in the Jardin des Plantes.

For tomorrow: the shot of Josette in her blue dress running to meet the Beast, a transparency on the road, and if possible another shot of Josette in the woods. The light will dictate the whole style of the final sequence beside the spring.

The frames we bring back from this strange Raray cannot be ordinary ones: good or bad, but not mediocre. Enthralling work.

September 28—8 a.m.

My whole face is now covered with swellings and scabs; an acid fluid seeps out of them, ravaging my nerves. I will be done with the location shots this morning, I suppose. Darbon offers to drive me back to Paris at eleven. What would I do there? Suffer in my room. R. cannot see me until seven-thirty. The dentist at six. I prefer to finish up our work and return with the others. Jeannot's boil is worse. Yesterday, once his make-up was removed, his face was livid. The glue stops the circulation. This struggle for the film is a cruel one. I wonder if we will have to break it off.

It would be ridiculous to lose sight of the rhythm of my destiny: no luck. Effort, and more effort. To obtain by a perpetual struggle what seems the easiest thing in the world. To expect opposition in every form. To admit it. To surmount it, no matter what.

This time, opposition takes the form of microbes. I recognize it—a poor disguise. I will overcome suffering, but if it persists, I can do nothing: dates are dates.

If Marais cannot work, impossible to struggle. If Marais can work and my own difficulties intensify, I shall arrange to take long-shots, letting Clément handle them—I am sure of his work.

4 p.m.

Worked in the rain, without lights, by torchlight, magnesium, and the English smoke producers. Raray is in the can. I persisted in the face of disastrous circumstances; I wanted to create, to force into existence, at all costs, *that accidental beauty I love.*

October 1—11 p.m.

This morning the lower half of my face was better, but the rest was itching and feverish. I was at Saint-Maurice by nine: a whole anthill of experts was swarming over the set, bringing it to perfection. Gradually ivy and nettles and weeds invaded the ruined architecture. The ground was covered with moss and dead leaves. Lights were hoisted up, swinging through the air, and concealed everywhere. A tarpaulin prolonged the studio to the alley wall; here the camera will be set up on its dolly. The studio door, taken off its hinges, opened onto a lane of trees. A mechanism opened and shut the magic branches. The château loomed up indistinctly, thanks to the smoke producers. The first shot was of moonlight on the corners of the stones. The merchant arrives in a mist, which the fans blow aside. The branches part, he enters. The branches close behind him.

Endless preparations. Alekan complains he does not have all the lights he needs. Darbon sulks. Clément is sick—coming down with the grippe. Tiquet, the cameraman, who arrived this morning, saves us by his fresh ingenuity. Jean Marais is made up—which takes four hours: the hands, the claws.

October 2—10 p.m.

At seven-thirty, rushes of the work at Raray. At this point, a disaster: the laboratory has scratched the negatives. Which means that I tremble as each frame appears on the screen. Luckily the negatives I like best are not scratched, but stains are visible. There must have been a mechanical defect the laboratory refuses to acknowledge and insists on attributing to the film. Yet the images of the day before were neither scratched nor stained.

October 4—8 a.m.

Yesterday, at a bistro in Epinay, Paulvé was having lunch with his staff and some reporters. Mounier tells me: "We're counting on your film to revive the French film industry." I answer: "Odd that I should be constantly attacked in France and at the same time should be 'counted on' to rescue the prestige of a country that castigates me. I'll do my best to make a film that pleases me and the people I like—I can't promise more than that."

Yesterday, for the first time, an essential prop was missing: the dead doe. The set director, whose job was to find one, hasn't dared turn up—I was waiting for him in the steet, opposite the studio. His only excuse: the strike at Les Halles. For in films you ask and you get—anything. We'll see if I have the dead doe this morning.

This structure which one erects neither in the present nor in the past nor in the future: a film.

October 5—9 a.m.

The struggle with fate continues. This morning I arrive in Epinay under a cloudless sky. We get to work at once. The fan is in its place. I shoot the sequence of the rose. Four takes, including the one of the dead doe, whose throat I cut open myself and over which I pour the hemoglobin. There are lovely patches of sunlight through the leaves. We stop at noon and have lunch. At one-thirty, just when we start again (at this rate, I would have my nine shots in the can), the electricity is cut off. Impossible to obtain any information by telephone. Except that the breakdown will last until six. I take the crew to Saint-Maurice in the car. I want to see the last rushes again, and to keep the whole set from being taken down as well as supervise the new set. After the rushes I chide Alekan, whose mania for half tones revolts me. The "artistic" style—whereas nothing equals the "sublimation" of the documentary. That is the style I want him to give me.

A profession of patience. One must wait. Always wait. Wait for a car to pick you up. Wait for the new lights to come. Wait for the camera to work. Wait for the branches to be nailed onto the palings. Wait for the sun. Wait for the shadows. Wait for the painters. Wait. Wait for the developing. Wait for the sound track to be spliced. Wait for the arc lights to stop smoking. Wait, wait, wait.

Sunday, October 7—8 a.m.

Ravaged by urticaria, impetigo, afflictions of every kind, I persist. I continue. And I love this persistence. I cannot say that it costs me anything. My work is the work of an archaeologist. The film exists (pre-exists). I must discover it, with pick and shovel, there in the shadows where it lies sleeping. Sometimes I spoil it by hurrying. But the fragments that are still intact gleam out of the darkness like fine marble.

When you think of the number of accidental circumstances which must coincide to produce a single usable take, it is astonishing ever to hear the cry "Print that!" Afterward this miracle of chance runs other dangers: the indifference of machines. If the current is cut off while the negative is in the developing bath, the work is lost. The continual apprehensions are agonizing. Retakes cost a fortune. The sets are down. The impulse is extinguished. I am discovering that a good deal is expected of this film—I must armor myself against the fear these expectations give me. It would intimidate me. I must work as I did when I made *Le Sang d'un Poète*, when no one was watching. That is the price of freshness.

We are all paying for five intolerable years. Five years of hatred, terror, waking up to nightmares. Five years of shame, of mud that has spattered our very souls. We had to endure. Wait it out. It is this waiting, this nervous tension that costs so much. It is this waiting which we must make up for, whatever the obstacles. France must shine, at all costs. I suspect America cannot understand what we must overcome, the difficulties of working with an unoiled machine, long out of order. Our manpower is what saves us—it is beyond all praise.

My beard is growing in white. I didn't realize it—but facts

are facts: I have a white beard. Not a serious matter. The serious matter would be to have a soul that matched. Thank God my blood is red. I will spend it, down to the last drop. I will save nothing.

Sunday, October 14—6 p.m.

Last night I was too sick to write. It is the first time sickness has triumphed on every front. During the night, with the night's amplification, I imagined that the boil on my neck was turning into a kind of phlegmon which would keep me from working. It is true that with these collaborators there would be no interruption, even if *I* had to stop: Marais would see to the acting, Clément the direction, Iberia the splicing, and Bérard would add his miracle. My creation is solid enough to work for a week without me—as Madame de La Fayette says, *par machine.*

This morning, a blood test. At five o'clock, R. I am very, very sick. At seven Dr. Chabannier gives me the results of the test: the sugar has returned and is determining this latest offensive of the microbes. I must start insulin injections again.

Tuesday, October 16

Without being at all conceited about it, I wonder if anyone else would do the work I am doing while suffering what I am suffering. I mean, I wonder if any professional filmmaker would prefer his work to himself to the point of exhausting all his strength. To live in this uproar of cameramen, electricians, dressers, make-up men, decorators, assistants, in this cyclone of dust and shifting furniture, my neck devoured by a malevolent creature, pierced by a star of pain that shoots its arrows into the nerves of my skull and shoulders . . . And a cold as well, the incurable cold that makes us laugh so much in the theatre, like the cuckolds and the deaf. Yet these are scarcely amusing matters. Without the devoted kindness of Jean Marais, who, sick as he is, nurses me and comes to Saint-Maurice to give me my insulin shots, I wonder what would become of me.

October 17—11 p.m.

After lunch I shoot the vestibule scene, when the sisters come in from the stable with the magic mirror. I finish up at six with the monkey Mila sees in the mirror instead of her own face. The monkey was delightful: I shot him behind a pane of glass in the mirror frame, in a nun's coif, a strawberry on a ribbon round his neck, perched on an open book à la Chardin.

October 20

Last night the unendurable made me almost happy. There was something of the hairshirt and the ecstasy of the monks about it. In *Le Sang d'un Poète* the statue says: "You have written that you entered mirrors and you didn't believe it." It would be absurd to write: "A poet must be a saint," and then to complain as soon as circumstances force us to prove it. I look at myself in the mirror. Hideous. Which doesn't bother me at all. The physical, the material no longer matter. It is the work and the beauty of the work which must replace them. The crime would be to make the film suffer because of *my* suffering, *my* ugliness. The true mirror is the screen, on which I can see the physical nature of my dream. The rest is indifferent to me.

I have, in addition, tracheitis. I cough, and the cough exasperates the pain of the open lesions. If I were well, perhaps the film would fall ill. I am paying. I am paying ready money. That is the ethic of *Les Chevaliers de la Table Ronde,* a play no one has understood, because at the time pleasure was the order of the day and everyone refused to make the slightest effort.—The work which devours its author is not a joke. It is the truth. The work hates us and seeks any criminal means to get rid of us.

October 22—evening

Filmed the scene of Marais slapping Mila. I had anticipated no more than one take, but in the excitement, the shock of the scene, Michel forgot his part. Five minutes before, poor Mila, to whom the strangest things keep happening, was hurrying from her dressing room to the set and tripped over her dress, fell, and scraped her right cheek. We managed to shoot even so, Mila bleeding, Marais pampering her, the dressers compensating for having to keep still at the moment of the slap.

October 23

Lymphangeitis. Boil on my neck. Impetigo beginning again. Bronchitis. Yesterday's scene retaken this morning. Beauty's room. I decide with Paulvé and Darbon to stop the film.

October 24

Face pain impossible to endure. This morning Paul asked Professor Martin to have me admitted to the Institut Pasteur. My appointment is for two-thirty; I wonder if I can wait till then. It is an agony for me to interrupt our work, but I have passed the limit. It is no longer possible. I am going mad.

October 25

I remember what Thomas Mann once wrote me, when I was in Toulon, suffering from typhoid: "You belong to the race that dies in hospitals."

I have been at Pasteur since yesterday. Professor Martin was kind enough to have me admitted instantly (his apartment building is next door to the Institut). Marais brought me to my room, then returned to the Palais-Royal for bedclothes, fruit, cigarettes, the notebook and pencils I use. Penicillin injections were begun at once. Penicillin and the atom bomb are the fashion now. The fashion will pass. The word "penicillin," for those who will some day read these notes, will produce the effect of the word "panorama" in *Père Goriot*. The atom bomb will become a Bengal light.

But in 1945 penicillin achieves extraordinary results. I am

given a shot every three hours. The morning one is the most painful, injected directly into the boils, but they cannot even treat my face and the impetigo until they have reduced these neck lesions. Meanwhile, my face itches less. A hospital is the only real clinic. I am in a kind of emergency surgery, under the most intensive care. Visitors can see me only from behind glass. I have no books. Except for these notes, I shall do no writing. I refuse to think about the film. This is a resting place, a parenthesis of calm.

Friday, October 26

Violent itching this morning, especially around the lower part of my face. On the other hand, my neck and shoulders have stopped hurting almost entirely. The painful penicillin injections in the boils have arrested the lymphangeitis zone.

All day long the newspapers telephone my secretary: "We understand Cocteau has grown a beard. Can he be photographed?" Stoicism of the journalist: complete indifference to the pain of others.

October 28—7 p.m.

I am notified that the insurance company regards me as a poor risk and refuses to insure my next film. I will write books, put on plays, and leave the testimony of *La Belle et la Bête* as I left that of *Le Sang d'un Poète*.

If the insurance company suspected the kind of inner fires which devour us in such undertakings, they would insure no one of our race and would underwrite only safe ventures.

October 29

To tell the truth, I have never been so happy as since I have been sick. The suffering doesn't count. I have lived, sustained by the kindness, the grace, and the warmth of my colleagues. I receive the reward of having chosen them. My constant obligation to set an example and to keep going was a kind of exaltation. I offered my cross to the film, and I am convinced that something of this effort has passed into the work. I left off when I realized that I had no more than death to give.

Besides, is it not *in my line* that my face should be destroyed, should swell, crack, be covered with scabs and hair, that my hands should bleed and seep, since I cover Marais's face and hands with a carapace so painful that the removal of his make-up resembles the torment of my bandages? All this accords with a certain spiritual style which is my own. The contrary would greatly disturb me.

October 29—10 p.m.

Alekan has heard rumors at the studio that everything I find splendid is regarded as a failure, badly lit—blancmange. He does not yet realize what I have grown accustomed to over the years: each time you try something new, people go blind, seeing only what resembles what they *have* seen. It has been decided, once and for all, that what is vague is poetic. Now, since to my eyes poetry is precision, I am leading Alekan toward the opposite of what these fools regard as poetic. And Alekan is uneasy, lacking my long familiarity with the struggle, my serenity in the face of the age's foolishness.

I can think of nothing duller than the "photographic consistency" of a film, a unity which specialists take for style. A film must distract the eye by contrasts, by effects which make no attempt to copy those of nature.

Tuesday, October 30

The skin of my face is still very sensitive, and I am afraid that the sulfamide dressings will give me another attack of urticaria. It would be better to return to Pasteur for the penicillin dressings, but the studio schedules make this impossible.

Yesterday I was brought (to whom does it belong?) the manuscript of *Le Grand Ecart*. I no longer recognized it because the school notebooks have been pasted on pages, numbered, sumptuously bound. All at once, turning a page on which the cover of a pale-green notebook decorated with a cock and scribbled with hieroglyphs had been mounted, I saw once again the Hôtel du Lavandou, the Pension Bessy at Pramousquier, Radiguet rolling his cigarettes and taking notes for *Le Bal du Comte d'Orgel*. I was flooded with happiness.

October 31

I read almost all last night and this morning the book Jouhandeau brought yesterday, as yet published only in an edition of four copies: *Essai sur Moi-même*. Closing the book, I thought of the remark Roger Lannes quotes from *Le Potomak*: "God made man in his image. Tempted by God as others by the devil, I cling to myself with all my might."

Jouhandeau's book is a book of love. Its title should be *Tristan and Tristan*. There is a "glory" around it, and Marcel can laugh at the conspiracy of silence some people are trying to organize around *him*.

Marcel says he has discovered his true equilibrium: he gets up and works at four every morning. No one bothers him. Everyone is asleep. He escapes the chaotic emanations of men. By the time they are stirring, he has finished his work.

November 2

I returned to the Palais-Royal last night. Paul and Jeannot had brought a car to the Institut Pasteur. I felt quite strong. But as soon as I was outside I realized I could scarcely stand up. A mountain of letters waiting for me at home; impossible to answer them. Last night I couldn't write a line. I am continuing this diary today, Friday, at two in the afternoon. The barber has just run the clippers over my face. He'll be back at six to shave me. —The insurance company wants me to be back at work tomorrow, which is madness. I'll try to get back to the film on Tuesday, though the Institut doctors prescribe fifteen days of country air. The main thing is to keep going.

November 7—8 a.m.

Colette, whom I visited yesterday and who is suffering from
lumbago, mentions an article in some American scientific journal the Polignacs brought her. The American scientists apologize
for causing, by their atomic research, a worldwide epidemic of
dermal diseases and furunculosis. Perhaps I am a victim of this
research, just as I once found myself rolling on the floor, in the
Rue d'Anjou, during a tidal wave in Japan which Claudel told
me about afterwards.

Back to work on the film. I am like a child at Christmas: I
have wakened too early, got up too early, unable to stay in bed a
moment longer.

November 7—10 p.m.

During the rushes I keep wondering how the brilliant and fresh
scenes can emerge from the chilly, dust-infested places where
we work. To work at Saint-Maurice until I fall asleep on my
feet, then to come home and fall asleep on top of my bed—that
is the rhythm I like. But I am always afraid of waking with
some new warning of the disease.

November 10—9 p.m.

I don't say: What beautiful work (I know nothing about that),
but: What good work I've done since yesterday morning.
Everything came of its own accord, assuming an unexpected
order. I felt neither my itching eye nor my fatigue. Actors,
technicians, cameramen were sustained by a single impulse
which seemed to proceed from my own heart. We worked on
the farcical scene of Marais and Auclair imitating the girls, after
they have locked the draper in the cupboard. First I took
images of the draper in the shadows—an eye, or the nose, or the
mouth revealed by a crack of light. This morning I began on
the Ludovic-Avenant horseplay. I constructed a steep track
from the ground up to the loggia. The camera moved up and

down, following their exploits. After lunch (Bérard had come, with Boris, Marie-Louise Bousquet, and an American journalist) I built a new track at the top of which the camera can pivot and sweep the entire room. This device allows me to film the boys at top speed, shifting from their own roles to the sisters', snatching up a hanging and using it as a train, perfectly anticipating the recorded voices of Mila and Nane, who must dub their lines when the boys imitate them. By this method I have reduced twelve shots to four.

November 12—10 p.m.

Harmonious work. The meal, the dream, the lights, the room, the linen hanging in front of the fire, the artists—everything was well oiled, easy, in order.

Rushes of the worthies and of the first day's work on the draper's farce. This is direct writing, unfiltered. Faults don't matter—they afford a certain relief. It was like *looking* at Mozart's music (in which the slightest detail, any four notes, can be isolated and whose movement *as a whole* is so admirable). Visually it resembles—until further notice—the overture to *The Magic Flute*.

November 13—7 a.m.

For five years I have been smothered, paralyzed by a hostile, aggressive, dangerous atmosphere. My talent for improvising in public had utterly vanished. Little by little I am coming to; I manage to think about a problem and to solve it in words, by myself, in my room. Perhaps I will recover that old contact— such a pleasant one—with the public. I wonder.

I look up (I am writing on my lap) and I see one of those accidental scenes which sometimes occur and which my work forces me to instigate again and again. A candle is reflected in the glass case containing the mask of Antinoüs. As a result, the left temple curls, hollows out, extends the hair and the beard into a white wound. The tall flame seems to emerge from the very center of the mind. The enamel eyes gleam, reflecting this flame which blazes up behind them. There is something divine in this optical phenomenon.

To reorganize chance. That is the basis of our work.

November 15—11 p.m.

Already, between four and five, Avenant has received from Diana (who will not be filmed until Monday) the white arrow which transfixes him. Marais dangled in the void, supported by Ludovic's hands. His pose required tremendous effort. An archer, on the scaffolding, aimed at his back, which was protected, under his cape, by a coat of mail and a layer of cork. The archer aimed straight, fearing an accident if he shot upward. Marais insisted; the arrow left the bow, ricocheted, slid along the fabric, and brushed the back of Marais's neck. The archer protests: "Next time it will go through his neck."

I refuse to do another take. But Marais finds a pose which tilts his back toward the camera, and the arrow is planted in just the right position. Each time, those watching recoiled, believing they saw the arrow kill the actor. In the preceding take, Marais breaks the glass and the window frame with his boot, knocks out a last pane with his bow, and must speak his lines when the window frame is empty. The first time, the frame didn't break properly. The second time, it bumped into the camera. The third time, Marais forgot his lines. The fourth time was perfect. Between each take, the prop men must put in the frame, set the panes, nail up the ivy. These endless efforts for one short scene allow me to get only four takes into the can.

November 21—11 p.m.

I telescoped five shots into one, hoping I could then shoot the rest (two shots in one). Unfortunately, Marais stumbles over a line, and there occurs that strange phenomenon of memory characteristic of actors: he stumbles a dozen times over the same line. The disaster is complicated by our chickens, which

Clément must cajole, caress, and each time convince to play their part, motionless, at certain specific places in the set.

Once, Marais overcomes the obstacle. But then it is Tiquet who gets his camera caught in a cable and cannot finish his pan shot. The simplest thing is to take a break, send the actors out for a walk, wait, relax, and after this intermission try one last time. Twice more Marais overcomes the obstacle. It is six o'clock. Alekan is setting up the lights for the next scene, and I stop the shooting for the day.

November 30—10 p.m.

We are working among a crowd of American visitors drawn by the spectacle of the special effects and crowding onto the rickety steps.

The young extras who play the part of the stone heads display incredible patience. Uncomfortably positioned, kneeling behind the set, shoulders in a kind of armor, they must lean their powdered, lacquered heads against the capitals and receive the spotlights directly in their eyes. I wonder if the camera will translate the intensity of the effect, its magical truth. These living heads *stare*, exhale smoke, turn, follow the movements of the actors, who do not see them, behave as the objects around us behave perhaps, taking advantage of our habit of supposing them motionless.

I film the merchant's arrival (skipping the candelabra, which I shall take tomorrow). The fire blazes. The clock chimes. The table is set, covered with dishes, goblets, pitchers (in the style of Gustave Doré), all on the verge of the horrible (in the style of the Gare de Lyon). Out of a chaos of roast meats, pastry, fruits, emerges a living arm which coils round the candelabrum.

Saturday evening, December 1

At six-fifteen, I shoot a scene which occurs to me when I notice the lion head which serves as a finial on the arm of a chair. The merchant's hand *sleeps* on this lion head. We hear the distant roaring of the Beast; the hand *wakes*. Monday, I will cut to the candelabrum with the candles burned down and smoking. From the candelabrum I will cut to Marcel's anguish and prepare his escape.

December 5

After lunch and until evening, the slow-motion sequence of Josette going up the monumental staircase, accompanied by the great crane on which the camera rises with her.

We wear ourselves out, waste time in details, last-minute changes. The dust raised by her quick movements (quick because we will print in slow motion) may look quite noble and sumptuous on the screen. Upstairs one of the caryatids turns his head to the right, the mailed arms raise the curtain, Josette proceeds down the corridor. All this very fast (slowed down to eighty frames).

December 16

Marais has kept on his make-up for fifteen hours. I no longer dared ask him to retake a scene. We receive visits at night in Beauty's room. But our visitors are soon bored. They cannot believe that our profession requires such an effort. They watch; they get tired; they leave. And the agony of the lights, of the alternating heat and cold, continues. But the thing *had* to be attempted once: a poet who narrates by means of a camera. I know people criticize me for exhausting myself over a film. People are wrong.

December 22

The torments continue. An abscess forming under a neglected tooth is driving me mad. Having worked until eight, I lie down at nine and at ten I wake up in such pain that I must get dressed and rush to the dentist. The night before last, I suffered so much from my rash and my tooth that I lost control of myself and spoiled my work. The caryatids were fainting in their armor. We carried them outside, where they revived, insisted on being repainted, fainted again. Returned in the morning to the Hôtel du Louvre, where I am given a miserable room next to a phone booth in which people keep shouting. Impossible to sleep. Thanks to this insomnia, I have blocked out a new scene which combines the takes, completing the sequence with a certain splendor. Yesterday I canceled the work of the day before and shot my new scene. Marais was splendid. The rushes show frames of great beauty.

Christmas

After the rushes, Bérard and I crossed the ruins of Beauty's room to put the finishing touches on the pool. My last set: poignant sadness. All the overwhelming work of a film dissolves, leaving us nothing but its reflection. The places where we have labored, suffered, struggled together become new places inhabited by tenants who treat us like visiting strangers.

Here is the spring, the filthy water, the rocks, the cave, the seeping wall, the winged horse that will watch the swans. Here is the place where I will once again become involved, suffer, and forget my suffering.

December 28—8:30 p.m.

Last night I shot the scenes of the dying Beast. I had fastened necklaces around the swans' throats. In an hour they had managed to rip them off. In their fury they produced arabesques, writhing like monograms. Chance granted me real discoveries with regard to style which would pose insoluble problems if we had tried to prepare them beforehand. The swans were filled with rage against this unknown Beast whose mane and paw hung down into the water. They attacked him, hissing. Marais, with his habitual *sang-froid*, did not flinch, defied their attacks. These swans attacking their sick master now dispossessed of his privileges added a strange grandeur to the scene. I love this last set of ours: the winged horse shimmers under the spring water; the moon illuminates a pool of ink.

The night before, Marais, lapping up this water, invented a striking imitation of an animal drinking. He thrust his muzzle into the water, snorted, spat; he actually *drank* that disgusting water—I know no other actor who would have done that.

December 31

The last day of 1945. Whatever happens to us in France, we must remind ourselves that we are in France and that the worst civil disputes are better than any occupation. I know what occupation means: I am occupied by microbes. These red patches I suffer from remind me of the gray moss which has vanished. How grateful I should be to those who could rid me of my microbes. Praise be to those who have rid France of hers. The rest is merely discomfort.

January 3—7:30 a.m.

In my little red room in the Palais-Royal I look at the Gustave Doré object which has just been cast in bronze for me. It is under the sign of this object that I have made my film, which it epitomizes and explains. The influence of an object over our deepest being is inconceivable. This group of Perseus, Andromeda, and the Dragon would embellish Beauty's room in the Beast's castle.

At the upper end of his steel lance, which transfixes the monster's gullet, Perseus, mounted on Bellerophon, almost standing in his stirrups between the steed's wings, sways above the scaly spirals of the dragon-woman. The art-nouveau pedestal looks like a breaking wave. Each time I walk into the room, the lance quivers. Horse and hero tremble. I must contrive the end of the film in this style, invent something just as unexpected, an analogous use of the clouds filmed in the courtyard.

January 4—7 p.m.

We will be working at night. The last night. I know nothing sadder than the end of a film, than a loving crew disbanding. Every technician is sensitive to this minor death. The work that still remains is difficult. The Prince and Beauty depart, flying up into the clouds. Beauty passes through the wall and enters her father's house. Tricks, but direct tricks, the only kind I like, tricks which I invent and over which I slave.

Yesterday I finished the takes of Prince Charming beside the spring. Marais was a prince, and he was charming. I filmed him, at the end, falling backward (reverse slow motion), so that he will rise suddenly with an other-worldly grace. But for all the work they put in and all the help they give, Alekan, Tiquet, and Clément are beginning to live *elsewhere*. Clément must scout locations for Noël-Noël's new film; Alekan is preparing Stroheim's film with Tiquet's help. We are no longer all imprisoned within the same dream. Each of us is half awake.

Next week, I shall begin editing. That will reveal the true rhythm of the work: my handwriting. Anyone could give me back a page of my script *corrected*, copied out, Palmer method or Spencerian . . .

January 6—4:30 a.m.

We have just finished the night scene: Beauty with the glove's shadow on her face. Using both cranes, we shot Beauty and the Prince flying against the night sky, over the set of the pool.

Duverger has had a splendid moviola installed in the cutting room. I can now begin at once on the work which had alarmed me because of the old moviola. The moviola is the apparatus which allows us to see the film, and to understand it, on a reduced scale, to stop it at any point, to turn it in any direction.

January 11

I have finished. That is to say, I am beginning. I have harvested the images. What remains is to dissolve them into each other, to give them a movement all the more subtle in that this tale rises to no peak and unrolls, without any real drama, in a deliberate rhythm of dreams. No occasion to move an audience, to provoke tears. We must please, at all costs, or displease. That is the whole point.

January 18

M. asks Paul, "Why is Jean making a film? It doesn't last." Astonishing remark. As if anything lasted, beginning with the world.

I am not a desk writer. I write when I cannot help writing. As little as possible. Writing dialogue bores me. But to set this great mill of dreams in motion, to struggle with the angel of light, the angel of machines, the angels of space and time—that is a task made to my measure. What does the result matter? I do not claim that what I have done is well done. I have done my best to prove that France can still do battle against giant forces. In fact, can do battle *only* against giant forces. That is her true task, her mission. If France persists in renouncing her privileges, still coveting what she cannot have and scorning what she owes herself, then we deserve our purple shroud. Let us die and wait for the future to come and pray on our Acropolis.

"Cinema is not an art." An absurd remark, made by the people who keep it from being one. The cinema will be an art only on the day the silk merchants no longer try to be silk-worms.

February 13

If the nations ask France: What are your arms? she can answer: I have none. I possess a secret weapon. And if she is asked what it is, France will answer that one does not divulge a secret weapon. If pressed, France risks nothing in telling her secret, for this weapon is inimitable. *It is her tradition of anarchy.* I rejoice that France does not recognize herself, that she denigrates herself. For a poet to recognize himself means to live poetically. For a prince to recognize himself means to live historically. Two faults which cause ridicule and cost dear. One cannot *be* and *seem to,* Erik Satie used to say. And he added the phrase I keep quoting: "What matters is not that you refuse the Legion of Honor; you must also not have deserved it."

The film industry opposes the *accidental,* the *unforeseen,* presenting a blank wall to *anarchy.* Last week Gabriel Pascal saw my film. He told me: "France is the only country in the world today where such an undertaking is possible." Whether my film pleases or displeases is another matter. I have been able to complete it because of the venturesomeness of a free producer, the kindness of my colleagues, the ingenuity of my crew, and that tradition of anarchy which still authorizes, among us, an accidental intrusion into order.

April 1946

At Saint-Maurice for the sound track.

A job properly done enthralls me. Rauzenat, the sound man, not only loves his job, he enjoys it. Some sound men produce their effects close to the microphone with fingers, earth, a straw, matches. Rauzenat works with his feet, his hands, his mouth. For a galloping horse, he slaps his belly, his chest. Shut up in the sound chamber, I hear what I see, and through the glass I make out Rauzenat executing a kind of ritual dance.

Today is the day for the music. I have refused to hear what Auric has composed, wanting to receive the shock of it without preparation. A long habit of working together gives me complete confidence in him.

We record from nine in the morning until five, in the

Maison de la Chimie. This operation is the most moving of all. As I have said before, it is only in the musical dimension that this film can really take wing. Désormières is on the podium. Jacques Lebreton arranges the instrumentalists and the choruses. The microphone is set up on a long pole in the center of the hall. Behind the orchestra, the screen will receive the film, which the half light and the makeshift projector make almost invisible.

And now the silence, then the three white flashes which announce the image, then the image and the wonder of that synchronization which is not a synchronization, since Auric avoids it, at my request, and since it must not occur save by the grace of God.

This new universe troubles, disturbs, enthralls me. I had composed my own music without realizing it, and the waves of sound from the orchestra contradict that music. Gradually Auric's score triumphs over my absurd discomfort. My music gives way to his. This music weds the film, impregnates it, exalts it, completes it. The spell of the Beast lulls us to sleep, and the spectacle of this sonorous penumbra is the dream of that sleep.

June 1, 1946

I write the last lines of this diary in the country house where I have just taken refuge from every kind of bell: door, telephone, studio . . .

I had decided to escape after the last work on the film. And yesterday (Friday) I presented it, in the Joinville projection room, to the studio technicians.

The announcement of the screening, written on the blackboard by the projectionist, revolutionized Saint-Maurice. Chairs and benches had to be added. Lacombe had changed his shooting schedule so that his artists and staff would be free.

At six-thirty, Marlene Dietrich took her chair beside mine, and I tried to stand up and say a few words. But the accumulation of all the moments which had led to this one paralyzed me, made me almost incapable of speaking. I watched the film, holding Marlene's hand and crushing it in mine without realizing what I was doing. The reels unwound, the film gravitated, sparkled—no longer part of me, solitary, insensible, remote as a star. It had killed me. It rejected me and lived its own life. In it I found only the memories attached to each piece of footage and the suffering it had cost me. I did not dream that others could be following the story it told—I believed them all plunged into my own imaginings.

The response of that roomful of workers was unforgettable. That is my reward. Whatever happens, I shall never again meet with the grace of that ceremony so simply organized by a little village whose occupation and artisanry is the canning of dreams.

My Room in the Palais-Royal

> *"I am over fifty, and death need not*
> *travel far to meet me. The performance*
> *is nearly over: I have only a few lines left . . ."*

My room, that narrow cell overlooking an arcade of the Palais-Royal, fringed with the sound of footsteps, has been so often described by journalists, magnified by photographers, that I wonder if it can really be mine, it has so little in common with the image they circulate. Doubtless, the most arresting piece of detritus that has washed up on this little beach with red walls is the Gustave Doré sculpture, a plaster group of Perseus, Andromeda, and the Dragon which Charles de Noailles gave me and which I had cast in bronze. It stands on a column between the fan window and a sliding blackboard which conceals a tiny study, a closet too cold to work in during the winter. Here I wrote *Renaud et Armide*, utterly sequestered, severed from the telephone and the doorbell, in the summer of 1943, on an architect's table over which—rescued from my room in the Rue

Vignon—hangs the big charcoal and red-chalk drawing by Christian Bérard of Oedipus and the Sphinx.

This blackboard-door and several others in the vestibule are used for chalking up addresses and chores, for my memory is riddled with holes. Visitors predisposed to the fanciful may suppose they see hieroglyphics here rather than a memorandum over which, every week, I pass an eraser.

To the right of my bed there are two heads, one a Roman marble of a faun (which belonged to my grandfather Lecomte), and the other, under a glass bell, of an Antinous so fragile that only the fixity of its enamel eyes could have conducted it here, down through the ages, like the white cane of the blind. A third head adorns that of my bed: Lipschitz's terra-cotta portrait of Raymond Radiguet, made the year of his death.

Here is the catalogue of the imagery suspended on the walls above the inundation of disorder: Delacroix's lithographs for *Faust*. Carjat's photograph of Rimbaud, taken the day of the sword-cane scandal. A collage by Picasso, in a butterfly case. Clairin's portrait of Sarah Bernhardt (sculpting). The original of Bérard's cover for *Opéra*. A large ink drawing of a woman by Picasso. A photograph of Mallarmé in his plaid shawl. A folded-cardboard die by Picasso, mounted in a green shadow box (see *La Fin du Potomak*). A sketch by Ingres for *Tu Marcellus eris*. Manet's dry-point profile of Baudelaire. My portrait drawn in Rome by Picasso and dated Easter 1917. Two ink drawings by Victor Hugo: one of Gavroche, under which Hugo has written, "Watching the guillotine"; the other a fantastic elaboration of his own initials. A charming watercolor of my mother by Vencker.

The rest—smothered under papers, books, unanswered letters, jars of salve, and medicine bottles—the rest is merely the debris of my tempest, vestiges of the countless apartments and hotel rooms in which so many treasures have been lost, strayed or stolen, and from which nothing remains. I rented this little chamber, wedged between the Théâtre du Palais-Royal and the block of houses adjoining the Comédie-Française, in 1941, when the German Army was marching on Paris. I was living then in the Hôtel Beaujolais, next door to Colette, and was not to move here—36 rue de Montpensier—until 1942, after the exodus. The friends whom I had wanted to make into neighbors by impulsively renting this curious tunnel had had to flee the building. I lived here six years under insult, stricken in my work and in my person. I stay on now out of fatigue, out of the impossibility of finding a suitable lodging, and also because of a charm (in the exact sense of the word) which the Palais-Royal works on certain souls. This charm consists of the Revolutionary phantoms which haunt the arcades, the bird-embellished silence which followed the celebrations of the Directorate, the almost Chinese position of a necropolis the place occupies among the ramparts of ancient, sordid houses listing like Venetian palaces, where Delphine de Nucingen led Rastignac to the gaming tables.

I know everyone here, his habits, his cats, his dogs. I walk among smiles, surrounded by the gossip of which I am a part. I eat in the little restaurants four steps down from the street. I meet friends here, and the ghost of Giraudoux, who came from outside but was one of us. I call out of my window to Colette crossing the garden with her cane, her foulard scarf, her broad felt hat, her fine eyes, her sandals.

I do not like leaving this room, yet I must. A harsh wind is driving me out. Wherever I go, under whatever sun, I shall regret my penumbra, and the glow the snow casts up like footlights from the ground in winter. And the spectacle I glimpsed the other day (one of a thousand): the hairdresser in the Galerie de Chartres had put out his wigs to dry in the sun. These wigs were attached to wax heads, and these heads to the pickets of the grille which by night shuts up the shades of Thermidor.

In the morning, when the grille opens onto corridors, galleries, colonnades, vaults, arches, lanterns, dovecotes, the prospects of Russian squares and Roman cities, stalls displaying foreign stamps, books on flagellation, medals of the Legion of Honor, you can play *boules* under the trees; from the garden into the gutters rolled just such heads in another game of *boules*; and there, too, paraded more than one company of ragged cocks that brandished them, like fists, at the stone-framed sky.

4

La Difficulté d'être

1946–1963

On est juge ou accusé. Le juge est assise. L'accusé debout. Vivre debout . . .

One is either a judge or a defendant. The judge sits, the defendant stands. To live standing . . .

Christian Bérard

André Gide

Self-portrait

Colette, by Jean Cocteau, 1945 (Collection Edouard Dermit)

On receiving an honorary doctorate of letters from Oxford University, 1956

With Edouard Dermit, 1958

top left: Wall of the Chapel of Saint-Blaise-des-Simples at Milly-la-Forêt, which Cocteau decorated in 1959, and where he is buried

left: Cocteau's signature with a wistful cat

above: Apse of the chapel of Saint-Pierre at Villefranche-sur-Mer, which Cocteau decorated during the summer of 1956

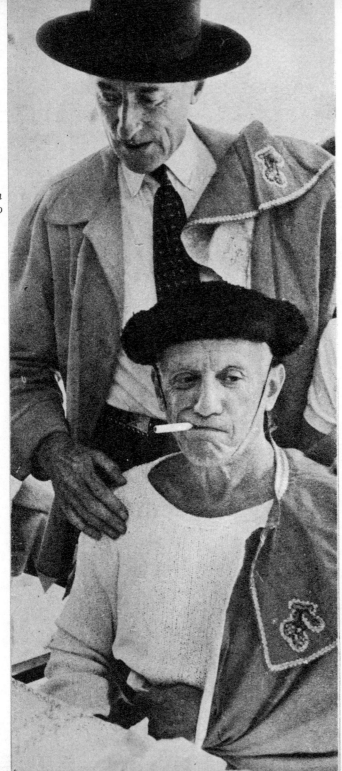

With
Picasso

Cocteau
working

Cocteau
speaking

CALENDAR

1946–1963

Except for vacations, Cocteau had always lived in Paris. Now, at fifty-seven, he acquired a house in the village of Milly-la-Forêt, near Fontainebleau, and here he began to gather around him the mementos and emblems of a lifetime. Outside, there was a walled garden, with marble busts, a moat, and an occasional deer from the adjacent forest of Fontainebleau. Inside, there was the mixture of theatre and elegance that always characterized Cocteau's ambient: leopard-skin carpeting on the stairs, on the wall Bérard's huge drawing of Oedipus' encounter with the Sphinx, a unicorn's horn, a crystal ball; it was almost possible to hear Auric's haunting music for la Bête's enchanted castle in the background. Interviewed for the radio by André Fraigneau, Cocteau was asked what he would take if the house should ever burn down, and replied without a moment's hesitation, "I'd take the fire!" Showing a reporter through the house, he led the way into the garden, where the moat water was violet-colored. "Voilà!" he cried. "Gossips are going to say, 'Cocteau even has his water tinted now!' The truth is, my neighbor uses the creek to wash his sugar beets!"

The international success of La Belle et la Bête led to more filmmaking with Jean Marais: adaptations of Victor Hugo's Ruy Blas, as well as Cocteau's own plays, Les Parents Terribles and L'Aigle à deux têtes, and then in 1950, the most ambitious and original movie he was ever to attempt under commercial conditions, Orphée. "Even those who see it without understanding it," he wrote to his friend and translator, Mary Hoeck, "keep pictures from it in their minds and think about it. This is what matters . . ."

He traveled more and more: alone to New York in 1949, and with a troupe of actors later the same year to Egypt and the Near East; to Greece, Germany, Spain, England. Old friends began to die: Bérard, Colette, Gide. In the spring of 1950, Cocteau and Gide had met for the last time in Sicily. "It was Gide's custom," wrote Truman Capote, "to dream away the morning hours propped in the piazza sun: there he sat sipping from a bottle of salt water brought fresh from the sea, a motionless mandarin shrouded in a woolly wintry black cape . . . Then one morning Cocteau, whirling a cane, sauntered upon the piazza scene . . . still anxious to please, still the rainbow-winged and dancing dragonfly inviting the toad not merely to admire but perhaps to devour him. He jigged about, his jingling merriment competed with the bell-music of passing donkey carts, he scattered rays of bitter wit that stung like the Sicilian sun, he effused, enthused, he fondled the old man's knee, caressed his hands, squeezed his shoulders, kissed his parched Mongolian cheeks . . . until at last he croaked, 'Do be still, you are disturbing the view.' "

At the same time, there were new friends, especially two who were to become permanent friends and very close. The first was a young Yugoslav painter named Edouard Dermit, who had come to the Milly household as a gardener but who soon became Cocteau's companion and eventually his heir. The other was Madame Francine Weisweiller, who, in 1950, invited Cocteau and Dermit to visit her house, the Villa Santo Sospir, on Saint-Jean Cap-Ferrat. Cocteau spent the summer "tattooing" the walls with murals; Madame Weisweiller's small yacht was soon christened Orphée II; and the next year Cocteau's last play, Bacchus, was dedicated "à Francine, qui pense avec le coeur."

He was now a world celebrity, a first-magnitude star, and

though a part of him loved and could never resist this "last infirmity of noble mind," it was an exhausting role. "One day," wrote his Palais-Royal neighbor Maurice Goudeket, "we were talking on the broad walk of the Place du Théâtre-Français, when a girl darted toward Jean, waving a little book. 'Monsieur, do you do autographs?' she asked, as if she had been in a dry-cleaner's shop asking, 'Do you do accordion pleats?' A few other young people followed the ingenuous collector's example. Jean did what they asked him, with good grace. After they had gone, he let his smile droop and he said to me, 'Do you realize that I have been at the top of the bill like this for more tha.1 forty years . . . And I shall certainly have to stay there until the end!' "

In 1954, after a trip to Spain, he suffered his first heart attack but was soon back at his old rounds. He designed a tapestry for the Gobelin workshop. He made potteries. He restored and redecorated a little waterfront chapel in nearby Villefranche. "In my youth I thought it was only an old bum sleeping under the dust and the fishermen's nets. Cleaned up, it turned out to be a marvelous little Romanesque church . . ." He spent a whole summer on scaffoldings, painting the walls himself, inside and out, issuing weekly bulletins to Paris newspapers.

The next year, 1955, he solicited admission to the Académie Française. Elected in March, he presented himself sous la Coupole, before eight hundred illustrious members and guests, on October 20. "The time is coming when there will be no more reading and writing," he declared. "Only a few mandarins will whisper their secrets in each other's ears. My wish is that this Academy will then protect those persons suspected of Individualism, and that our doors will always be open to the Singular pursued by the Plural . . ." Lanvin made his uniform. He had two swords, one designed by Picasso, the other by himself, with a Toledo blade and a Cartier hilt of ivory, rubies, and gold. His portrait was on the cover of Paris-Match. La Table Ronde devoted an entire issue to his lifework. Even Jean Genet was seen at the ceremonies. "It will be," said Cocteau, "my last scandal."

In the autumn of 1959, he undertook his last film. Half autobiography, half myth, alternately grave and farcical, it was called Le Testament d'Orphée, ou ne me demandez pas pourquoi. In addition to writing and directing it, Cocteau played The Poet, with Edouard Dermit as Cégeste-Radiguet, and assorted old friends, including Picasso, Dominguín, Jean Marais, and Madame Weisweiller, in bit parts.

Early in 1963, he collaborated in a full-length television documentary of his own life. It had just been finished when another heart attack disabled him, on April 22. For many days he lay ill in his Palais-Royal room and was finally removed to Milly. There he seemed to recover and by the end of the summer he had new work plans. Another chapel, in Fréjus, up the coast, was to be decorated; and for Jean Marais, he was going to translate George Bernard Shaw's The Devil's Disciple. To his old friend and literary executor, Jean Denoël, he wrote: "I'm staying on in Milly until October 15 . . . After that, it's still a mystery . . ."

On the morning of October 11, a reporter informed him, by telephone, of the death of Edith Piaf. "Mais alors, ils s'en vont tous, ils me laissent tous," he cried. "They're all going, they're all leaving me." A few minutes later, back up in his room, he himself collapsed with another heart attack. He died at one o'clock that afternoon, and was buried on October 15 at a tiny chapel on the outskirts of Milly which he had decorated in 1959 with drawings of medicinal herb flowers. "Il n'y aura que lui," said his friend Marcel Jouhandeau, "pour avoir une tombe aussi belle, loin des cimetières . . . Only he will have so lovely a grave, far from the cemeteries."

A Letter to Americans

Paris–New York (Air France),
January 12–13, 1949

Americans,

I am writing on the plane that is taking me back to France. I have spent twenty days in New York and done so many things, seen so many people, that I cannot tell whether I lived there twenty days or twenty years. I know: you cannot judge a whole country by one city, America by New York; my stay was too short to entitle me to such comparisons. But sometimes our first glimpse of a face tells more than a long study of what is inside.

*

New York is an open city—wide open. Arms, faces, hearts are open, streets, doors, and windows. The consequence, for the visitor: euphoria, a jet of oxygen in which ideas cannot ripen but dance like dead leaves.*

I have said it before: you refuse to wait, to keep others waiting. In New York, everyone is ahead of time for appointments. Tradition and novelty repel you equally: your ideal would be an *instantaneous tradition*. The new is at once on the curriculum. From that moment, it ceases to be new. You classify it, attach labels . . .

I shall never forget what I saw at the Museum of Modern Art**: in a spotless schoolroom, fifty little girls painting away at

* No trees in New York. Trees are suspect: they look as if they were dreaming.

** Under the guidance of Monroe Wheeler, this museum is a model of order and beauty. Among other marvels I rediscovered Rousseau's *Sleeping Gypsy* and Picasso's *Guernica,* the latter still waiting to take its place in a new Spain.

tables covered with brushes, pots, tubes, bowls, staring into space and sticking out their tongues like the clever animals that ring a bell, tongues lolling and eyes vague. Teachers supervise these young creators of abstract art and slap their wrists if what they paint *represents* something and dangerously inclines toward realism. The mothers (still at the Picasso stage) are not admitted.

*

In France, a man passes with no transition from the status of a schoolboy to the status of an old man. In America, harsh struggle obliges a man to live, from childhood till the day he dies, in *middle age*—an age detached from his mother. In marriage, the American rediscovers a mother, before whom he bows his head.

When a New York couple invites me to dinner, when the elevator flings me into their vestibule, the wife, the lady of the house, comes to the door. Stooping, anonymous, the husband takes cover behind her.

*

In the seat beside me, a woman whose face is hidden by a beard of orchids has fallen asleep with a copy of *Life* open on her lap. This publication, I believe, has the widest circulation in the country. Closing my own eyes, I can see what happened last Sunday all over again: *Life* had asked to do a story, accompanied by "eccentric" photographs. When I told the reporters that neither my age nor my situation as a poet (i.e., a worker) authorized "eccentricity," they replied that such photographs were the custom, the rule, the only kind their readers were interested in. Being a guest in New York, I complied with their request, suggesting some themes likely to satisfy them and to compromise me only insofar as I allow myself to be compromised.

We worked from three in the afternoon until seven. I took

dinner with Jacques Maritain. *Life* and I resumed from eleven until five in the morning. At around two there was a break for sandwiches and ginger ale. That was when the photographer amazed me by asking, "What can a man somewhere in Massachusetts, leafing through *Life* in a barber shop, make of such photographs? Won't they be a little too much?"

"But these extravagances aren't my idea," I answered. "They're yours!" Their anxiety alternated with their certainty that such pictures were the only ones that would "work." Then came the tremendous problem of the text—how could we explain the inexplicable? I told them to say that the pictures they had taken were perfectly ordinary ones, that the camera had been playing tricks on them, that unfortunately—apologies—the machine was becoming dangerous to the human image. I suggested they add a plug for Rolleiflex. For instance, *The Rolleiflex thinks*.

*

In Hollywood, after endless arguments and despite his reluctance to compose music for a film, Stravinsky was about to reach an agreement with Mr. G.—when Mr. G. declared that Stravinsky would also have to pay his arranger. "What arranger?" Stravinsky asked. "The one who will arrange your music."

This habit of arranging everything is your method. A work must not, at any price, remain what it is.

*

Of course I know your answer: "What business is it of yours—a European, a man of the Old World?" Of course I know it is absurd to preach when I deserve to be preached to. I know our faults better than I know yours. But there still exists, on our side of the Atlantic, a disorder which admits of surprising births, a compost heap in which our cock anchors his claws

and which must not be confused with a garbage dump, a fatal
mistake our government almost always makes.

I know we live in a barnyard and you in a bathroom. But is
that not a good reason for an exchange of visits? That is my
dream, the dream of a man of the old French barnyard, of the
artisan who produces his object with his own hands and carries
it, under his arm, to your city.

Is it not time for despecialization? Is it not time to entrust
your machines to us, to see if we can humanize them, and to
humanize yourselves by diminishing their privileges—in short,
to stem our individualism and to stimulate yours? To advance
together, hand in hand, against false ethics and bad habits?

A few days ago Richard Wright spoke to the French, as I am
speaking to you, and the things he said are not pleasant for
anyone to hear. I know that trumpet of the Bible, that trumpet
dear to the black people. When Louis Armstrong puts it to his
lips, it utters an angel's cry. What does that cry mean? What I
am trying to tell you. What I have learned on my visit to New
York. A cry of anguish and of love.

*

Americans,

I must now express my gratitude to you. New York has received me more as a friend than as a guest. The minute I set
foot in your city, I felt that lightness of air in which the skyscrapers spread their nets. They rose about me like hives from
which a golden honey flows. I repeat: everything is wide open
in New York. Nor is this because New York hasn't "suffered"
(a polite cliché). Suffering never made anyone beautiful. The
French have not been made beautiful by it, and it is because
our wounds are ugly that they will heal. No, your good graces
are immediate, your kindness indigenous: never, in all my
contacts with the most various circles, did I have to hear a man
slander his neighbor. Scandalmongering does not exist in New
York, and if it exists it does not make a spectacle of itself.

*

By day, New York's sky is maritime: the wind, the snow, the sun alternate at top speed. You freeze or you scorch. At night, Broadway looks like a woman covered with jewels and shaken with twitches. Your streets are jammed with yellow taxis whose electric diadems pursue each other in a slow cortege swathed in the incense of mysterious vapors rising from the pavement. Yesterday I contemplated your Nighttown, riding inch by inch to the theatre where I was to present my film *L'Aigle à deux têtes*.

My English is too poor to express the difficult nuances my profession demands of me. I therefore had to walk out on the stage and speak French, and I asked Jean-Pierre Aumont to come along and translate for me. From the first moment, I lost every scrap of embarrassment. The audience carried me, carried me away. It understood my sentences so immediately that its applause made the translator useless. When I asked Jean-Pierre to translate what I had said, he would answer: "There's no need to." The audience burst into laughter, and one man shouted, "Yes, yes, translate!" and a Frenchwoman translated from her seat. The atmosphere was the kind we have always longed for in France, where our elite audience is forever on its guard, afraid of being ridiculed.

*

Americans,

It is my love that addresses these lines to you. It is my gratitude for your reception which implores you not to read them carelessly, not to confuse them with a newspaper article, an aesthete's work. Not to read me while your radio broadcasts a program called "Music to read by."

In a world of universal management, our French liberties are shrinking. I believe I have explained what still protects us. But your example would be a crushing one, if you acknowledged that your liberty means only that you are free not to be free, that you thus consent to be managed, to be stripped of your freedom.

I address you as a free man—one of the last, speaking in all the solitude that freedom implies. I cannot claim the suffrage of any group, any school, any church, any party. My tribunal is in this ether the propellers are ravaging now, a tribunal surrounded by cruel stars and by sleeping men, each of whom, on terra firma, has his own milieu, his own opinion. I have neither opinion nor milieu. I address myself, as always, to those who seek to be free, and who must, as I do, expect a slap at every turn, and who wonder, when they receive a compliment instead, if they have not made some mistake.

Good night.

Jean Cocteau

Working in the Theatre

The theatre is a furnace; in it the unsuspecting are slowly roasted or incinerated on the spot.

The public is like the high seas; the nausea it produces is called stage fright. And no matter how often you tell yourself: it's just the theatre, it's just the public, nothing does any good. You resolve not to let yourself be trapped again. You go back. It's the gambling table. You bet what you have. And the torture is exquisite. Unless you're a fool, you suffer. But you're never cured.

When I direct a play, I become a spectator. I correct badly. I love the actors, and they delude me. I hear something besides myself. By the dress rehearsal, my weaknesses leap to my eyes. It is too late. Afterwards, suffering from an almost oceanic discomfort, I prowl the ship—the hold, the cabins, the passageways. I dare not look at the sea. Much less get wet: once I went out front, I would sink the boat.

I stand in the wings, listening. Behind the set, a play is no longer painted; it draws itself. I leave. I lie down in the women's dressing room. What my actresses leave behind, changing souls, creates a fatal void. I am suffocating. I stand up. I listen. How far along are they? I snoop at keyholes . . . Yet I know this sea is subject to rules. Its waves roll and unroll at my orders. A new audience uncoils its springs at the same effects. But if one of these effects is prolonged, the actor enters the trap. It is hard for him to refuse the bait of laughter. This cruel laughter must wound him—he propitiates it. "I suffer and I make them laugh," he tells himself. "I come out ahead." The bait is offered quickly and quickly taken, the author forgotten. The ship is adrift, a derelict. Once actors listen to these sirens, drama turns to melodrama, the thread that stitched the scenes together breaks. The rhythm is lost.

For me, *remote control* is a contradiction in terms. The imponderables escape me. What can I change? Here are the performers who correct themselves and perfect the machine; here are the ones who live onstage and try to conquer the machine. Diderot missed the point—he had never lived in the wings.

I know authors who supervise their actors, write them notes. They obtain a discipline. They paralyze. They lock a door that can open at a puff of wind.

There are two great races confronting each other on the stage. Such authors prevent the first from enriching its trajectory by some find; they waken the second from its trance. I prefer to risk their chemistry, either way: it is the red or the black that comes up.

Writing this paragraph, I seem to be back in Marcel André's dressing room, arguing. Yvonne de Bray and Jean Marais are onstage. Their natures correspond: what is it that allows them to respect a dialogue they *live*, forgetting that a wall is missing from the room they are in? Marcel André is talking. I listen to him. And I listen to the silence of the building. He keeps his ears cocked for the timbre which will fling him into the performance. We only half exist.

Delicious moments, which torment me, which I wouldn't exchange for anything.

Orphée (Orpheus, *first performed June 17, 1926*)

Originally this play was to be about Joseph and Mary, about the gossip they endured on account of the angel (the carpenter's apprentice), about the slander of Nazareth when faced with an inexplicable pregnancy, about the couple's obligation to flee because of this village slander.

The plot led to so many misapprehensions that I gave it up and substituted the Orphic theme, in which the inexplicable birth of poems would replace that of the Divine Child.

The angel was now to appear as a glazier, and I note here the strange coincidences which accompanied the Pitoëff production in June 1926:

Because Marcel Herrand wanted to work on the play the night before opening night, we rehearsed in the vestibule of my apartment, Rue d'Anjou. Herrand had just said the line: "With these gloves you will pass through mirrors as if they were water," when there was a tremendous crash at the other end of the apartment. A huge mirror in the bathroom had fallen out of its frame: the shattered fragments covered the floor.

Glenway Wescott and Monroe Wheeler, who had come up to Paris for the opening, were stopped on the way to the theatre by a collision, a broken window, and a white horse that thrust its head into their car on the Boulevard Raspail.

A year later I was having lunch with them in their very isolated house on a hillside above Villefranche-sur-Mer. They were translating *Orphée* and told me a glazier would be incomprehensible in America. I cited *The Kid*, in which Chaplin plays a glazier in New York. "It's rare in New York and rare in Paris," I told them. "You almost never see one." They asked me to describe a glazier for them, and were just seeing me to the gate, crossing the garden, when, contrary to all expectation and likelihood, a glazier came walking along the deserted road, then vanished around a bend.

Orphée was performed in Mexico City, in Spanish. An earthquake interrupted the Bacchantes scene, demolished the theatre, and injured several persons. When the theatre was rebuilt, *Orphée* was put on again. Suddenly the stage manager announced that the performance would have to stop. The actor playing Orpheus could not leave the mirror. He had died in the wings.

From *Orphée*, scene i:

EURYDICE: Orpheus, my poet . . . How nervous your horse has made you! Remember how you used to laugh, how you kissed me and held me in your arms? You had a wonderful job. You were covered with glory. People couldn't wait to read your poems, and all Thrace recited them by heart. You celebrated the sun . . . you were a priest, a leader. But since the horse—that's all over. We live in the country now—you've given up your job, you refuse to write. You spend your life coddling that horse, questioning that horse, waiting for that horse to answer. It's foolishness.

ORPHEUS: Foolishness? My life was beginning to spoil, to stink of success and death. Now I put the sun and the moon in the same bag. And what's left is night. Not other people's night—my own! This horse sinks into my night and rises out of it: like a deep-sea diver. He brings back sentences. Can't you tell that the least of his sentences is more wonderful than any poem? I'd give my complete works for just one of those little phrases in which I hear myself—the way you hear the ocean in a seashell. Foolishness? What do you expect, my darling? I'm discovering a world. I'm changing my skin. I'm tracking the unknown.

EURYDICE: And now you'll quote the famous sentence again.

ORPHEUS (seriously): Yes. (He returns to the horse and recites.) *Madame Eurydice reviendra des Enfers.*

EURYDICE: It doesn't mean a thing, your sentence.

ORPHEUS: Yes, it does. Put it up to your ear. Listen to the mystery: *Eurydice reviendra,* that just means Eurydice will return—but *Madame* Eurydice! *Madame Eurydice reviendra—* that *reviendra,* that future tense! And the end: *des Enfers—* from the underworld. You should be happy I'm talking about you!

EURYDICE: You're not talking . . . (Pointing to the horse) it's him.

ORPHEUS: Not him, not me, no one. Who knows? Who's talking? We bump into each other in the dark; we're up to our necks in the supernatural. We're playing hide-and-seek with the gods. We know nothing, nothing, nothing. *Madame Eurydice reviendra des Enfers—*that's not a sentence, it's a poem, a dream poem, a flower from the other side of death.

Les Chevaliers de la Table Ronde (The Knights of the Round Table, *first performed October 14, 1937*)

For this drama, in which I seem to break with a sort of Hellenomania, it would be absurd to depend on the original fable with any exactitude, the source of a work of this order being precisely imprecision, and exactitude no longer finding a place in it except in the secret forms of number, balance, weights and measures, spells, charms, etc. . . . .

It seems to me more interesting to say how this work was born. I am not fishing for compliments when I say that I do not hold myself accountable. Inspiration does not necessarily come down from some heaven. To explain inspiration, we must sift the human darkness, and doubtless nothing flattering would result. The poet's role is a humble one. He is at the orders of his night.

In 1934 I was ill. One morning I awakened, unaccustomed to sleeping, and I watched this drama unfold from beginning to end, though plot, period, and characters were quite unfamiliar to me. I should add that I found them unprepossessing.

It was three years later, when Markevitch affectionately forced my hand, that I managed to draw the work out of the limbo in which I had been keeping it, the way we sometimes prolong our dreams when we are ill, floundering between dawn and daylight, inventing an intermediary world which protects us from the shock of reality.

Once the play was written, I did some research, discovered my mistakes as a fabulist, and decided to stand by them.

Except for the talking flower, which came from a newspaper item (a plant in Florida emitted waves like those of a radio station), the entire work was given to me, I repeat, by myself. We need not regard this gift as any particular privilege.

What strikes me, looking at *Les Chevaliers* from outside, is the chief character, the invisible Ginifer, the young demon who is Merlin's servant.

This character appears only in the form of those characters in whom the wizard's power incarnates him; sometimes they are the characters themselves (Gawain, the Queen, Galahad), sometimes phantoms. We shall see that if the phantoms risk doing harm, they can also assume charms all the more dangerous for affording only a phantom joy. This is the case of Arthur, bewitched by the false Gawain and bored by the real one. But life is not a dream, as the play proves, unfortunately, and once the castle is disenchanted—I was going to write *disintoxicated* —it will be less frivolous for some, more solid for others, and in any case uninhabitable for those who do not regard Earth as an Eden.

From *Les Chevaliers de la Table Ronde*, Act III:

ALL: The Grail! The Grail! I see it . . . do you? There it is, there, there!

GALAHAD: Do you see it, Arthur?

ARTHUR (in ecstasy): I see it.

GALAHAD: What shape is it?

ARTHUR (still ecstatic): No special shape . . . you can't describe it . . .

GALAHAD: Do you see it, Blandine?

BLANDINE (in ecstasy): I see it.

GALAHAD: What color is it?

BLANDINE: Every color . . . you can't tell what color it is . . . Oh!

GALAHAD: Segramor, Gawain, do you see it?

SEGRAMOR AND GAWAIN (together): I see it.

GALAHAD: What does it smell like? Where is it?

GAWAIN: Lovely!

SEGRAMOR: It glows . . . It's nowhere . . . it's everywhere. It keeps moving.

GALAHAD: It is within you. You see it once you are in harmony with yourself. Now that you all see it, my task is done.

ARTHUR: Galahad, why do you ask us to explain the Grail? Galahad, is it not you who should be explaining it to us?

GALAHAD: I cannot see it.

ARTHUR: You!

GALAHAD: I shall never see it. I am the one who makes it visible to others.

Les Parents Terribles (first performed November 14, 1938)

I remember the days when "Boulevard Theatre" reigned supreme. No one ever heard of a director. The "realism" of Lucien Guitry, of Réjane, was the realism of the stage, as emphatic as the excesses of the sacred monsters of the drama: Sarah Bernhardt, Mounet-Sully, de Max. In those days the theatre reached me by way of programs, titles, posters, my mother's departures in a red velvet dress. I imagined a theatre, and that imaginary theatre influenced me.

At Montargis, I tried to write a play which, instead of serving as a pretext for a director, would serve as a pretext for great actors. I have always preferred, for my plays, sets which *act*: a door through which disaster could enter and exit; a chair on which fate could sit down. I have always loathed the superfluous, and avoided it in all its forms. What I had to do, now, was write a modern, naked play—to give actors and audience no chance to catch their breath. I eliminated telephone, letters, servants, cigarettes, fake windows, even the family names, which limit the characters and always ring false. The result was a vaudeville plot, a melodrama, character types which, though each was consistent, contradicted each other. A series of scenes —each one, in fact, a complete action—in which personalities and peripeties are, moment by moment, *in extremis*.

A popular theatre—one worthy of a public without preconceptions—would be a theatre of this order, the exposure of works incapable of living without decorative subterfuges.

*

None of my plays had so much difficulty reaching the boards. It was written for Jouvet. Jouvet imagined it would be a *succès d'estime* and make no money. We must not blame him for lack of foresight; his estimation proves he understood my enterprise better than the nearsighted fools who take it for a boulevard play.

The success this play always enjoys derives from one fact: each of its tenants believes he recognizes those on the other floors. It was unforeseeable. And the laughter it provoked amazed me, for I read it as a tragedy; I was as unconscious of its humor as families that argue are aware of their disputes. For that, one must observe this family through the keyhole. Which happens.

La Machine à Écrire (The Typewriter, *first performed April 29, 1941*)

The play is a disaster. At first, when I thought I was ready to write it, another inspiration seized me and dictated instead *La Fin du Potomak*. I tried to get back to it, but I was taking dictation badly. After the first act I listened only to myself. Once the play was done, I sat down and rewrote the whole thing. Then I took the advice of the actress-manager for whom I had written the play, and spoiled the end, which I now bitterly regret. This play serves me as an example. I shall never be my own master. It is my nature to obey. As for these lines I am writing now, a week ago I had no idea I should have to write them.

Of all the problems which entangle us, the problem of fate and free will is the most obscure. What? the thing is written in advance and we can write it. We can change its ending. The truth is different. Time does not exist: it is our seam, the fold in our fabric. What we call the consecutive is, in fact, simultaneous. Time spins it out for us. Our work is already done—it nonetheless remains for us to discover it. It is this passive participation which astonishes. And with reason. It leaves the public incredulous. I decide, and I do not decide. I obey, and I direct. This is a great mystery. *La Machine à Écrire* was not a bad play to begin with. The fluid evaporated from me. I was free. But I am no longer free to efface the stain I have made. It is there.

L'Aigle à deux Têtes (The Eagle Has Two Heads, *first performed in November, 1946*)

Commissions suit me. They set limits. Jean Marais dared me to write a play in which he would not speak in the first act, would weep for joy in the second, and in the last would fall backwards down a flight of stairs.

*

For some time I had been seeking the causes of a certain degeneration of the drama, inquiring into the prevalence of a theatre of words and production over an active theatre. I attributed these causes to the cinema, which, on the one hand, forces us to see our heroes interpreted by young actors and, on the other, accustoms these young actors to speak in low voices and to move as little as possible. As a result, the very basis of theatrical convention is dissolved—the Sacred Monsters have vanished, who by their tics and their timbres, their listing façades and indefatigable lungs, created the high relief indispensable to the proscenium and the footlights, to a stage which devours almost everything. These aged Hippolytes, these ancient Hermiones went out of fashion, alas; and without caryatids to carry them, the great roles disappeared too. What replaced them, without our even realizing it, was the word for the word's sake, the *production*. Words and production then assumed a significance of which the Bernhardts, the Réjanes, the Mounet-Sullys, and the Lucien Guitrys had no notion. On the boards where these ancestral beasts had once prowled, the production . . . produced itself, and the sets spoke no louder than these extinguished voices.

*

I had decided (something in me, to be precise, had decided) to create a work in which psychology would play no part, or would be replaced by a heroic, a heraldic psychology. In other words, the psychology of my heroes would bear no more relation to a genuine psychology than the lions and unicorns of a tapestry to real animals. Their behavior (the lion laughing, the unicorn bearing an oriflamme) would belong to the theatre as these fabulous beasts belong to escutcheons. To psychologists, such a work would necessarily be invisible, illegible. To make it visible, I required sets, costumes, Edwige Feuillère, Jean Marais. I required them so that the stamens and sepals of the work would function and so that the vehicles—I mean, the spectators—would carry my pollen.

*

Everyone has heard of the amazing death of Ludwig II of Bavaria, the riddle it poses and the countless texts which attempt to solve it. I decided, rereading some of these, that it would be interesting, and favorable to a grand theatrical *gestus*, to invent a historical occurrence of this nature and then to write a play to discover its secret.

These books about the King's death had steeped me once again in the atmosphere of that family which, being unable to create a masterpiece, chose to *be* one, even the kind that ended in disaster, appropriately enough.

I had to invent plot, setting, characters, and heroes capable of putting the public on the wrong scent and at the same time of flattering that craving to *recognize* which is the form of knowledge the public prefers, doubtless because it demands the least effort.

Remy de Gourmont's fine study in his *Portraits littéraires* suggested the style of my queen. She would have the naïve pride, the grace, fire, courage, elegance, the sense of destiny of the Empress Elizabeth of Austria. I even borrowed one or two remarks attributed to her.

The real disaster of these princes, superior as they are to their role, is that they are more *ideas* than they are *beings*. Moreover, it is not rare for another idea to kill them. I therefore decided to dramatize two colliding ideas and their obligation to *become flesh*. A queen of anarchist inclinations, an anarchist of royalist tendencies—if the crime were postponed, if they were to speak to each other, if there were no stabbing on the gangway at Lake Geneva: our queen would soon become a woman; our anarchist, once again a man. They betray their causes to *become* one. They form a constellation, or, better still, a meteor which blazes a second and disappears.

*

It must be understood that art does not exist as art, as detached, free, rid of the creator, but that it exists only if it prolongs a cry, a laugh, or a groan. That is why certain canvases in a museum make signs to us and live with an anguish all their own, while others are dead, exhibiting merely the embalmed corpses of Egypt.

Bacchus (*first performed December 20, 1951*)

When I finished this play, I anticipated that something would happen, but I did not guess what it would be. I had even said, laughing, to Mme Weisweiller, in whose house I was working: "Be sure your boat is armed—we'll have to beat a retreat."

I should have taken my cue from an apparently comical event which reveals the medieval style of our age.

Father Christmas was burned in effigy in the main square of Dijon. The Church accused him of being a dangerous and German custom, likely to lead children into error. If the poor children believe this fable, they will have to be burned alive as heretics.

What I did foresee was an imperialist attack against *Bacchus*, but it was impossible for me to anticipate the direction from which it would come, from what window the sniper would fire, since my play offered a great many targets.

The sniper, unexpectedly enough, was François Mauriac, an old friend. We had tempered our first weapons together, and it would have seemed unthinkable to me that he might turn one of his against me.

For a long time I had wanted to write this *Bacchus* of mine. It came to me as a play, a film, a book—I returned to the play, for the theatre suited the story best. I had heard it from Ramuz. The custom still survives, in the harvest season, around Vevey.

This custom dates from the Sumerian civilization, about 3,000 B.C.:

Documents describe the ceremonies performed on the occasion of the dedication of the temple of the god Ningirsu. The rejoicing populace indulged in revels originating in an ancient agrarian cult. For seven days a state of general license prevailed—civil laws as well as

moral ones were suspended. No authority was mani-
fested. A slave replaced the king, enjoyed the royal
harem, was served at the king's table. Once the festival
was over, the slave was sacrificed to the gods, who would
forgive the city its sins and confer abundance upon it.
On the temple steps, mystery plays were performed
which were transmitted to Babylon and throughout
Mesopotamian history. Berosus attended such a play in
the third century. Rome itself was to see the celebration
of these strange festivals which date back to the earliest
times and which Christianity preserves in its carnival
season.

—J. Perenne, *Civilisation antique*

*

My first version described a dictatorship in which a village
idiot became a monster. I soon abandoned this—it was too
crude, and besides, it resisted me. I tackled the theme of the
confusion of the young surrounded by dogmas, sects, obstacles.
In the conflict of servitudes and sentiments, the young struggle
for their freedom, their chaotic freedom which ricochets among
the obstacles raised against it until it is crushed by them. The
young can prevail only by cunning or by taking power for themselves. They lack the skill which cunning requires. They drive
straight on—and this clumsy straightness, this audacity, this
exaltation of heart and senses is a disservice to a society in
which cunning is rewarded, in which secrets intersect, com-
mingle, unite.

*

Sartre and I discovered that both our new plays took place in
sixteenth-century Germany when it was too late: he had just
finished *Le Diable et le Bon Dieu* in Saint-Tropez, and I had
written my first act in Cap-Ferrat. We decided to meet in
Antibes. Our plots had nothing in common. I could continue

my work. Since our documentation was related, Sartre suggested books, which I added to those that were helping me to know Luther. Others reached me from other sources.

The problem was to take my notes, put my papers in a drawer, forget about them, and to relive the essentials in the mouths of my characters. It is these old sentences presented from a new angle which seem subversive. They have been attributed to me, and it is fair to say that they coincide with what was happening in 1952. But the coincidences became apparent to me only long afterwards. Some of them I discovered only because of laughter or applause during the performance.

Once the play was finished, I gave it to Jean Vilar. A conflict of dates made our collaboration impossible; I took *Bacchus* to Barrault. In a month I had worked out the direction, the set, the costumes. The actors of the Marigny troupe, overwhelmed with work because of their repertory system, supposed my text would be easy to learn. They soon discovered that the tongue-twister style I used to keep the phrases from running together obliged them to respect every syllable. Otherwise, the fabric would unravel. The actors took a liking to these grammatical calisthenics. Barrault was a Cardinal of tremendous presence: one heard a Prelate out of *La Chartreuse de Parme*; one saw a young Cardinal out of Raphael.

We performed (1) for an audience of professionals, whose reaction was very favorable; (2) for a fashionable audience, whose reaction can be imagined; (3) for the public and the critics. Our triumph was the kind in which personalities lost their separateness, in which the public left its individualism in the coatroom, caught up in a collective hypnosis our critics detested. Our critics assumed an individuality in the opposite direction and cut themselves off, in a spirit of contradiction. As we might have expected. But invisibility demanded more than that, to achieve its ends. On opening night, François Mauriac, impelled by some blinding, deafening force, believed he saw

and heard a work which was not mine, took offense, and left
the theatre in a spectacular fashion during the curtain calls for
the actors and myself. The following Sunday, while I was resting in the country, I guessed that Mauriac would write an
article and I amused myself by writing an "answer" to it.

The next day the article appeared. An "open letter"—a
cowardly aria testifying to a total incomprehension of the world
I live in. The indictment of a fable that had nothing to do with
mine, or with me.

A man who is attacked in the foremost newspaper in France
must defend himself, even if he is reluctant to do so. I touched
up my original reply and published it under the title "*Je
t'accuse*" in *France-Soir*. I could not blame Mauriac for his
atavisms, for his Bordeaux origin. As a matter of fact, he has
remained one of those children who want to mingle with the
grownups. You know the kind—you can find them in any hotel.
No matter how often they're told, "It's late, go upstairs to bed
now," they refuse to obey, and get in everyone's hair. (Mauriac
once told me as much himself: "I'm an old child disguised as an
Academician.")

So I merely blamed him for having made up his mind before
he came to the theatre, for usurping the prerogatives of a priest,
for sitting at God's right hand.

*It is a municipal law you cite, nor do you know which is the
universal one.*

*God is not your colleague, nor your fellow-citizen, nor your
companion; if He is in any fashion communicated unto you, it
is not in order to reduce Himself to your littleness, nor to give
His power into your hands.*—Montaigne.

*

Why do you write plays, the novelist asks me. Why do you
write novels, the playwright asks me. Why do you make films,
the poet asks me. Why do you draw, the critic asks me. Why do

you write, the artist asks me. Yes, why, I ask myself. Doubtless, so that my seed will be sown where it may. I know little enough of the spirit that is in me, but it is not a tender one. It cares nothing for sickness, knows nothing of fatigue. It profits by my talents. It seeks to give its form to the trumpets. It compels me from all sides. It is not inspiration, it is expiration—that is the word. For this spirit, this breath, comes from a zone in man where man cannot descend, were Virgil himself to lead him, for even Virgil did not venture there.

*

Three Friends

Christian Bérard

"Thank you, Lord, for lending me Madame my mother." These were the words Saint Louis spoke at the deathbed of Blanche of Castille. I think of them each time one of the passengers on my voyage falls overboard. Many have fallen and I remain on deck, watching the indifferent waves devour them.

The loss of Christian Bérard leaves me sick at heart, suffering, in the void he creates, from the soul's *mal-de-mer*.

He lived his times with an intensity so rapt, a disorder so apparent—chaos was the meshing of his gears—that we supposed, yet again, that broad Olympian face to be immortal.

It is the same trick each time, and each time it works. Our absurd and paralyzing stupor is doubtless the result of habit—the habit of not admitting that death is our natural condition, the habit of regarding life as a permanent state.

So there was Bérard finishing his work on the décor for *Les Fourberies de Scapin* at the Marigny Theatre. Standing between the first rows, his dog's leash round one wrist, he revised the costumes, watched the set go up. Like smoke, like an alley cat, like a specter of all the cities where we spent our vacations, this set, piece by piece, *takes the stage:* here are the stairways and their iron railing, here the urinal and its lantern, here the sky and the pearl-gray sea, here the houses hanging from poles like the laundry in Marseilles, in Sicily, here the dome of the little church, here . . . and Bérard falls. Jouvet, Barrault in costume (a lunar Scapin), and the stagehands carry him on their shoulders between the empty rows: it is the cortege of a Shakespeare hero, and the cortege will continue to Père-Lachaise, where with a shock of terror and delight we saw him buried next to the grave of Raymond Radiguet.

*

Jouvet had telephoned the news at five in the morning. When I reached the Rue Casimir-Delavigne and walked into the courtyard, a flashbulb exploded—the photographers were already there. A reporter stood in my way, insisting: "Say something about Bérard," and when I protested, "I'm half dead—let me alone," he exclaimed, "That's a good headline, I'll use that." The concierge's little girl was hopping on one foot in the hall, chanting, "Monsieur Bérard is dead, Monsieur Bérard is dead!" I went up the six flights. A few close friends greeted me in the vestibule. Bérard was in his bedroom, in the tiny closet that served as a bedroom: the walls are red and covered with newspaper clippings, photographs, the thousand trifles he pulled out of his pockets. Bérard was lying under shapeless blankets, in the posture and overcoat of a man persecuted by fatigue who has fallen asleep in a heap without the strength to undress. We could not touch the body until the medical examiner arrived.

People usually said that Bérard's eyes were what made his face beautiful. Now his eyes were closed. A purplish reflection from the walls glowed on his cheeks and the burning bush of his beard. His broad face smiled—the face of Ingres's *Jupiter*, of a Neptune, astonishing in its majesty. The tumult, the cyclone of gestures and laughter which accompanied his appearance gave way to the serenity of the sleepers in his early pictures. Pictures in which he painted sleep while his colleagues painted dreams, huge effigies mixed with sand and wax, human dikes on the brink of the dream tide, sentries of silence.

How often we had seen Bérard lying fully dressed like this and forced him to get up and come with us, still smeared with sleep, charcoal, and chalk. It was out of this deep sleep that Jouvet wrenched him, every morning, to immerse him once again in his labors: Bérard would rub his face with a towel soaked in eau de Cologne and amble to the theatre.

Staring now at this false sleeper, this marvelous machine that had broken down, I remembered circumstances I had never noticed, occasions disguised by habit, episodes that only a shock can loosen from the tree, making them fall at our feet.

For instance, I can see Bérard at Milly, slaving away, in the room where I was writing my film *Orphée*, on costumes for the character of Death. These were his last fashion studies, for, as he said, "Death should be the most elegant woman in the world, for she is concerned only with herself."

That perpetual search for truth which seems mad because everyone is content with a vague madness and treats as madmen those who approach the truth—one need live only a few minutes with Picasso to make contact with it. Bérard merely followed in its wake. He lacked that divine ferocity which falters, rights itself, and proceeds only by accidents. Bérard's heart went out to the accidental, and from it he drew a charm, a ceremonial, a cortege. Picasso proceeds only by accidents and delivers them to the public without sweeping up—in all the intensity of impact.

Yet it is true that these two men, different from each other as they are, have each achieved on the stage (*Parade, Mercure, La Machine Infernale*) certain cries in which song is not yet formed, in which artifice and reverent fraud play no part.

*

I am writing these lines in my country house, in Milly. A very mild February deceives birds and trees alike: the former sing, the latter sprout. A few months ago Christian Bérard lived here, preparing my film *Orphée*. All that remains of this long visit is some fifty drawings, by which we must improvise, at all costs, a performance under his inspiration.

We are "in places full of his power." His red beard still blazes here, for it is true that Bérard blazed, that he loved the fire which ravages and revives—to the point of abandoning a house which fell still, which no longer blazed. It was not drama that he loved, sought, provoked, but an atmosphere of intensity, without which he lost interest and vanished in a cloud. In an atmosphere of intensity he breathed, moved, strolled from room to room, draped in a bathroom full of stains, paint, and holes. He could not paint without involving his own person, without a kind of struggle during which he mopped his face with the same rag with which he rubbed his canvas, without erasing and shading and blowing his nose on his bathrobe, in short without contracting, between his body and his work, a terrifying mythological marriage. Even as Bérard passed into his work, so his work passed into him. This exchange of sweat and ink left the floor strewn with all the superfluities with which decorative painters overtax their undertakings. All that remained intact was a beauty almost impoverished, stripped of its finery. Bérard preserved only what served, which is to say, the total absence of stupidity which seems to me the privilege of the beautiful.

*

André Gide

> "In the final accounting, our different figures manage to produce the same sum."

In 1918 I had just published *Le Coq et l'Arlequin*. Gide took umbrage: the young, he feared, would forsake his enterprise and he would lose his constituents. He summoned me like a school-boy to the principal's office and read me an open letter he planned to send me, or rather to publish.

I have been sent a good many open letters. In Gide's I figured as a squirrel, and Gide as a bear at the foot of the tree. I skipped certain steps, and from branch to branch. In short, I was reprimanded, and the reprimand was to be given in public. I told Gide I intended to reply to the letter—openly as well. He sniffed, nodded, and said that nothing was more valuable, more instructive, than such exchanges.

Naturally, Jacques Rivière refused to print my answer in the *Nouvelle Revue Française*, where Gide had published his letter. It was a harsh one, I admit; in it, I pointed out that Gide's windows in the Villa Montmorency did not look straight across, but offered instead a view of the back side . . . Time passed. Gide kept aloof. He knew how to forget injuries, especially those caused by his own pen. One day he telephoned and asked me to take care of (let's call him) Olivier. This disciple, Gide said, *was bored with his library*. Would I initiate him into the Cubist painters, the new music, the circus I kept praising for its huge band, its tumblers, its clowns.

I complied, reluctantly: I knew Gide and his almost feminine jealousy. As a matter of fact, young Olivier delighted in tor-menting Gide, filling his ears with my praises, declaring he spent every minute of the day with me and had learned *Le Potomak* by heart. Gide told me all this only in 1949, just before I left for Egypt, and admitted that he had wanted to kill me. This was the complication which produced the various hostilities in his *Journal*. At least, it was what he attributed them to.

*

I don't like writing letters, and I write very short ones. I have noticed that no one reads letters: when you come across an old letter and reread it, you find that you had read what you were looking for in it, and that the rest is new. Doubtless, it was the brevity of my letters that led Gide to write me short ones, but his charming, corkscrew hand and his tinted envelopes delighted me: I knew the sentences would not be indifferent.

All my life I have received exquisite letters from Gide which quite failed to *correspond* to all his obsessive "open" communications, his public letters, notes, and annotations. His affection, I venture to say, was expressed better in his letters than by his presence. Perhaps this was the consequence of his Protestantism —he preferred encoding to encountering.

*

Gide never admitted that I had had the devil's own time convincing him to read Proust, whom he regarded as a society author. No doubt he resented the fact that I had managed to convince him, once Proust filled the *Nouvelle Revue Française* with his marvelous flyspecks.

On the day of Proust's death, Gide whispered to me *chez* Gallimard: "I'll never have more than a bust here."

*

I am very fond of Paul Valéry, but he belongs to a race which is not mine. He is, no doubt about it, the only alchemist who succeeds in turning lead to gold. For which Gide admired . . . and resented him.

Valéry confessed that for him the poem was a matter of artisanry, not inspiration. But the problem is more serious, for inspiration is merely expiration: things do not come from outside but from inside, and neither Gide nor Valéry had the true courage to excavate themselves. Theirs is, in all their enterprises, a kind of higher trifling, a game which accounts both for their success and for the resistance to it.

By their method of total consciousness, playing with the unconscious, Gide and Valéry stand together. But Valéry, even when he plays, reaches or at least touches more secret regions, and this was why Gide resented him and failed to see the similarity of their undertaking.

*

Gide met General de Gaulle at a dinner in Algiers. He did not open his mouth once during the dinner, but as he left the table he approached the General and said, "Mon Général, I should like to know when you first felt tempted to disobey." He regarded disobedience as a schoolboy prank and not as the sign of all greatness.

*

He was gay, brisk, nimble, and delighted in all the trifles which make dialogue possible. He adored language, and pronounced his words with obsessive care, sucking and scouring the consonants, seeming to rip the vowels out of some remote matrix. I remember, for instance, how he chose to tell me that he, too, was writing an Oedipus; separating the syllables with tremendous care, he announced: "There seems to be a veritable Oedipemic."

*

What I like best in Gide's oeuvre is what the Gideans always care least about: to my mind, La Porte Etroite and Robert are closer to his person than the works in which he exploits immorality. When I asked Jean Genet why he refused to meet Gide, he answered, "His immorality seems very suspect to me. Either you are a judge or you are a prisoner—I don't like judges who lean lovingly toward their prisoners."

*

Colette

> *"She is unique. She always was.*
> *She always will be."*

Everything is monstrous in art, and Madame Colette is no exception to this rule. The monsters must have tamers. Without tamers, they would devour us. Maurice Goudeket has always been the tamer of that delicious monster Colette.

A masterpiece cannot help being a catastrophe in a world where smug mediocrity circulates freely. Genius? A sublime vice of the soul's senses, a moral depravity analogous to the sensual kind. What are Great Works, I ask you, if not the *enfants terribles* of a marriage between sense and the senses?

At first, all this seems absurd with regard to Madame Colette, whose singularity is never paraded: the wolf appears under a peasant kerchief. But we shall never wash Madame Colette clean enough of that false bonhomie in which her legend tricks her out. We can never praise Maurice Goudeket enough for having solved this great enigma: when God tires of writing His daily prose, suddenly it contracts, crystallizes, becomes a poem. And, in all this terrestrial prose, are not geniuses the poems of God? Alien to the intellectualism of our age, Madame Colette is nothing if not a monster, and if this monster frightens no one, it is because Maurice Goudeket has seen to it that she does not.

Let us hail Maurice, then, not without having hailed, too, the other Colette, Colette *fille*, whom the maternal monster intimidated to the point where she could not write her letters; and since the mother failed to recognize this timidity in her daughter, I would watch mother and daughter call to each other, grope for each other: a loving game of blindman's buff or hide-and-seek.

*

A tiny wooden bridge served as her desk. Under this bridge, Colette seemed to flow motionlessly, like certain rivers. The current consisted of sheets, shawls, and the surge of legs she could never decide where to stow to keep them from hurting less. Day in, day out, whereas I had once watched the combative bust of the Countess de Noailles struggling with death, springing out of her bedclothes to vanquish it, I saw Madame Colette flow gently toward hers under that tiny bridge on which was piled, as on the Rialto or the Ponte Vecchio, a lovely chaos of fruit, flowers, bouquets of pens, and mountains of papers through which she leafed, vainly seeking something she wanted to show us, calling Maurice to help her, shuffling the blue pages under the blue lamp which made the ghosts of the Palais-Royal say to each other: "Vanish. Colette is at work."

*

Between the cloud of dust that was her hair and the foulard knotted round her neck, glowing in that triangular face with its pointed nose and circumflex mouth, Colette's eyes: the eyes of a lioness in captivity, a spectator of her own spectacle, observing her observers, paws crossed one over the other, motionless, with sovereign disdain.

Madame Colette reserved this gaze of a pensive carnivore for those who passed in front of her cage, a cage her sick leg had erected around her; and since these persons, once their curiosity had been satisfied, never knew what to say, the roles were reversed, and it was the lioness who tossed them the tidbit of a few words, until the keeper Maurice appeared and directed them to the exit. Moreover, Maurice gradually reduced this procession—for Colette could not say no, and accepted the complicity of the little offerings (flowers or chocolate) which such visits invariably included. In my apartment it is the Siamese cats that receive offerings and caresses. But since my neighbor no longer had animals around her—doubtless, according to Nietzsche's principle that one keeps either a disease or a dog, both having to be cared for and taken out—it was more difficult, if one wanted to see Colette at close range, to seduce her housekeeper Pauline.

I have occasionally witnessed these absurd visits, the house rules having been broken in Maurice's absence. Nothing could have been more comical than that amiable purring of Colette's in contrast to the furious hand on the knob of her cane and, in my direction, a shipwrecked glance pleading for help.

Once I was sent for—my collaboration was needed. A film on Colette was being shot, and I was requested to "make conversation." Yet no sooner had the solemn word "Camera!" been uttered than Colette, like animals that freeze as soon as you want them to be . . . animated, turned to a statue, retreated into herself, and to get a single word out of her I had to drag her at the end of a rope, using all my strength. Tête-à-tête, everything changed. The eyes lit up. The curves became points. A strange machine began to hum. I can never emphasize this point enough: Madame Colette's greatness proceeds from the fact that an incapacity to separate good from evil preserved in her a state of innocence which it would be unworthy to confuse with that conventional, artificial, deliberate "purity" that bears no relation to the alarming purity of nature itself.

I have seen Madame Colette in pain, yet refusing aspirin as if it were the devil's own pill, insisting that there occur within her body, unaided, those mysterious amalgamations and dosages of herbs and "simples" which the synthetic reconstitutions of science imitate only superficially and without possessing their virtues . . . The peasant in her realized that whatever appears mad in nature has its own secret sense, and that to correct the most insignificant number produces deadly errors in the sum. And do not suppose that she bore any resemblance to the kindly old saint people tried to turn her into. It would be an insult to her legend to think of Madame Colette as mealy-mouthed. The velvet paw soon showed its claws, and each swipe left its mark, which generally appeared on those who dared attack persons her heart respected.

The cult of friendship made her ferocious. For instance, if her eyes happened to fall on some insult written about me, she pulled back as though at the approach of a foul-smelling beast, wrinkled her brow, flared her nostrils, pursed her lips, and the bullets of her splendid eyes riddled the void where the cowards were hiding. Rolling her *r*'s, she would murmur, "*Quelle horreur . . . mais quelle horreur!*" And, shaking her mane, she excommunicated the offending article with a flick of her freckled wrist.

*

At Père-Lachaise, what occurred on August 7, 1954, was not a matter for gravediggers but for gardeners, for the passage from one realm to another, for the collaboration of earth and flesh.

After Radiguet died, Romain Rolland wrote me: "How can one let go of life, after having thrust such a talon into it?" Yet it was not a talon that Madame Colette thrust into life. Rather, she pressed life to herself like a full-blown bouquet of roses, whose petals, suddenly, began to fall . . .

La Corrida of May 1

To be or not to be . . . Flamenco, that is the Spanish question. Not singing, not dancing, Flamenco is a style, a way of life. Flamenco rhythm, in all its forms, is uneven, variable, free. This characteristic is of immense significance. The use of the plumb line, the symmetrical rhythm adopted to its cost by our age, always provokes platitude and death. The gypsies observe an instinctive cult of the uneven, to the point where a woman will wear only one sleeve, a man roll up one trouser leg. This wisdom suffused with a limping rhythm is one of the secrets of their incredible vitality. It corresponds to that of the great poets, Góngora and Lorca among others.

The source of the gypsy river must have been in India; perhaps a meander flowed, as their name suggests, through Egypt. Gypsy music does not derive from a rhythm, but from a syntax. That is why a gypsy may be more or less inspired but cannot be mediocre. He speaks a language.

I came into contact with the gypsies through Alberto Puig (pronounced *Pooch*). He is the uncle of this mysterious people who seem to spit flowers of flame and to stamp on them to put them out. In Granada, Lorca's gypsies live in caves dug in the mountainside. Once they camped in the Alhambra, where Washington Irving rented them rooms. The amazing murmur which rises from Granada by night consists of their clapping hands, and of the long sobs they tear from their throats with the gestures and grimaces of the Apostles around the Holy Sepulchre.

*

People express themselves in Spain with incredible freedom. Censorship begins with the written word—a terrible censorship that stunts the growth, the realization of a whole community of writers and thinkers. Moreover, Spain is a nation of great writers without an audience. She scorns, one of her poets says, what she does not know. He speaks of Castille, but his words apply to all of Spain.

The juices of this dark stew simmer under a lid. From century to century the lid pops off, the pot boils over, and so terrible are these explosions that Spain frightens herself. The Spanish are all incendiaries. Today Spain is calm because the Spanish people are afraid of burning down their own house. But a Spanish calm is merely a respite between two fires.

*

Spain is much more superstitious than religious. Only the Madonna of one's own parish is acknowledged; the others are insulted. Loving insults, which help us understand the way Picasso lovingly and magnificently insults the human face. The Spaniard fears his clergy and is always on the verge of setting fire to the churches. But today, he thinks, like Henri IV, that Spain is well worth a Mass. He chooses the lesser of two evils. That, at least, is the conclusion I draw from remarks I hear exchanged in the street without fear and without repression.

*

The Spanish use an untranslatable word to express the fact that a thing, a person, an action, a style is the contrary of elegant. This word is *curci*. I know of no analogous term in French. From Perpignan to Gibraltar, one is either *curci* or Flamenco. Perhaps Don Juan de Marana deserved the epitaph which embellishes his tomb in Seville: *Aquí yace el peor hombre que fué en el mundo* [Here lies the worst man who ever lived]. Perhaps—but he surely was not *curci*, he surely was Flamenco. The same is true of Don Juan Tenorio, whose sacrileges delight the Spanish because there is nothing *curci* about them, because his audacity remains Flamenco to the very end . . .

*

> "The corrida and the Flamenco
> are a language spoken with
> the body."

On May 1, 1954, the last day of the Feria of Seville, during which no bull had been dedicated, Dámaso Gómez paid me the homage of his. I learned the next day that Domingo Ortega had planned, the day before, to dedicate one of his bulls to me, but had not done so because he judged the animal unworthy. That is the Spanish style. Moreover, Gómez was paying homage not to a distinguished foreigner but to a poet, instinctively entrusting to a poet's hands, as well as his *montera*, his lucky or unlucky star. A dread responsibility, which I had not experienced when two other bulls were dedicated to me in Barcelona, and which was to flood me with unaccustomed emotion.

My point of view could not be that of an *aficionado*, but only that of an amateur who seeks the continuity of drama regardless of school and despite the decadence deplored by the specialists.

My point of view is therefore one which forgets the rules and the aristocratic anarchy by which they are transformed and survive, one which envisages only the tragedy, i.e., the role of death. For, whatever happens, death remains the heroine of the tragedy of which the matador is the hero to whom she delegates an ambassador extraordinary—this animal sacrificed in advance whose mission is to negotiate their wedding (the strangest and most obscure nuptials in the world).

What then is this ambassador? A huge mass which suddenly looms up, always the same yet always different, his frontal weapons sometimes widespread, sometimes curving, deadly weapons of an energy inconceivable from a distance, amazing when one approaches even those stuffed heads that decorate the staircase of a Spanish inn. This dark surge of guts unattainable save by a keyhole the Spaniards call the eye of the needle, this male who asserts his privileges by a long paintbrush and the double sack of his testicles, this combat tank, moves on slender legs and the devil's own hoofs. Sometimes it seems that the ambassador's legs cannot support him: he skids, kneels. Then the crowd is indignant and insults the academy in which the naïve and somber diplomats are trained. Great beasts were sent against the beast fighters of old; modern fiancés receive ambassadors that are less massive, less capable of cunning.

*

As for the singularity of a *corrida*, is it not the consequence of the fact that its very principle is inconceivable? To force an animal to defend a lost cause with the excuse that it does not already know it is lost! The bull is raised to be a victim. Once he enters the arena, the light blinds him, and he wonders, rightly, where he is. Already the torero has shed his sumptuous chasuble, draping it over one of the plaza's shady balconies, but even stripped of this sacerdotal ornament he remains a flower, and our dreary fashions have not been able to deflower his suit (we saw the last white chasuble with scarlet roses, which belonged to Manolete, at the house of the famous *rejoneador*, the mayor of Jerez, Alvaro Domecq).

Then, from far away, men wave capes, at which the bull charges. Somehow these clowns manage to disappear, sometimes intriguing him by leaving a flutter of cape behind them, a proof of the human presence behind the barrier. It was not a dream then, the bull thinks, and turns away, and notices another distant cape fluttering. (The color of the cape has nothing to do with it. It is sufficient that the cape moves, and naïve of the British Society for the Prevention of Cruelty to Animals to ask that a green muleta be substituted for the red one. Moreover, the ring attendants in their red trousers perform their functions quite invisibly around the picador's gyrations.) The bull now pursues the second cape, while the third and fourth ones dupe him still better, for the adversary remains visible, but the recollection of the phantom curtains hurls the victim against an empty fabric behind which he supposes the man hidden as he was behind the boards. Woe to the matador who does not spirit himself out of the way fast enough; in Seville I saw Miguel Angel, kneeling, gored right in the mouth because of his overeagerness to defy fate. This time the animal is no longer deceived—he is offered a horse, a real horse. Here is fresh meat covered with old mattresses. Here is a patient Rosinante. Here is something to rip open. But the farce grows still more deadly: while the bull attacks the mattresses and crushes the innocent ribs, the picador thrusts into his shoulders nine centimeters of steel, a wound from which the bull's strength seeps away—flowers in a vase.

The farce of the banderillas will be less painful, but the gold and satin targets dancing in front of the beast vanish after having decorated him with a fierce bouquet of hollyhocks (unless the man fails to scale the barrier fast enough, for now the bull begins to suspect he is being hoaxed).

*

Body arched, chest forward, slippers dragging on the sand, muleta trailing over the sand, the torero defies the ambassador: "Ho, ho, toro!" The bull, motionless, fascinated, listens. He watches his strange provocateur, the hierophant who charms, who commands, who speaks and sometimes imagines he hears an answer (when this happened to Joselito, he took to his heels), employing all the liturgical movements of a priest. The matador begins the *faena*—a series of passes which shrink the circle of the arena around the pair to the size of a wedding ring. The poor dupe will recognize the deception, will submit to it like the victim demanded by the Greek oracle.

Why does this Iphigenia's fate revolt no one? Why is it that our nerves accept it, that an entire nation subscribes to it? This could never happen without a secret which transfigures a crime into a rite and transcends it, a secret which the *corrida* of May 1 whispered into my ear.

In reality there is neither a struggle nor a duel between man and beast—there is the creation of a couple isolated by the silence of a double hypnosis, unified by the institution of an ancestral sacrament over which no rule has any further dominion.

A woman unhappy in love once confided to me, "When I suffer too much, I visit my dentist"—the physical pain relieved her of a moral one. If the picador depletes the animal's energy too much, he increases instead of reduces the matador's risk. Pain can waken the beast from the hypnosis of love, as a shout from the public can waken the man. A mortal silence must precede this sacrifice, in which the hypnosis is the result of an extraordinary effort, I insist—the effort of the man to think as a beast, of the beast to think as a man, an effort which makes the couple blind and deaf to all that is not itself. The danger is not the murder of one of the partners in the dialogue—the danger is that this murder will break the thread which binds them to each other, will disrupt what death expects of them: either because the torero kills the ambassador, or because the ambassador kills the torero, or because they perish together as happened in Linares, or because the ambassador proves ineffectual, in which case a harmless *manso* takes him out of the ring to be executed offstage, or because the bull takes advantage of the pause during which the torero exchanges his artificial sword for a real one and imprudently drops the thread of the hypnosis.

Moreover, whether or not they marry, the White Lady grants mercy to none of her ambassadors extraordinary. The secret, once confided, costs them their life, and the Lady's equipage of mules covered with netting and plumes drags them off, once she has secured their silence. I think of that ear offered to the matador—a bloody ear filled with the roar of the crowd, like a shell filled with the roar of the sea; I think of that hairy conch brought to Manolete, which he kisses and which receives his last sigh.

Hatred is absent from a *corrida*. Here, only fear and love rule. Granted, a woman in love with a torero may become, without realizing it, jealous of the beast, i.e., of the White Lady, and may attribute this sentiment to a world of servitudes which turn the man from her, which render her power ineffectual. We must not forget that in this dream he incarnates, the torero is open to obsessions which cut him off from the world. I mentioned Joselito, who heard a bull speak to him, and I instance Dominguín, who over and over saw in the same place in the ring a man in black who stood up and called him a murderer, when he was obliged to perform in Linares after the drama there.

Let us note, further, the strange voluptuousness with which the couple, man and beast, coil round each other, touch and caress each other. As if the successive spirals of a long *faena* owe their perfect curves to the dark encirclement of a wave employed to polish a masterpiece.

For a moment, the nuptial phenomenon no longer functions. The bull respectfully stands aside, leaving alone on stage the great tragedian Belmonte. No part of his great black body now plays the slightest part—he draws away like a modest supernumerary whose role as confidant obliges him to be there, and who tries to be so as little as possible.

*

I shall abide by that spectator's ignorance which is like the innocence of the *espontaneo* who leaps blindly into the ring and faces the animal anywhere, even in the middle of the arena, on the very ground the torero yields to him. I have seen such a man holding his guts and his pants together with both hands. Let us jump down ideally into the ring. Let us approach the couple and see what is happening, regardless of schools, of fashions in bullfighting. Here nothing operates now but the law of insects, the law according to which the female couples with the male and devours him. But which is the male? Apparently two males confront each other, no erotic contact brings them together, yet certain toreros confess that the *estocada* provokes an ejaculation. The great mystery of the Fiesta lies precisely in this paradox of adversaries alternately feminized and resuming the prerogatives of their virility.

Here is how a little girl, in Seville, described the *corrida*: "They killed the cow because she wanted to eat the lady's dress." Just as this horned beast represented a cow for her, so the matador—his plait, his sequins, his satin, his pink stockings, his red train—represented a beautiful lady. Nor was she so wrong. For if the torero wears the brilliant colors of the male, and the bull the modest dress of the female, according to the laws of the animal kingdom, at the end of the act of love the male must change sex and, by his grace and his dancer's garb, become once more the predatory, murderous female. And the bull must reassume his male prerogatives, even as he is being stripped of them by the picadors, the banderillas. This is the great enigma. The beast is embellished with a bouquet of hollyhocks and a mantle of blood, as if it were parading its pride at the very moment it accepts death at the hands of a being so weak the bull could vanquish him by one last little charge. But no, the wedding continues according to an immemorial code, and since the ambassador has not killed, he must die by the hand of one who is in the true sense of the word the *bride/ groom*, a hand transformed by the White Lady's spell. The gesture of Luis Miguel Dominguín, leaning one elbow on the bull's forehead—is that not proof of the quasi-feminine domination the matador exercises?

The bull is Hercules vanquished by Omphale, and we can thereby understand the woman's costume Omphale inflicted upon Hercules, and why she reduced him to spinning, to arming himself with a distaff, whereas she put on his lion skin. Dominguín would never dare rest his elbow between those horns, were he not sure of his charm, of his utter domination. At that moment, the exchange of sexes is clear. It is the lovely lady, for whom the little girl took the matador, who rules over a great submissive beast.

*

Thus is performed a ceremony which, we must acknowledge, for all our repugnance to the literary, strives to imitate either by the horn or by the *estocada* that penetration whereby our

solitudes seek to delude themselves and to achieve, in an act
deflected from any procreative goal, a kind of fugitive victory—
a triumph over the number 2, the sign of death.

We are never done destroying ourselves once the mechanism
of thought begins to function. The testifying object tells us that
despite the acceptance of the sacrifice, the lovely insect, gilded
and feminized, plants its sting and experiences, with astonishment, at that very second, the spasm of love which releases an
arrow of sperm without even stretching the bow, or to be
plainer about it, without an erection taking place.

I account for all this quite inadequately on account of a sick
body. Only, in the ring, I understood it wonderfully, and I
knew I would cease to understand it upon awakening, as occurs
in the dizzying and immediate adventures into which nitrous
oxide plunges us and from which our awakening severs us—
leaving only the memory of a memory and the stupor of losing
the freedom of multiplicity.

I know, moreover, to what scandal I expose myself by describing in this way the final act of what is customarily taken for a
duel. No matter. This is what was given me to understand
during the period when I held Gómez's *montera* on my knees.
My body no longer existed. My mind became that couple and
penetrated certain secrets I should have been quite incapable of
divining without the phenomenon which transformed me into
the act.

*

Dámaso Gómez killed.

The spell was broken. He became once again a lunar prince,
dressed in lovely colors. A young man safe and sound, who
mounted the barrier and asked me to return his black cap. And
it was not his *montera* I tossed him from my bench, but a
boulder that was crushing my chest without my realizing it and
of which I became conscious only upon awakening.

The fact remains that I shall never forget May 1, 1954, and

the considerations which have proceeded from it. May the experts forgive me and find in my words no more than the inconsequential audacity of the *espontaneo,* who leaps into hell like an angel and then gives himself up to the police. I know that the penalty for trespassing upon the precincts of classicism is likely to be an immediate goring . . .

Perhaps my effronteries will afford some justification for the new bullfighting technique in which means have become ends, in which the premises entertained are too serious to resort to the strategies of sport. Surely the phenomenon which transforms a flower of Seville into a wasp of Toledo must derive from the secret arcana of nature . . .

Diary of an Unknown Man

> *"I know poetry is indispensable,
> but to what?"*

I have left Paris. Paris cultivates the method of Primitive tortures: its victim is smeared with honey, whereupon the ants devour him. Luckily, the ants also devour each other, which allows time to escape.

I have abandoned the roads covered with gray snow, and reach the garden of this Villa Santo Sospir whose walls I have tattooed like a living person; the place is a true haven, so effectively has the young woman who owns it palisaded the grounds with solitude.

The air is looking its best. Lemons drop into the grass. My regime begins—gradually the soul's skin clears.

*

Once the artist was surrounded by a conspiracy of silence. The modern artist is surrounded by a conspiracy of noise.

*

I am probably the most notorious poet in France and the most unknown. Sometimes this saddens me—fame intimidates, and I want to arouse only love. My sadness is the consequence of the mud which covers us, against which I rebel. I scoff at such sadness, realizing that my visibility, created out of absurd legends, protects my invisibility, envelops it in gleaming armor that is proof against any blows.

When people suppose they are wounding me, they are wounding a stranger I have no desire to know; when they thrust pins into a wax image of me, that image is such a poor representation their witchcraft mistakes its man and has no effect. Not that I boast of being unassailable, but a curious fate has found the means of safeguarding the vehicle I am.

*

The mail arrives: a bundle from Paris. A hundred envelopes drop out, postmarked from every country. My pessimism is limitless—I will have to read all these letters, answer them! I have never had a secretary. I write my own letters, open my own door. And people come in. Is it a fatal desire to please that impels me, or the dread of being forsaken? And the struggle begins, between the fear of wasting time and the guilt of letters which remain *on sufferance*, in the true sense of the word.

If I answer, there will be an answer to my answer. If I stop answering, there will be reproaches. If I avoid answering, there will be grievances.

After which I go to bed. Instead of escaping into reading, I escape into sleep, into dreams of an extreme complication, their unreality so realistic I sometimes confuse them with reality.

*

It is rarely admitted that one can be a poet and a painter, that one can change branches on the same tree. I just heard Charles Chaplin say on Radio Nice that he liked living in

France because a man like me could create a poem, a novel, a ballet, sets, costumes, plays, films, a chapel, without being asked to justify his activities, and without having to specialize . . . Free, that is the word. I am free (insofar as the night self that rules me warrants). For, alas, I long to be a composer, and what Beethoven in a letter to his publisher about *Fidelio* calls "the science of art" prevents me.

*

Art is born of the coitus between the male and female elements in all of us, elements more nearly balanced in the artist than in other men. Art is the child of a kind of incest, the lovemaking of self and self, a parthenogenesis. That is why marriage is so dangerous for an artist: it represents a pleonasm, the monster's effort toward normality. How many geniuses appear to be "poor specimens" because their creative instinct, satisfied in another domain, allows sexuality to function in the domain of the purely aesthetic, inclines it toward sterile forms.

*

A tradition cannot live if it does not evolve, if it does not embrace confusion. It would exhaust itself, come to the end of its curve; I expect that the present chaos in all the arts is merely the preamble of new rules which will rest on other premises. We cannot assign responsibility, cannot lodge accusations: we can acknowledge that everything is moving, changing, that everything observes the law of nodes and waves.

*

All of us contain in ourselves a night we scarcely know or do not know at all. This night tries to emerge from us, yet resists emerging. That is the drama of art, a real struggle between Jacob and the Angel.

*

Every work, poem, or painting, executed according to the methods of half sleep—that is, born of the marriage of conscious and unconscious—requires a Champollion to discover the secret of its script, to teach that secret not only to others but to the artist himself. Every true work expresses itself by hieroglyphics, by a language both living and dead, a language that must be deciphered. Heretofore, those who read or look have made the same mistakes as the experts who, before Champollion's discovery, saw nothing but picturesque figures in the hieroglyphs, which they interpreted arbitrarily.

It is this secret language, different in the case of each artist, which submerges their works in a great solitude.

*

The night of which I speak is not to be confused with the night which Freud invited his patients to enter. Freud was a modest housebreaker: he absconded with a few mediocre pieces of furniture and some erotic photographs. He never consecrated the abnormal as a transcendence; nor did he hail the great disorders. He devised a confessional for bores.

Freud's key to dreams is a naïve one, by which the simple baptize themselves complex. His sexual obsession necessarily seduced a leisure society of which sex is the axis. As the American investigations show, the plural remains plural when it becomes singular enough to avow the vices it invents. The same stupidity presides over the admission of vices and the display of virtues.

Freud is accessible. His inferno (his purgatory) is made to the specifications of the majority. He seeks—and in this he is my exact opposite—only visibility.

The night which concerns me is different. It is a cavern of treasures, opened by daring and a *Sesame*. Not a doctor or a neurosis. A dangerous cavern, if the treasures make us forget the *Sesame*.

It is in this cavern, this de luxe derelict, this living room at the bottom of a lake, that the great soul is enriched.

*

Bad morals are one of the few things people attribute to others without a moment's thought. Purity of heart and respect for one's neighbor no longer exist except in India and the Oriental countries for which France is a pinhead on the map and the white race crude and uncivilized. The heart's intercourse is naturally suspect to livid savages like ourselves, who trust only those whom business and eroticism make comprehensible to us. That is why I shall not discuss here my adoptive sons of the flesh, concerned only with the sons who spring from my brain, like Minerva from Jupiter's.

I have often said that Picasso is a couple and that no household ever fought so much, broke so many dishes. Perhaps Genet is right and my paternalism turns into maternalism when I commit the imprudence of adopting young souls who replace the true sons fate owed me but has not permitted me to have.

Yet though these adoptive sons do not concern me here, there is one so alien to the world of letters that he is almost more of a lyric creation; I speak of the former lightweight champion Al Brown. Struck by the analogy between his methods and mine, I undertook the strange task of extricating him from a catastrophe of drugs and alcohol, of proving, once he was back in the ring, that intelligence, provided the athlete uses his own, is a weapon capable of replacing strength. Besides, there was a kind of poetry in this black man, a poetry which exasperated the crowd, which scorns poetry in whatever form it can detect it. It pleased me to advise Al Brown and to watch him translate my moral combat to the physical realm. Anything but handsome, Al Brown glowed with a kind of sorcery, and ultimately the fans had to acknowledge the mystery of his successes.

After a long and painful cure, and despite the incredulous

smiles of the professionals, Al Brown, scrupulously following my advice, won eleven victories in a row. I taught him to give his adversaries confidence by a few childish tricks (for example: drinking soda water out of a champagne bottle before the fight) and, once these naïve athletes were off their guard, to go for the chin with the speed of a cobra. It was his famous left hook that made Al Brown invincible, even if, exhausted by twelve rounds, he appeared to be defeated and won the match on points: his method consisted in becoming a ghost, never being where his adversary thought he was, trying for a knockout only when he was certain of inflicting it.

How often I saw him disappoint the public by avoiding a massacre! When I except him from the race made illustrious by Raymond Radiguet, then, when I think of the kind of living death from which I rescued him, and of his demise in Harlem as a poor faithful animal who returns to his nest to die, I wonder if this whole strange career is a version of zombieism, if I must not add Al Brown to the list of my imaginary characters. Perhaps he actually died in Montmartre or during the terrible cure at Sainte-Anne, perhaps I resuscitated him by voodoo spells. Certainly the referees kept an eye on me during each fight, convinced that I exercised some hypnotic power over Al Brown, that I was controlling the fight from my ringside seat. They had noticed that the ex-champion never took his eyes off me, and it is true that he rubbed his chin a second before delivering his knockout blow, informing me by this sign that I could make my bets with the reporters.

Of course I know nothing about voodoo and have never attended its rites. And I have no idea how much credence we should attach to zombies, if they are a reality or a fiction. But no fiction is born out of frivolity, and I should never dare assert that we can dismiss the macabre phenomenon of such resurrection. Al Brown's methods astonished by their indifference to the rules, or at least to the rules of a modern style of boxing the crowd demands—a style as spectacular as that of wrestling.

Al Brown respected the old rules of the *noble art*, and dismayed his adversaries by a kind of dance, saving himself from their blows and risking only those of his own which he considered indispensable. He said his delicate wrists made obligatory feints which would make him invisible, and it was this talent for vanishing from a colossus like Angelmann which provoked, among managers, a kind of superstitious terror. I have heard him called "the poet of the ring"—a supreme insult aimed at me; I have heard elegant women screaming "Kill him! Kill him!" to stupefied young brutes who could never touch him. His final victory silenced all objections and obliged his public to account for it by the inexplicable. From this it was only a step to witchcraft and to the claim that Al Brown was no more than a marionette and that I was pulling the strings.

Attempts were made to keep me from taking a ringside seat, and the night he was carried out on a stretcher, though the referees declared him the winner on points, I was afraid I would be lynched. Al Brown explained to me later that San Chili had soaked his hair in a sleeping drug, so that after twelve rounds of close work he knew he would have to win a mathematical victory by the calculating use of his left hook. The night of this match against the man who had once stolen the title from Al Brown in Spain by inadmissible means, experts of good faith went so far as to claim I had bribed the referees.

I presume, moreover, that fearing the risks of a fight with a young English boxer, Al Brown was subject to a childish scare, which is why he asked me to write an article declaring that the experiment was over and that I was withdrawing him from competition. The same press which had mocked my undertaking now reproached me for concluding it and for obliging "the black wonder" to sign up with the Cirque Amar, touring in an act that was half boxing, half dancing.

P.S. The night before his death, Cerdan had promised me to look after Al Brown, who did not have enough money to pay for a seat at Cerdan's fight. Knowing how sick he was and that I

could not go to New York, the reporters of *l'Équipe* had me
record on tape my memories of a faithful friendship. Al Brown
died listening to this tape in a Harlem hospital.

*

I have never had any discretion, nor can I boast of that, for I
don't even know what discretion is. I dive into action head first,
come what may. Erik Satie used to say that people were always
telling him as a young man, "You'll see, later on." "I'm fifty
years old," he told me, "and I've still seen nothing."

*

When I admire a painter, people tell me, "Yes, but that's not
painting." When I admire a composer, people tell me, "Yes,
but that's not music." When I admire a playwright, people tell
me, "Yes, but that's not theatre." When I admire an athlete,
people tell me, "Yes, but that's not boxing" (I heard this after
each of Al Brown's fights), and so on. Then I would ask, "But
what is it?" My interlocutor hesitated, eyes fixed in space, and
murmured: "I don't know . . . it's something else."

I have finally realized that this *something else* is, after all, the
best definition of poetry.

*

What happens in a poet's soul is as remote and incredible as
the behavior of the Mongols under the rule of Kublai Khan,
grandson of Genghis Khan. That is why poets are regarded as
liars, just as Marco Polo was regarded as a liar till his dying
breath. Venice called him "The Liar" and mocked his memories
by calling them dreams. Nor did he tell much. It was coal, most
of all, that drew the laughs: a black stone that burns like wood.

Nothing more dignified, more savage, than the amazing
dialogue between Marco Polo on his deathbed and the notary-
priest who attended him. This priest, imploring him to confess
his lies—to confess that his discoveries were nothing but lies—

says among other things: "How could our Lord Jesus Christ have come down to earth if it were a round ball?" Marco Polo was then sixty. As a young man, he had lived in China at the court of Kublai Khan, who did believe him and asked, for instance, many questions about the Pope. Even during his Genoese imprisonment, Polo lost his temper with Rusticiano, to whom he was dictating his memoirs, because the poet interpolated tales of chivalry in which women dress up as men and fight the infidels.

In Venice, Marco Polo wrapped himself in that great sad cloud in which solitary souls seek a refuge against the society which rejects them. But with regard to the accusation of lying he remained intransigent. He persisted gently, but he persisted.

*

"Not to be admired.
To be believed."

Keats's cat story has never, to my knowledge, been transcribed; it journeys from mouth to mouth, changing as it travels. Several versions exist, but its atmosphere remains unchanged. Here are the facts.

In order to dine with his friend the vicar of the village of F., Keats had to ride through a woods, and lost his way by nightfall, when the labyrinth became inextricable. He decided to wait for sunrise, to tie his horse to a tree and search for some nearby woodcutter's hut where he could take shelter till daylight.

He prowled about, not daring to lose sight of his horse altogether, until he noticed a light, which he headed for. It came from a ruin unmarked on any map—the ruin of an ancient amphitheatre, arches, rows of crumbling stone, fragments of wall, gaps, briars. The strange light shifted as he headed toward it, circling the strange place. Keats drew near, slipped behind a column, and peered through one of the gaps.

What he saw rooted him to the spot with amazement and terror. Hundreds of cats invaded the amphitheatre and took their places side by side like the crowds in a Spanish arena. They swarmed over the stones, miaowing until suddenly a sound of tiny trumpets was heard, and the cats fell silent, motionless, turning their phosphorescent eyes to the right, from which came a cluster of lights—torches carried by fifty cats, booted and spurred, and preceding a cortege of magnificently costumed cats, pages and heralds blowing trumpets, bearing banners and standards.

This procession crossed the amphitheatre and circled it. Then appeared four white and four black cats with sabers and felt hats, walking on their hind legs like all the others and carrying on their shoulders a tiny coffin surmounted by an even tinier crown. More cats followed, two by two, bearing gold cushions to which were pinned medals and orders whose diamonds sparkled in the torchlight, the moonlight. Drums brought up the rear of the procession.

Keats thought: "I'm dreaming. I've fallen asleep on horseback and I'm dreaming." But dreams are one thing, reality another. He was not dreaming, and he knew it. He was lost in the woods at night, watching some rite men are forbidden to see. Keats was frightened. His presence, discovered, would cause this host of cats to leave the amphitheatre and tear him to pieces. He shrank back into the darkest shadows. The heralds blew their trumpets, the banners floated, the coffin passed by, all this in a kind of silence intensified by the proud little trumpets.

After circling the amphitheatre, the procession moved on. The trumpets faded away, the lights dimmed, and the cats left the rows of seats. Several leaped through the gap in the wall against which Keats was pressed, trying to remain invisible. The ruin became, once again, a ruin, occupied by no more than moonlight.

It was then that an idea occurred to Keats even more dangerous than the spectacle he had just witnessed: *no one would ever believe him*. He could never tell this story. It would be considered a poet's lie. Now Keats knew that poets do not lie. They testify. And Keats knew that people imagine poets lie. Keats grew wild at the thought that such a secret would remain his property, that he could never be rid of it, share it with others. It was a catafalque of solitude.

Keats shook himself, returned to his horse, and determined to get out of the woods. He succeeded, and reached the vicarage, where all hopes of seeing him had been given up. The vicar—a man of considerable culture whom Keats respected—had gone to bed; he got up and served Keats dinner himself, his servant being asleep. Keats ate in silence. Surprised by his abstracted attitude, the vicar asked if he was feeling ill. Keats said that he was not ill but under an influence he could not reveal. The vicar pressed him affectionately, insisted on an explanation. Keats changed the subject, fell silent. Finally the vicar managed to persuade his guest to admit that he refused to speak because he feared he would not be believed. The vicar promised to believe whatever Keats told him, but the poet demanded that he swear to it on the Bible. This the vicar refused, but declared that his promise as a friend was just as valid as his oath as a priest. "I'm listening," he said, and leaned back in his armchair, puffing on his pipe.

Keats was about to speak, then changed his mind, overcome once more by fear. The fascinated vicar had to respect his silence in order to loosen his tongue. At last Keats closed his eyes and told the story. The vicar listened in the shadows. The window was open, the stars bright. The fire crackled on the hearth, where the cat seemed to be sleeping. Keats described the ruin in the woods, and the strange spectators of the strange spectacle performed there. From time to time he glanced at the priest who, eyes closed, sucked on his pipe.

The thing happened the way a thunderbolt falls, without either man's realizing it or understanding what had transpired.

Keats had come to the procession, the torches, the trumpets, the banners, the drums. He described the costumes, the hats, the boots. "Four white cats," he said, "and four black ones, bearing a coffin on their shoulders. The coffin had a gold crown on it."

No sooner had he spoken this sentence than the cat sleeping in front of the fire leaped up, fur bristling, and exclaimed in a human voice: "Then I am King of the Cats!" and leaped out the window.

*

The enmity of cats and dogs is a myth. Bring them together in the country and they befriend, they adopt each other. Martin, one of Moulouk's puppies, nurses the kittens of my old cat, who sleeps in her corner. Last night, in Monte Carlo, Colette showed me how swallows and bats collaborate in their thieving. Hatred feeds on lack of contact, dissolves upon intimacy. Ignorance awakens it. This is true of the animals we dare not bring together: they feel the absurd hatred animating peoples whose customs and languages differ. From his houseboat, Moulouk contemplates without hatred the rats hurrying along the bank.

*

From the sexual point of view, a normal man should be able to make love with anyone, anything, for the instinct of the species is blind; it functions *en gros*. This accounts for the ambiguous behavior described as lower-class vice, especially on the part of sailors. Only the sexual act itself counts. An animal is unconcerned by the circumstances which provoke it. I am not speaking of love.

Vice begins with choice. Depending on the subject's heredity, intelligence, nervous fatigue, this choice is refined to the point of becoming inexplicable, comical, or criminal.

*

My friend Pobers, professor of parapsychology at the University of Utrecht, went on an expedition to the Antilles to study certain telepathic phenomena frequent among the common people in those islands. The women, if they wanted to communicate with a husband or son in the city, addressed themselves to a tree, and the father or son brought home what he had been asked to bring. One day when Pobers had observed this phenomenon and asked the woman why she used a tree for the purpose, he was astonished by her answer, which may contribute to the solution of the entire problem of our atrophying instincts. Here is the question: "Why do you speak to the tree?" And here is the answer: "Because I'm poor. If I were rich, I'd use a telephone."

A poet's answer. We recognize its childish logic, its exactitude which is denied to poets yet which is our armory, its unexpected method which would have obliged us to be burned alive in the Middle Ages, its contempt for a progress we subscribe to only from fatigue and without prostrating ourselves before its taboos.

*

I have never been handsome. Youthfulness is my form of beauty. My bones are good, though the flesh is poorly organized around them. Besides, the skeleton alters, and ultimately for the worse. My nose, which used to be straight, hooks like my grandfather's. I noticed on my mother's deathbed that her nose, too, hooked. Too many inner storms, sufferings, crises of doubt, rebellions put down by will, slaps of fate, have wrinkled my forehead, hollowed a deep groove between my eyebrows, which are twisted now, creased the lids, softened the hollow cheeks, lowered the corners of the mouth, so that if I lean over a mirror the whole facial mask hangs shapeless from the bones. My beard grows in white. My thinning hair is just as refractory to the comb. My teeth overlap. In short, above a body neither tall nor short, emaciated and equipped with hands admired because they are long and expressive, I bear a thankless head. It gives me a false pride which originates in a determination to overcome a reluctance to show myself as I am . . .

My childhood is interminable. Which makes people imagine I remain young, whereas youth and childhood have nothing to do with each other. Picasso says: "*It takes a very long time to become young.*" Youth drives away our childhood. In the end childhood reasserts its rights.

My mother died in "childhood." She did not fall into it: she was a very lively old child. She recognized me, but *her* childhood situated me in *mine*, without, of course, the two childhoods coinciding. An old little girl, surrounded by her little girl's acts, questioned an old little boy about his school, told him to be a good boy the next day.

Perhaps I inherit this long childhood, disguised as maturity, from my mother, whom I resemble; it is the cause of all my misfortunes. Perhaps the invisible makes use of it. It has led me, without a doubt, to certain discoveries proper to children, in whom the sense of the ridiculous does not exist. The remarks of children that people quote are close to the dissociations of poets, and I know many I should be pleased to have made.

No one is willing to admit this amalgam of childhood and old age in us, except in the form of senility, yet I am constituted of just such an amalgam. Sometimes people reproach me, scold me without realizing they are adopting toward me the style of families toward their children.

Such is man. Such is the vehicle whose use is not an easy one. It is natural that this human vehicle should annoy that night which tries to take shape, to *form itself,* and which I hamper out of imbecility.

I wonder if I can be otherwise, if my *difficulty of being,* these defects which impede my progress, are not my progress itself. My progress and my regret that I have nothing more. A fate I must accept as I accept my own physique. Whence these bursts of pessimism, of optimism, whose conjugation leaves its mark upon me, the systole and diastole of a universal rhythm.

And this inclines us to mourn the dead, to rejoice in new births, whereas it is our true condition *not to be.*

Our pessimism emanates from this void, from this non-being.

Our optimism, from a wisdom which counsels us to take advantage of the parenthesis this void offers, to take advantage of it without seeking an answer to the riddle man will never answer for the good reason that there is no answer, that our celestial system is no more durable than our somatic sky, that duration is a legend, that the void is not void, that eternity dupes us by offering a time that unrolls, whereas in reality the lump of space-and-time explodes, motionless, far from the concepts of space and time.

*

All in all, man gives himself airs, and no one dares claim that our system functions in a pinhead, perhaps, or within some other organism. Only Renan has dared, in a tiny, grim sentence: *Il se pourrait que la vérité fût triste.*

*

Erik Satie once said (speaking of Ravel): "What matters is not that you refuse the Legion of Honor; you must also not have deserved it." Membership in the Académie-Française, in the German and American Academies, a doctorate from Oxford, countless official honors have rained down on me, which, far from making me proud, have put me on my guard, for they must correspond to sins against solitude which I have committed and against which fate warns me under an illusory aspect of honors.

Once these prizes are handed over on the dais where we sit next to the pop singer, Miss Europe, and the bicycle racers, we shall be forgiven them only by the rigorous indiscipline of the bad student, carrying to extremes what society reproaches us for and which is nothing but ourselves, that true self by which we differ from the rest and sit next to no one.

*

Our machinery is dismantled a little more every day, and each morning a man awakens with new fetters. I see this in myself. I used to sleep the night through. Now I wake up, get out of bed, begin to work. That is the only way I have of forgetting my ugliness: to be beautiful at my desk. The face of my writing is my true face. The other is a shadow, a fading shadow. Quick, let me shape my features out of ink, to replace those which are forsaking me.

*

Writing is an act of love. If not, it is merely writing. It consists in obeying the mechanism of plants, of trees—in projecting our sperm far from ourselves. The world's luxury is in loss. One seed germinates, another falls to the ground, barren. So it is with sexuality. The center of pleasure is very vague, though very intense. It urges the race to perpetuate itself. Yet functions blindly. One dog rapes my leg; a bitch fights another tooth and nail. Certain plants, once high, now stunted, still produce for their seeds a parachute which drops to earth before it can open. Women in certain Pacific atolls deliver their babies in cow dung so that only the strongest will survive; to avoid overpopulation, these islands favor what we are in the habit of calling "immoral behavior."

Soldiers, sailors, laborers who indulge in such behavior see no crime in it. If they do, it is because vice has marked them down. Vice, I have written, begins with choice. I have seen American sailors in Villefranche to whom lovemaking suggested no specific form and who managed to make anything, anyone serve. The notion of vice never occurred to them. They acted blindly. They yielded instinctively to the very vague laws of the vegetable and animal kingdoms. As for the blind desires of the flesh, I know little enough about them, but since I choose to frequent the young, from whom I have much to learn, the world has decided differently. Moreover, I consider such transactions, after a certain age, depravity, permitting no exchange and equally laughable with regard to either sex.

I lead, in short, a monk's life. A life incomprehensible in a city whose inhabitants think only of rubbing against each other, of seeking such pleasures even in dancing, of attributing it to everyone, of regarding any friendship as suspect.

No matter. The more deceived about us others are, the more we are disfigured by lies, the more we are protected and taught to live in peace. Enough that those who know us esteem us. What we are to the rest is nothing to us.

A lady I had invited to lunch served me up such a description of myself that I had to excuse myself from the table. "You are sharing," I told her, "a meal with someone I do not know, someone I have no desire to know."

*

Jean Genet, whom we shall one day regard as a moralist,* paradoxical as this now appears, for we are in the habit of confusing the moralist with the man who preaches morality, made this poignant remark to me a few weeks ago: "It is not enough to watch our heroes live their lives and to pity them. We must take their sins upon us and accept the consequences."

Which are my true heroes? Feelings. Abstract figures no less alive for that, figures whose requirements are extreme. This is what I realized listening to Genet and witnessing the ravages

---

* Genet is a moralist in that he possesses a morality and never departs from it. Moreover, Genet is a fabulist. He makes his animals speak. He invents (he expresses) the psychology of animals who possess none or who possess one so subtle they can express it only by silence and violence. As for his being a thief: Colette calls me a bad idler; Genet is a bad thief. Theft is his *violon d'Ingres*.

inflicted upon his soul by the crimes of the Egyptian *Querelle.*
He acknowledged himself responsible for them, rejected any
excuse of irresponsibility. He was ready, not to contemplate an
indictment of his book and its boldness, but to submit to the
indictment which a higher justice would bring against his characters.*

Thus he sheds for me a great light upon the endless indictment in which I myself am engaged. Thus he explains why I
feel no need to rebel against it. This indictment brought against
words, attitudes, ghosts must be endured—it is only fair—by
the author, who must appear in court between two policemen.
The situation of an author who judges is inadmissible—the
author who sits on his own tribunal and who leans compas-
sionately toward the guilty. A man is on one side of the bar or
the other. That is the very premise of our commitment.

If I were not of the race which is accused and incapable of
defending itself against accusation, how ashamed I should have
been to look in Genet's eyes when he confided the secret of his
torment. Moreover, would he have confided in me if he had not
long since recognized me, and at first glance, by those signs by
which outlaws recognize each other?

*

An artist cannot expect help from his peers. Any form which
is not his own must be intolerable to him. I saw Claude Debussy taken sick at the orchestral rehearsals of *Le Sacre.* His
soul discovered the score's splendor; the form he had given to
his own soul suffered from a form which did not observe its
contours. Hence, no help. Neither from our peers nor from a

* To identify Jean Genet before a Court of Justice (1942), I
testified that I regarded him as the greatest writer in France. The
Occupation newspapers gloated over this, of course, but a Parisian
magistracy is always in terror of repeating a famous ineptitude, of
condemning Baudelaire. I saved Genet. Nor do I wish to alter my
testimony.

public incapable of accepting a violent break with habits it is beginning to adopt as second nature. Where will help come from? From no one.

*

Wilde rightly remarks that technique is merely individuality. The technicians who worked on my film *La Belle et la Bête* praised my "technique." I have no such thing. Because there is no such thing. No doubt we call *technique* that moment-to-moment balance the mind instinctively achieves in order to keep from breaking its neck. All of which is summarized by Picasso's great remark: "One's *métier* is what cannot be learned."

*

The mechanism which imposes upon us the beauty of a picture, or, more correctly, the combination of lines and volumes capable of moving us, results from a phenomenon analogous to what triumphs over our intelligence when sexuality speaks. A kind of psychic sexuality provokes a moral erection comparable to the sexual one in that it functions without our control and gives immediate proof of the effectiveness of the forms and colors likely to convince a secret part of our organism. If this moral erection does not occur, the pleasure a work of art affords is of a merely Platonic or intellectual order and without the slightest elective value. It will be no more than a dilettante's choice, an opinion unsubjugated by the inevitable. I suppose that a precise consciousness of what happens within the spectator overwhelmed by a work would shame those who conceal their sexual secrets or reveal them only in a form in which the confession is expressed by enthusiasm.

Moreover, I know persons who must vaguely experience such things, since modesty keeps them from expressing their enthusiasm and obliges them to maintain a cold reserve in the presence of what excites them most. The example of such modesty is not

so rare as is imagined. It explains why, for example, those trans-
fixed by an artist's arrows take care not to let him know it,
whereas those merely grazed often write to an artist who in-
terests them more than he moves them.

A work of art which is the consequence of an ethic and not
an aesthetic presents all the properties of a presence, all that a
presence implies of a particular nature belonging to no one else,
or at least belonging to a category suggested by a phrase com-
monly used when sexual pursuit is in question: "That's my
type." Such a work possesses a sex and an age, a weakness or a
strength likely to satisfy the requirements of a moral zone
which corresponds, in sexual matters, to the skin. One might
then say of a work of art: "I've got it under my skin," as a man
will say of a woman, or a woman of a man. It remains to be
seen whether the work becomes an independent person or
whether it is so closely referable to the artist that it is the artist's
psychic flesh which is exposed in the work.

Of course, I am not referring to the bodies and faces physi-
cally represented in the work, bodies and faces which may be
pleasing or displeasing to the spectator, but to the body and the
face which the work itself constitutes, beyond all representation
and by the sole virtue of its equilibrium. We must therefore
eliminate the lovers of the *Mona Lisa* or of Michelangelo's
David and consider only the very rare persons in love with a
work without taking its *pretext* into account. I refer then to
those persons whom the least comma in a sentence, the lightest
touch of a paintbrush, the merest indentation of a sculptor's
finger will put in a state where a higher sexuality prevails. The
work of art is then capable of awakening a psychic desire which
may be carried to the point of exclusive possession, the theft of
the object itself by the man or woman who lusts after it.

In most cases, the judgments made about art (and sometimes
without the judge realizing the fact) are influenced by the
artist's signature and the guarantee this signature represents.

Our judges resemble those spectators who acclaim a famous tragedienne before she opens her mouth. Can we blame them, when the mere appearance of this actress is elevated upon a cothurn of legend? The merest sketch signed Matisse rests upon a mass of previous works which sustain it and confer a certain prestige upon it. But this is not the realm which concerns me— a realm, rather, where love begins with an irresistible attraction, a positive force requiring no previous reflection.

The artist's role is therefore to create an organism with a life of its own derived from his and not intended to surprise, to please or to displease, but to be sufficiently active to excite certain secret senses responsive only to signs which will represent beauty for some, ugliness and deformity for others. And all the rest is no more than picturesque and arbitrary . . .

*

The goal of every artist must be his own extremity.

*

The other evening, during a conversation, you learned your age. *Learned*, because you count poorly and had not established even the slightest relation between the date of your birth and the present year. Something in you was stupefied by this discovery. The contagion spread, perniciously, to the entire organism, until you told yourself: *I'm old*. No doubt you would have preferred to hear someone tell you "You're young" and to believe the flattery.

Intrepid and stupid, you had to take sides. This limits the difficulty of being, since for those who embrace a cause, whatever is not this cause does not exist.

But all causes solicit you. You are not willing to renounce any. To slide onward, among them all . . .

Shift for yourself, then, intrepid as you are . . . Intrepid and stupid, onward! Risk being, to the end.

*

And the book I am writing—has it completed its trajectory, its curve? I who boast, in these very chapters, of never caring about this, of discovering the fact only by a shock, a surprise—for the first time, I question myself. Could I go on speaking to you and still keep this journal, which is not one, in the fashion of a journal, according to what happens to me? That would be to tamper with its mechanism. I should not be writing the book which comes to me but another which I would be forcing. I submit to the cheat of railroad stations where you run alongside the train, trying to postpone breaking the cord tied around your heart and around the heart of those departing. I am torn now between the force of habit and that fatality which forces me to break off. I used to picture us so clearly, youth like my youth, standing on a streetcorner, sitting in a park, sprawling on a bed, elbow on a table, talking together. And I am leaving you. Without leaving you, of course, for I have stirred enough of myself into my ink for the pulse to beat inside it. Don't you feel it under your thumb holding the corner of these pages? Surprising if you didn't, for it throbs even under my pen, making that fierce, inimitable clamor of my heart recorded in *Le Sang d'un Poète*. "The poet is dead. Long live the poet." That is what his ink exclaims. That is the message of his muffled drums. That is the illumination of his funereal candles. That is what shakes the pocket where you put my book, and what makes the people you pass turn their heads, startled by the sound.

You take this book out of your pocket. You read. And if you can read without anything distracting you from what I write, gradually you will feel that I inhabit you, and you will bring me back to life. You will even risk making, unconsciously, one of my gestures, your face will look like my face. Naturally I am speaking to the youth of a time when I shall no longer be here in flesh and blood, when my blood will be mixed with my ink.

That is the whole difference between a book which is only a

book and this book which is a person turned into a book. Turned into a book and calling for help so that the spell can be broken and the person reincarnated in the person of the reader. That is the hocus-pocus I ask of you. Understand me. It is not so difficult as it seems at first.

Glimpsed, Judged, Remembered
by a Jury of His Peers

W. H. Auden:

"To enclose the collected works of Cocteau one would need not a bookshelf, but a warehouse, and how even then could one catalogue such a bewildering assortment of poems, plays in verse, plays in prose, mythologies, natural histories, travels, drawings, tins of films, phonograph records, etc.? . . . He has always been a poet in the Greek sense: a maker who forgets himself in a complete absorption with the task in hand . . . The lasting feeling that his work leaves is one of happiness; not, of course, in the sense that it excludes suffering, but because, in it, nothing is rejected, resented or regretted . . ."

Charles Chaplin:

"Cocteau could not speak a word of English, neither could I speak French, but his secretary spoke a little English, though not too well, and he acted as interpreter for us. That night we sat up into the small hours, discussing our theories of life and art. Our interpreter spoke slowly and hesitantly while Cocteau, his beautiful hands spread on his chest, spoke with the rapidity of a machine gun, his eyes flashing an appealing look at me, then at the interpreter, who spoke unemotionally: 'Mr. Cocteau —he say—you are a poet—of ze sunshine—and he is a poet of ze—night.'

"Immediately Cocteau turned from the interpreter to me with a quick, birdlike nod, and continued. Then I would take over, getting deeply involved in philosophy and art. In moments of agreement we would embrace, while our cool-eyed interpreter looked on. Thus, in this exalted way, we carried on through the night until four in the morning . . ."

Colette:

"When Jean Cocteau came to visit me in Saint-Tropez, in the summer of 1936, the car that brought him stopped on the little road in front of my gate, and out bounded the poet who signs his works with his first name and a star. He was simply dressed, and thin as only those who pass through mirrors can be. A purple silk scarf was knotted tight around his throat, and he was wearing a floppy Tuareg straw hat into which he had stuck bunches of black chicken-feathers. That was how he dressed for Provence, which after all sees all kinds. But at her first sight of him, the woman who tends my garden recognized him—besides, everyone knows black chickens bring bad luck—and she jumped up, screaming 'Lucifer! Lucifer!'

"As if to prove how right she was, a moment later she was won over, declaring him to be 'such a nice man' and offering him a glass of ice water, a flower, volunteering then and there to bake him some of her cookies you have to eat right out of the oven, piping hot . . ."

Jean Genet:

"We deny Jean Cocteau the stupid title 'enchanter': we declare him 'enchanted.' He does not 'charm.' He is 'charmed.' He is not a wizard, he is bewitched . . ."

André Gide:

"Not that I do not admit, as I have long since admitted, the correctness of your maxims, but some of them seem to me less relevant to the man you are than to the man you want people to think you are . . ."

Marcel Jouhandeau:

"I can never forget that I was lying flat on the floor of my room, overcome by despair, when Jean entered my life in 1927. We had never set eyes on each other. Someone had told him something, and without knowing me except by my first books, he had immediately rushed to help me."

Marianne Moore:

[Reviewing an English translation of *La Machine Infernale*]: ". . . One has the sense of something submerged and estranged . . . of valor in a fairy tale, changed by hostile enchantment into a frog or a carp that cannot leave its pool or well . . . M. Cocteau, in refusing to be answerable to any morality but his own, is in the Greek sense impious and unnatural. But he is a very fine inhabitant of the world in which ichor is imagination, in which magic imparts itself to whatever he writes."

Katherine Anne Porter:

"I [saw] him in 1952 in Paris, at the performance of *Oedipus Rex*, looking very elegant in his own idea of black tie, intoning the poetry while Stravinsky conducted his own music, and it was enchanting. But by then obviously it had become a tradition for Paris audiences to whistle and jeer at Cocteau, so this audience worked up a slovenly little imitation of a riot at one point. The performance stopped. Cocteau rose to his feet and said, 'If you have no respect for me and my work, at least respect Stravinsky who is a great composer!' The audience was quiet. He sat down again, and smoothed out the pages he was reading from, in perfect stillness, but his face looked as if he might shed tears . . ."

Raymond Radiguet:

[Aged sixteen]: "Jean Cocteau will always be eighteen years old."

Rainer Maria Rilke:

"Tell Jean Cocteau I love him—the only one who plunges into the myth which lies open to him and from which he returns tanned as from the seashore."

Gertrude Stein:

"Lipschitz had told Gertrude Stein a thing which she did not know, that Cocteau in his *Potomak* had spoken of and quoted The Portrait of Mabel Dodge. She was naturally very pleased as Cocteau was the first French writer to speak of her work. They met once or twice and began a friendship that consists in their writing to each other quite often and liking each other immensely and having many young and old friends in common, but not in meeting."

Igor Stravinsky:

"His conversation was always a highly diverting performance . . . and his personality is generous and disarmingly simple. Artistically, he is a first-rate critic and a theatrical and cinematographic innovator of a high order . . . His best caricatures are as good as any but Picasso's . . ."

Sources and Asides

For the selection and arrangement of the foregoing text, I alone am responsible; but for the immense privilege of working with literally thousands of Cocteau's original pages as freely as though they had been my own, I must now—and eagerly—thank M. Edouard Dermit, Cocteau's testamentary heir, who, in January 1967, generously accorded me carte blanche to make an "autobiography" out of the lifetime writing of his great friend. It is in partial acknowledgment of this trust that I have asked M. Dermit to accept, on behalf of his own sons, aptly named Jean-Cégèste and Stéphane-Orphée, one half of the dedication of this book.

The other half I would like to offer to Monroe Wheeler, who remained Cocteau's closest American friend for nearly forty years and who, along with Glenway Wescott, has been my principal source of personal recollection of Cocteau the man, as well as of unpublished letters and precious, inscribed books.

For further kindness, forbearance, and assorted advice, I want also to thank the following: Natalie Clifford Barney, Jean Chalon, Richard Howard, Robert Giroux, Colette de Jouvenel, Marcel Jouhandeau, Michael Lebeck, Margaret Nicholson, Katherine Anne Porter, Jean-Marie Simon, Roger Straus, Jr., and Hal Vursell.

To several dozen others, with whom I am not personally acquainted, yet from whose published writing I have taken the liberty of borrowing a glimpse or an insight to set off Cocteau's own story, I have made formal acknowledgment at the appropriate place below, but I would like to add a grateful bearhug here to each, as well.

Lastly, I must take a sentence to record my thanks to Jean Cocteau himself, not only for the joy which his work continues to give me, but for five different days in my private calendar when something he wrote was more salutary, more life-giving, than anyone or anything else I had access to.

R.P.

All the material for Jean Cocteau's text has been drawn from the following:

1918　*Le Coq et l'Arlequin* (Editions de la Sirène)
1920　*Carte Blanche* (Editions de la Sirène)
1923　*Le Grand Écart* (Grasset)
1924　*Le Potomak* (Stock)
1926　*Lettre à Jacques Maritain* (Stock)
　　　　Le Rappel à l'Ordre (Stock)
1927　*Opéra* (Stock)
　　　　Orphée (Stock)
1930　*Opium* (Stock)
　　　　Le Livre Blanc (Editions du Signe)
1932　*Essai de Critique Indirecte* (Grasset)
1935　*Portraits-Souvenir, 1900–1914* (Grasset)
1936　*Mon Premier Voyage*
1946　*La Belle et la Bête: Journal d'un Film* (Janin)
1947　*La Difficulté d'être* (Paul Morihien)
1948　*Reines de la France* (Grasset)
　　　　Le Sang d'un Poète (Marin/Editions du Rocher)
　　　　Théâtre I and *II*: reprinting *Les Chevaliers de la Table Ronde, Les Parents Terribles, La Machine à Ecrire, L'Aigle à deux têtes* (Gallimard)

1949 *Lettre aux Américains* (Grasset)
      Maalesh (Gallimard)
1950 *Oeuvres Complètes, Vol. X:* reprinting *Le Numéro Barbette* (Editions Marguerat)
1951 *Jean Marais* (Calmann-Lévy)
      Entretiens autour du Cinématographe (Editions André Bonne)
1952 *Gide Vivant* (Amiot-Dumont)
      Journal d'un Inconnu (Grasset)
1953 *Démarche d'un Poète* (Bruckmann)
1955 *Colette* (Grasset)
      Discours de Réception à l'Académie-Française (Gallimard)
1956 *Le Discours d'Oxford* (Gallimard)
1957 *La Corrida du 1er Mai* (Grasset)
1959 *Poésie Critique I* (Gallimard)
1960 *Poésie Critique II* (Gallimard)
1962 *Le Cordon Ombilical* (Plon)
1963 *Beauty and the Beast*, with an afterword by Jean Cocteau (Macmillan)
1964 *Jean Cocteau: Entretien avec Roger Stéphane* (RTF et Librairie Jules Tallandier)

Professional Secrets: Epigraph: *Lettre aux Américains*, p. 49.

Part I: Title: *Le Prince Frivole*, from Cocteau's second collection of poems, published in 1910, when he was twenty-one. His first, *La Lampe d'Aladin*, had appeared in 1909, and the third, *La Danse de Sophocle*, in 1912. Cocteau later excluded them all from his bibliography, calling them "*trois niaiséries*, three silly trifles." ** Epigraph: *Le Coq et l'Arlequin*, p. 11.

Calendar: 1889–1900: *Jean Cocteau et son temps*, by Pierre Georgel (Paris, 1965), p. 6.

Chapter 1: Epigraph: *Journal d'un Inconnu*, p. 143. **
      Text: *Jean Cocteau: Entretien avec Roger Stéphane*, pp.

46–8, 45, 48–9; *Portraits-Souvenir*, pp. 26–8; *Entretiens avec Roger Stéphane*, pp. 45–6; *Portraits-Souvenir*, pp. 24, 28–9; *La Difficulté d'être*, p. 16; *Portraits-Souvenir*, pp. 31–5.

Chapter 2: Epigraph: *Essai de Critique Indirecte*, pp. 148–9. ** Text: *Portraits-Souvenir*, pp. 62–75.

Chapter 3: Text: *Portraits-Souvenir*, pp. 49–55, 82–3, 84, 89–90, 86–8, 41, 37–40, 44; *Entretien avec Roger Stéphane*, p. 59.

Chapter 4: Epigraph: *Le Grand Écart*, p. 13. ** Text: *Portraits-Souvenir*, pp. 105–7; *Le Livre Blanc*, pp. 16–18; *Portraits-Souvenir*, pp. 111–12; *Le Livre Blanc*, pp. 18–21; *Portraits-Souvenir*, pp. 114–15.

Calendar: 1900–1914: *Entretien avec Roger Stéphane*, pp. 65, 67; *Dialogues and a Diary*, by Igor Stravinsky (Doubleday, 1963), p. 44; *La Difficulté d'être*, p. 50.

Chapter 5: Text: *Portraits-Souvenir*, pp. 123, 125–33, passim, 152–3; *Reines de la France*, pp. 134–8; *Portraits-Souvenir*, pp. 154–63.

Chapter 6: Epigraph: *Le Potomak*, p. 24. ** Text: *Portraits-Souvenir*, pp. 211–14, 220–2, 186, 197–204; *Démarche d'un Poète*, p. 13; *Poésie Critique I*, pp. 122–5, 127–8, 130–2.

Chapter 7: Text: *La Difficulté d'être*, pp. 68, 47; *Le Coq et l'Arlequin*, p. 61; *La Difficulté d'être*, pp. 68–71; *Le Coq et l'Arlequin*, pp. 61–6, 62, 66–8.

Chapter 8: Text: *Portraits-Souvenir*, pp. 179–86.

Part II: Title: *Le Rappel à l'Ordre* is from a collection of essays published in 1926. The "order" Cocteau has in mind would be the sort he imputed to Radiguet, "who taught us to write 'like everyone' " (*La Difficulté d'être*, pp. 34–5). In other words, the genuinely new does not necessarily look that way, and it will be the instinct of the truly revolutionary artist "to contradict the avant-garde," as did Radiguet's own novels, as well as those Cocteau

wrote under his influence. ** Epigraph: *Le Potomak,*
p. 53.

Calendar: 1914–1923: *Le Potomak,* p. 8; *La Difficulté d'être,*
p. 48; *Journal, 1889–1939,* by André Gide (Gallimard,
1948), p. 473; *Jean Cocteau,* by Roger Lannes (Pierre
Seghers, 1945), p. 26; *The Autobiography of Alice B.
Toklas,* by Gertrude Stein (Harcourt, Brace, 1933 and
Arrow Books Ltd, 1960), pp. 206, 175; *Plain-Chant,* in
Poèmes 1916–1955 (Gallimard, 1956), p. 56; *Dessins*
(Stock, 1923); *Conversations with Igor Stravinsky,* by
Igor Stravinsky and Robert Craft (Faber, 1959), p. 88.

Chapter 9: Epigraph: *Portraits-Souvenir,* p. 243. ** Text: *La
Difficulté d'être,* p. 48; *La Corrida du 1ᵉʳ Mai,* pp. 163–
4, 171–5; *Entretien avec Roger Stéphane,* p. 40; *La
Difficulté d'être,* pp. 169–77; *La Corrida du 1ᵉʳ Mai,* pp.
205, 166–9, 175–6, 170–1; *Maalesh,* pp. 30–1; *La
Corrida du 1ᵉʳ Mai,* pp. 199, 164, 202, 197, 177–80; *La
Difficulté d'être,* pp. 50–1.

Chapter 10: Epigraph and text: *Le Rappel à l'Ordre,* passim; *La
Difficulté d'être,* pp. 26–8.

Chapter 11: Epigraph: *Lettre aux Américains,* pp. 69–70. **
Text: *Oeuvres Complètes,* Vol. X.

Chapter 12: Epigraphs: *Le Rappel à l'Ordre,* p. 247; *Lettre à
Jacques Maritain,* pp. 18–19. ** Text: *La Difficulté
d'être,* pp. 33–4; *Entretien avec Roger Stéphane,* pp.
81–3, 87, 83–4, 92–4; *La Difficulté d'être,* pp. 26, 36.

Calendar: 1923–1929: Berenson and Crommelynck quoted in
Diary of an Art Dealer, by René Gimpel (Farrar, Straus
& Giroux, 1966), pp. 247, 262; *Entretiens avec André
Fraigneau* (Bibliothèque 10/18, 1965), p. 71; *Opéra,* pp.
90, 13: *Orphée,* p. 74; *Correspondance 1915–1963,* by
Francis Poulenc (Editions du Seuil, 1967), pp. 68–9;
Glenway Westcott, from an unpublished letter of Octo-
ber 6, 1925, to Bernardine Szold; *Portraits-Souvenir,*
p. 233.

Chapter 13: Epigraphs: *Lettre à Jacques Maritain*, p. 7; *Opéra*
("*Le Paquet Rouge*"), p. 90. ** Text: *Lettre à Jacques
Maritain*, passim; *Portraits-Souvenir*, pp. 135–6, 147,
150–2; *La Difficulté d'être*, pp. 117–19; *Journal d'un
Inconnu*, p. 54; *Entretien avec Roger Stéphane*, p. 94.

Chapter 14: Epigraph: *Gide Vivant*, p. 65. Text: *Le Livre
Blanc*, pp. 15–16, 9–14, 35–41, 41–5.

Chapter 15: Epigraphs: *Les Chevaliers de la Table Ronde*, in
Théâtre II, p. 176; *Opium*, p. 175. ** Text: *Opium*,
passim.

Part III: Title: *Le Sang d'un Poète* is from Cocteau's first film,
made in the spring and summer of 1930. He often used
the image of a poet's blood being his ink, and in one of
the best evocations of him ever recorded, Claude Mauriac
quotes him as follows: "One day I asked Colette how it
was she had never written anything you could exactly
call a masterpiece, in spite of her immense talent. She
marched me over to a mirror and said, 'Look at yourself.
I want to enjoy life, to have good legs and a healthy
body . . . You haven't even kept enough flesh to sit
down on!' She understood that I have become a mere
fountain pen, that my very blood has turned to ink . . ."
—*Conversations avec André Gide* (Albin Michel, 1951),
pp. 72–3. ** Epigraph: *Le Cordon Ombilical*, p. 15.

Calendar: 1929–1936: *Les Années Faciles*, 1929–1934, by Julien
Green (Plon, 1938), p. 129; *Make It New*, by Ezra
Pound (Faber & Faber, 1934), p. 245; *Opium*, p. 263;
Les Mémorables, Vol. II, by Maurice Martin du Gard
(Flammarion, 1960), pp. 412–13; *Portraits-Souvenir*, p.
140; *La Jumelle Noire*, by Colette (Ferenczi, 1934), pp.
205–7; *Portraits-Souvenir*, p. 243; *Entretiens avec André
Fraigneau* (Bibliothèque 10/18, 1965), p. 120.

Chapter 16: Epigraph: *Le Sang d'un Poète*, p. 106. ** Text: *Le
Sang d'un Poète*, pp. 97–9; *Entretiens Autour du Cinématographe*, pp. 14–16; *Le Sang d'un Poète*, pp. 104, 99–100,

15–16, 100–1, 14, 102, 104–5; *Entretiens Autour du Cinématographe*, pp. 70–1.

Chapter 17: Epigraph and text: *Mon Premier Voyage*, pp. 9–227, passim.

Calendar: 1936–1940; W. H. Auden: *Flair*, February 1950, p. 102; *Conversations avec André Gide*, by Claude Mauriac (Albin Michel, 1951), pp. 63–5.

Chapter 18: Epigraph and text: *Journal d'un Inconnu*, pp. 57–66.

Calendar: 1940–1946: *Journal de Guerre et d'Occupation* (1939–1948), by Ernst Jünger, translated from the German into French by Henri Plard (Juillard, 1965), p. 122; *Cocteau par Lui-Même*, by André Fraigneau (Editions du Seuil, 1957), p. 187; *Paris de ma Fenêtre*, by Colette (Editions du Milieu du Monde, 1944), pp. 135–6; *Les Années Perdues*, by Lise Deharme (Plon, 1961), p. 148; *Jean Marais*, p. 111; *The War Years*, by Harold Nicolson, edited by Nigel Nicolson (Atheneum, 1967), p. 440.

Chapter 19: Epigraph: *Le Sang d'un Poète*, p. 22. ** Text: *Beauty and the Beast* (Macmillan, 1963), p. 35; *La Belle et la Bête: Journal d'un Film*, pp. 7–235, passim.

Chapter 20: Epigraph: *La Difficulté d'être*, p. 11. ** Text: *La Difficulté d'être*, pp. 149–55.

Part III: Title: *La Difficulté d'être* is from a book of autobiographical essays published in 1947, for Cocteau's fifty-sixth birthday. Literally, it means "the difficulty of being," and comes from Fontenelle's reply when, at the age of one hundred, he lay dying and his doctor asked him what he felt. "But," adds Cocteau (p. 193), "Fontenelle only felt that way in his final hours. I have felt that way all my life." Three lines from a poem by W. H. Auden make an inadvertent but beautiful gloss:

> for the funniest
> mortals and the kindest are those who are most aware
> of the baffle of being . . .

—from "Tonight at Seven-Thirty," in *About the House* (Random House, 1965), pp. 30–1. ** Epigraph: *Journal d'un Inconnu*, p. 210.

Calendar: 1946–1963: *Cocteau par Lui-même*, by André Fraigneau (Editions du Seuil, 1957), p. 134; *La Table Ronde*, February 1955, p. 162; Letter of April 9, 1950, to Mary Hoeck, in *Jean Cocteau*, by Margaret Crosland (Peter Nevill, 1955), p. 194; *Observations*, by Truman Capote (Random House, 1959), pp. 59–60; *Bacchus*, p. 7; *The Delights of Growing Old*, by Maurice Goudeket (Farrar, Straus and Giroux, 1966), pp. 198–9; *Arts Spectacles*, September 19, 1956; *Discours de Réception de M. Jean Cocteau à l'Académie-Française* (Gallimard, 1955), p. 60; Letter of September 19, 1963, to Jean Denoël, in "*Candide*," October 17, 1963; *France-Soir*, October 17, 1963.

Chapter 21: Text: *Lettre aux Américains*, pp. 9, 15–17, 61–2, 18–21, 25, 27–30, 33–7, 50–1, 93–5.

Chapter 22: Text: *La Difficulté d'être*, p. 56 ff.; *Journal d'un Inconnu*, pp. 48, 54; *Opium*, p. 58 ff.; *Orphée*, p. 24 ff.; *Théâtre I*, pp. 71–3, 174; *Jean Marais*, pp. 106–7; *Théâtre I*, pp. 181–2; *Jean Marais*, pp. 107–10; *La Difficulté d'être*, pp. 66–7; *Jean Marais*, p. 110, *Théâtre II*, p. 302; *La Difficulté d'être*, p. 273; *Théâtre II*, pp. 301–2; *La Difficulté d'être*, p. 274; *Journal d'un Inconnu*, pp. 83–92, passim; *La Difficulté d'être*, pp. 63–4.

Chapter 23: "Christian Bérard": Text: *Maalesh*, pp. 9–11, 14–17, 11–13. ** "André Gide": Epigraph: *Gide Vivant*, p. 65. ** Text: *Journal d'un Inconnu*, pp. 110–12; *Gide Vivant*, pp. 37–9, 56, 33, 60–1; Footnote: *Journal d'un Inconnu*, p. 112, and *Poésie Critique I*, p. 230. ** "Colette": Epigraph: *Colette*, p. 60. ** Text: *Colette*, pp. 27–30, 31–8, 53–4.

Chapter 24: Text: *La Corrida du 1ᵉʳ Mai*, pp. 132–5, 130–2,

136–8, 104, 11–12, 53, 56, 64, 73–8, 82–93, 99, 101, 96–7, 104–7.

Chapter 25: Epigraph: *Discours de Réception à l'Académie-Française*, p. 31. ** Text: *Journal d'un Inconnu*, pp. 19–20, 33–4; *Poésie Critique I*, pp. 9–10; *Opium*, pp. 137–8; *La Corrida du 1er Mai*, pp. 57–8, 196; *Démarche d'un Poète*, p. 25; *Journal d'un Inconnu*, pp. 39–40; *Le Cordon Ombilical*, pp. 61–6; *Journal d'un Inconnu*, p. 208; *Discours de Réception à l'Académie-Française*, pp. 23–4; *Démarche d'un Poète*, p. 33; *Journal d'un Inconnu*, pp. 147–51; *Jean Marais*, p. 64; *Opium*, pp. 136–7; *Le Discours d'Oxford*, pp. 18–19; *La Difficulté d'être*, pp. 37–8; *Journal d'un Inconnu*, pp. 35–7; *Poésie Critique II*, p. 213; *La Difficulté d'être*, pp. 242, 229–31, 267–8; *Maalesh*, pp. 23–4; *Entretiens Autour du Cinématographe*, p. 56; *La Difficulté d'être*, pp. 225, 227; *Démarche d'un Poète*, pp. 27–9, 7; *La Difficulté d'être*, pp. 272, 263–65.

A Jury of His Peers: W. H. Auden: *Flair*, February 1950, pp. 101–2; Charles Chaplin; *My Autobiography* (Simon & Schuster, 1964), p. 385; Colette: *Oeuvres Complètes*, Vol. X: *La Jumelle Noire, 5ième Année* (Flammarion, 1950), pp. 465–6; Jean Genet: *Empreintes*, Mai-Juin-Juillet, 1950, p. 24; André Gide: *Incidences* (Gallimard, 1924), p. 64; Marcel Jouhandeau: *Jean Cocteau: L'Amitié Faite Homme* (Editions Dynamo, 1963), p. 8; Marianne Moore: *Predilections* (Viking, 1955), p. 129; Katherine Anne Porter, from an unpublished letter of January 11, 1957, to Monroe Wheeler; Raymond Radiguet: *Oeuvres Complètes*, Vol. 2 (Club des Libraires de France, 1959), p. 258; Rainer Maria Rilke, from a letter to Madame Baladine Klossowska, quoted in *Démarche d'un Poète*, p. 11; Gertrude Stein: *The Autobiography of Alice B. Toklas* (Harcourt, Brace, 1933, and Arrow Books Ltd, 1960), p. 206; Igor Stravinsky and Robert Craft: *Dialogues and a Diary* (Doubleday, 1963), pp. 44–5.